Family Law

for Every

CANADIAN

M A R T H A   A .   M C C A R T H Y

Prentice Hall Canada Inc.

Scarborough, Ontario

for doug and madelyn
  who continue to teach me about the beauty and peace of family

and in memory of jack weir and josephine mccarthy
  who gave me logic, perseverance and faith

Canadian Cataloguing in Publication Data

McCarthy, Martha A.
    Family law for every Canadian

Includes Index.

ISBN 0-13-742768-9

1. Domestic relations – Canada.
I. Title.

KE539.M32 1997   346.7101'5

C97-930562-4   KF505.ZA2M32 1997

© 1997 Prentice-Hall Canada Inc., Scarborough, Ontario
A Division of Simon & Schuster/A Viacom Company

Prentice-Hall, Inc., Upper Saddle River, New Jersey
Prentice-Hall International (UK) Limited, London
Prentice-Hall of Australia, Pty. Limited, Sydney
Prentice-Hall Hispanoamericana, S.A., Mexico City
Prentice-Hall of India Private Limited, New Delhi
Prentice-Hall of Japan, Inc., Tokyo
Simon & Schuster Asia Private Limited, Singapore
Editora Prentice-Hall do Brasil, Ltda., Rio de Janeiro

ISBN 0-13-742768-9

Acquisitions Editor: Sara Borins
Managing Editor: Robert Harris
Production Editor: Kelly Dickson
Substantive Editor: Bruce McDougall
Copy Editor: Kelli Howey
Production Coordinator: Julie Preston
Text/Cover Design: Sputnik
Cover Image: Doug Ross
Page Layout: Arlene Edgar
Art Director: Mary Opper

1 2 3 4 5   W   01 00 99 98 97

Printed and bound in Canada

Visit the Prentice Hall Canada Web site! Send us your comments, browse
our catalogues, and more. **www.phcanada.com**

Every reasonable effort has been made to obtain permissions for all articles
and data used in this edition. If errors or omissions have occurred, they
will be corrected in future editions provided written notification has been
received by the publisher.

Contents

ABOUT THIS BOOK

This book is intended to be an easy reference on all subjects relating to the law of the family. It provides a detailed overview of all issues that arise on the formation and breakdown of intimate relationships. The first chapter, "Formation of the Family," addresses marriage, birth, adoption, surrogacy, alternative fertilization and name changes. The balance of the chapters describe the rights and obligations of married, common law and same sex couples. Some specific chapters discuss violence in the family, domestic contracts, alternatives to litigation, the conduct of a legal action and options for settlement. Since all of these areas also describe the attitude and procedure of Canadian family law generally, they should be of equal interest to those who are entering a relationship or are currently involved in one as they are to those who are considering separation or have separated.

The idea is to provide all of the information you need to manage the interaction between your personal life and the law. If you are embarking on a new relationship or wondering about your rights and obligations in a current relationship, this book should provide you with the background to decide whether you need a marriage contract or a cohabitation agreement; and to understand how the law perceives your relationship. If you are involved in or contemplating a common law or same sex relationship, it is especially important that you understand that the current law of your relationship is likely to change substantially in the near future. This book will help you do that, and will tell you your options to create rules for your relationship so that you will not be held hostage to unpredictable law reform. If you are separating or separated from your spouse, this book will give you an overview of the law relating to property, matrimonial homes, spousal and child support, child custody and access, and settlement options. It should help you figure out whether the issues that arise in your situation are ones that you can negotiate alone, or whether you will require the help of a lawyer. In the event that an amicable settlement eludes you, the discussions of mediation, arbitration and litigation will provide you with all of the facts required to make informed decisions about how to resolve outstanding issues, while managing the process cost-effectively and keeping your focus on the big picture.

If your situation is relatively simple, this book may be all you need to appreciate, discuss and resolve the family law issues that arise in your life at any given time. However, in most cases, you will need the assistance of a lawyer. If you can resolve matters in principle, it is a good idea to retain a lawyer to draft an enforceable and comprehensive agreement. If you are considering litigation, it is simply indisputable that legal assistance is necessary. The outcome of family law litigation can affect your life forever, and it is worth spending the time and money on getting the right resolution. For these reasons, the old adage is especially applicable in family law: "He who represents himself has a fool for a client."

This isn't to say that you don't need this book if you are involved in a heated dispute or are contemplating litigation. To the contrary; it is anticipated that this book will be equally helpful to you in such a situation. All legal services are performed at hourly rates. If you rely on your lawyer to educate you—to advise you of your options on an interim basis, or to explain the meaning of exclusive possession—you are paying a substantial premium for that knowledge. Also, not all lawyers focus on cost-effective service, and the background that this book provides and the tips on saving legal fees should arm you with an ability to control the cost of legal advice. This book is therefore not intended to make you into your own lawyer; it is meant to empower you—to help you understand and manage this fundamental part of your life.

So, if you're embarking on a new relationship or trying to understand an old one: good luck, and may you find happiness in your family and fairness in the law. If you're separating, or considering separation: keep your chin up and your focus on the things that really matter. In all cases, I hope that this book provides you with everything you need to take charge of the issues and obtain the best possible resolution.

ACKNOWLEDGMENTS

When my husband and I got married, I started my speech by saying that I wasn't going to promise to be brief, so if anyone needed a drink or a seat, they should get one. Those who were there continue to joke about how long I took to mention each important person in my life, and they won't be surprised to see that I am having the same problem with the acknowledgments for this book.

I owe substantial gratitude to the people who made this book happen, including Jerry Levitan who chose me for the project and Sara Borins who had the creative vision to talk me into it. Malcolm Kronby is truly the perfect mentor. He has been the source of so much of my knowledge about family law and such a shameless promoter of my capacities that he truly made this book possible. David Kent and Simon Chester gave generously of their time on all sorts of tactical and publishing issues, and I cannot and probably have not thanked them enough. Mark McMackin did all of the background research, without which I could not have even started to write, and I thank him for undertaking that all-consuming drudgery. Mark Opashinov gave me organized and efficient answers to a multitude of nitpicky questions in the final days—or did that turn into months?—of revision. I am grateful to Joanna Radbord who provided substantial background by assisting me with a previous conference paper, and who took the time to read the draft manuscript and give me her detailed comments. My thanks and affection to Bruce Ryder and Nicole Tellier who bless me with their infinite knowledge and support. Ricki Andersen and Lenie Ott are the two best librarians in the world, and I am thankful that, for years now, they have always cheerfully agreed to find me the most obscure information anyone could ask for.

My law clerk Angela Brooks is my constant support, and she diligently managed my practice for the many hours that I neglected it in favour of this book. My secretaries Nicola Allison and Rosa Ionadi kept track of fifty different drafts of each chapter, managed headers and footers and tables of contents, and kept me calm during all of the ups and downs of this project. Without these three women to back me up, I am sure that I would be an unhappy, disorganized lawyer.

My law firm, McMillan Binch, encouraged me to write this book, notwithstanding that it was a sacrifice for the firm and a personal advantage for me. This is not the first time that I have benefited from the selfless attitude of my employers, and I am grateful for all of the opportunities that I have been given as a member of the firm.

Special thanks to my editors, Bruce McDougall and Kelli Howey, who showed extreme patience in the face of my obsessiveness. Thanks also to Robert Harris and everyone at Prentice Hall Canada.

At the centre of everything, there is family. My parents gave and gave and continue to give. Of course, as my father readily points out, they conceived me, changed my diapers and put me through law school, and so they are the only ones who literally made this book possible. More important, they taught me all of the good things about family, and my desire to emulate and please them continues to motivate me. My brothers Peter and Patrick are my best friends and soul mates, and along with Doug and Maddy, are the recipients of my purest, strongest love. My in-laws, Bob and Joyce, are so perfect that they defy the term. My two grandparents, Justin McCarthy and Madelyn Weir Foy, are the vivacious and learned role models every grandchild needs, and they continue to add meaning and focus to my life.

Finally, in the interests of brevity, I wish to thank, praise and express my love for the two Amys, Suzy & Johnnie, Mary Bea, Kimmy, Schmel, Scott & Jo, Emp, Les & Andy, Stephen & Mary, Colleen & Michael, Meredith & Sasha, Nancy, Robert, Kelly, Herschel, Sue & Andrea & Megan, and Norah.

INTRODUCTION

For nearly ten years it has been my privilege and opportunity to work with Martha McCarthy. In that time she has become a knowledgable and effective advocate, but more than that, she has retained the compassion that first motivated her to specialize in what is, I think, the most challenging area of legal practice. A family law lawyer encounters all of the factual, evidentiary and interpretive problems that arise in resolution of legal disputes, but must also manage the emotional load when love turns to failure of love. And unlike the "closure" that ends a commercial dispute, the parties to a family dispute usually remain linked, at least through their children. The best lawyers in this field combine traditional legal skills with psychological insights, and a deep desire to solve rather than perpetuate or exacerbate the problems of their clients.

That's what makes this book different from any other exposition of family law for the general public. Ms. McCarthy goes beyond a lucid and up-to-date explanation of legal principles. She offers counsel in behaviour and relationships. This, then, is not just a book to be referred to in a time of crisis; it will be consulted and found useful before, during and after the actual encounter with a family law issue. The focus is, as it should be, on solving the problem in a bilaterally beneficial and cost-effective manner.

In her clarity of organization, her depth and range of subject, and her sensitivity, I suspect that Ms. McCarthy's book may become the Dr. Spock of its field. She deserves nothing less.

Malcolm C. Kronby, Q.C.

CHAPTER ONE

Formation of the Family

IN THIS CHAPTER: Cohabitation, Marriage;
Formal Requirements of Marriage, Void and Voidable Marriages,
Birth; *Registration, Paternity,* **Adoption;** *Agency and Private Adoption,*
International Adoption, Stepparent and Family Adoption, **Alternative**
Fertilization; *Sperm Banks and Fertility Clinics, Self Insemination,*
Surrogacy, Foster Children, Stepchildren, Abortion, Name
Changes; *Changing Your Name, Changing Your Name After Marriage,*
Changing Your Name After Divorce, Changing Your Child's Name

BEFORE WE TALK ABOUT RIGHTS AND OBLIGATIONS OF FAMILY MEMBERS AND WHAT HAPPENS WHEN THE FAMILY BREAKS DOWN, WE SHOULD CONSIDER THE BASIC FACTS ABOUT THE BUILDING OF FAMILIES. SINCE THE LAW DIFFERS DRAMATICALLY FROM PROVINCE TO PROVINCE ON MANY OF THE FOLLOWING SUBJECTS, THIS CHAPTER PRESENTS A BASIC OVERVIEW. WHEN YOU GO ABOUT FORMING YOUR OWN FAMILY, YOU WILL UNDOUBTEDLY RUN INTO THE LAW OF THE FAMILY IN YOUR PROVINCE.

COHABITATION

Two people of the same or opposite sexes cohabit when they share a common residence or residences, have an intimate relationship, share household responsibilities and are financially interdependent. Whether a couple cohabits is a question of fact. The number of years required for cohabitation depends on the particular aspect of the law involved. For spousal support rights to accrue to a couple, for example, they must live together for a specified number of years which varies from province to province; some provinces do not give support rights to unmarried couples at all. Same sex couples have support rights only in Ontario, although this is currently subject to appeal. A couple may be cohabiting and have a right to employment benefits and insurance protection after only one year. For income tax purposes, however, two people are considered to cohabit if they live together for one year, although the tax statute recognizes only opposite sex couples. A comprehensive discussion of the meaning of the term cohabitation is found in Chapter 9, "Common Law Couples." Chapter 10, "Same Sex Couples," also addresses the issue.

MARRIAGE

Each province makes its own rules about the formal requirements of marriage. The following general principles apply with minor variations across the country.

Formal Requirements of Marriage

For their marriage to be valid, a couple must meet the following requirements:
• the parties must be of the opposite sex;

- both parties must be of the provincially prescribed age of consent (in Nova Scotia and PEI, 16; in Alberta, Manitoba, Ontario, Quebec and New Brunswick, 18; in British Columbia, Saskatchewan, Newfoundland, and the Territories, 19). If either party is under the age of consent, a parent must consent on their behalf or a judge must make an order allowing the marriage to proceed;
- both parties must have the mental capacity to understand the nature of the ceremony and its consequences;
- both parties must consent to the marriage without duress or misunderstanding;
- the husband and wife may not be too closely related by blood or marriage. In Ontario, for instance, a woman can't marry her daughter's ex-husband or her ex-husband's uncle. These rules are called "prohibited degrees of consanguinity," and they vary provincially. A list is available where marriage licences are issued;
- neither person can be married to someone else. A person who has been married before must prove that he or she is divorced, with a Divorce Certificate if the divorce was granted in Canada, or if the divorce was granted in a foreign jurisdiction, with a lawyer's opinion in the form prescribed by the province. (For a foreign divorce opinion, a lawyer will charge about $100.) Failure to disclose a prior marriage or prove a valid divorce constitutes bigamy and may be subject to criminal prosecution;
- the couple must publicize banns or obtain a marriage licence within a prescribed time before the wedding; and
- in most provinces, the couple must exchange vows using prescribed language, and they must be pronounced husband and wife in standard form.

Void and Voidable Marriages

A marriage that fails to meet any of these requirements is void. A void marriage was never a valid marriage and is dissolved by annulment. A voidable marriage occurs when a marriage meets all formal legal requirements, but one spouse demonstrates some incapacity (usually sexual in nature) that gives the other the option to obtain an annulment. If the spouse doesn't seek an annulment, the voidable marriage remains valid.

Both void and voidable marriages are dissolved by annulment. Divorce only dissolves a valid marriage. Annulment is discussed in Chapter 13, "Divorce, Religious Divorce and Annulment."

Spouses in void and voidable marriages—and their children—have the same rights and obligations as parties to a valid marriage except in Quebec (where property division is permitted only if you were innocent to the invalid marriage, and where spousal support is available only in limited circumstances and for a period of no more than two years). Only the method of dissolving the marriage differs.

FYI

The federal **Divorce Act** *provides a single set of rules for divorce across the country, including custody of children and support. However, the provinces have also enacted statutes that deal with these issues, so one federal and one or more provincial statutes often apply to the same situation.*

BIRTH

Registration

Each province keeps its own birth records and imposes different rules about birth registration. In general, a medical practitioner must send a notice of birth to the provincial registrar within a few days of a child's birth. The notice identifies only the child and the mother. Within thirty days of the birth, the mother must submit a prescribed document, usually called a Certificate of Live Birth, that becomes the registration of birth. The mother's marital status must be included in this document.

The mother must mail the Certificate of Live Birth to the appropriate provincial ministry with the required form and fee. The province then issues a Birth Certificate. Only the parents or the child may apply for a Birth Certificate.

To meet the requirements of the law regarding registration, the child must carry the husband's surname or a hyphenated form of the mother and father's surnames if the mother is married to the father and was living with him at the time of conception. If the mother is unmarried, she is not required to disclose information about the father unless she and the father agree, and the father acknowledges that he is the parent. If they agree and file the required documentation, the child may be given the father's surname or some combination of the parents' names. If no father is disclosed, a baby must carry the mother's surname.

If a child is later adopted, the birth records are amended to show the adoptive parents as if they were the natural parents, and reference to the child's pre-adoption name is removed.

Cases of alternative reproduction raise more problematic issues involving birth records. In the cases of insemination by donor and in-vitro fertilization, the individuals who will raise the child will be shown as the parents only if they are married. If the sperm has been donated, the donor might successfully challenge the presumption of paternity created by the birth registration if he brings an application before the court (except in Newfoundland, Quebec and the Yukon, where the law specifically provides that a sperm donor is not the father unless he is married to or living with the mother). Unmarried couples do not have automatic rights for the father to register, and so if the "social father" is not the sperm donor, he will not be shown on the birth records.

- A surrogate mother, who carries a child on behalf of another person, is registered as the mother of the child despite the circumstances of the conception and/or birth. If the surrogate mother is married, her husband will be presumed to be the father. These results occur regardless of the source of the ovum (surrogacy is discussed in more detail later in this chapter).

- If a child's social father is also the sperm donor, he may be recorded as a parent if he files the birth registration form and acknowledges that he is the father. This would give him standing as a parent, and the surrogate's husband would no longer be regarded as the child's father.

- If the social father is recorded as the father on the birth records, the social mother can adopt the child by stepparent adoption, discussed later in this chapter. If the social father is not recorded on the birth records, both social parents must undergo the full procedures for adoption, discussed below under Agency and Private Adoption.

- To give a child a surname different than either the mother's or father's, one spouse must legally change surnames before the birth, or the child and/or the parent(s) may seek a formal name change at any time after the birth, as discussed later in this chapter.

Paternity

The issue of paternity arises in claims for child support in defence to a claim for custody or access or simply to establish the identity of a child's biological father. Under children's or family law statutes in all provinces, courts may order blood tests, or the people involved in a paternity dispute may agree on them. Usually a man will consent to a blood test once the issue is raised, since a court can be critical of his refusal to do so and will usually order the test anyway.

A paternity test usually involves blood testing, which costs about $400. A blood test cannot conclusively prove that the man is a child's father; it can only prove the man is not the father. The results of the blood test are expressed as a probability of paternity. In most cases in which paternity is assumed, the probability of paternity exceeds ninety-eight percent. If the result is questionable or inconclusive (a result of eighty percent or less) the court may require DNA tests. DNA testing costs about $1000 and provides entirely accurate results.

A person who is declared to be a father must pay child support just like any other father and is entitled to make claims for custody or access. All defences relating to the circumstances of the conception are irrelevant.

FYI

Since 1982, the Canadian **Charter of Rights and Freedoms** *has formed part of Canada's Constitution. The Charter guarantees everyone certain essential rights and liberties, such as freedom of speech, freedom of religion, and equal protection under the law. If a law is found to violate the Charter, it is unconstitutional and must be modified or repealed. In recent years, the Charter has been used to change provincial and federal statutes that were perceived to be discriminatory.*

ADOPTION

Adoption laws and procedures could fill a whole book. The following discussion summarizes the general principles of the three types of adoption available in Canada. If you are contemplating adoption, this section will give you an idea of the procedures and considerations involved. You will then be ready to do further research or obtain professional assistance.

Agency and Private Adoption

Through the process of adoption, a person who is not biologically a member of a family becomes one under the law. There are two approaches to adoption in Canada. An agency adoption is facilitated by a public agency specializing in adoption; while a private adoption is arranged through a private agency or by an independent facilitator. Public agencies have very few newborns available, and typically handle adoptions of children with special needs. Private agencies primarily handle adoptions of healthy newborns. Independent facilitators—usually lawyers or social workers with the appropriate adoption licences—act for potential adoptive parents and for birth mothers looking for adoptive parents, and assist with matchmaking before the child is born.

Regardless of the licensed authority that manages the adoption, most of the legal process is the same. But the cost can vary substantially, ranging from $2000 to $20,000, depending on agency fees, legal fees, and whether any of the birth mother's expenses may be paid under provincial law.

There are two stages of eligibility screening in adoption. The first involves an assessment by the public or private agency of the adoption application. The assessment is based on age, health, marital status, family structure and stability, employment status and income. In the last thirty years, there has been a marked decline in the number of children available for adoption, especially newborns, and the demand for children now far exceeds the number available for adoption. As a result, public and private agencies apply these initial criteria strictly. They usually eliminate older and financially disadvantaged parents or consider them to be eligible only for special needs children. Many suitable parents who simply do not exhibit the same desirable characteristics as other applicants are also eliminated at this stage.

Facilitators and agencies will accept applications for adoption from gay men and lesbians, as long as they describe themselves as single (except in British Columbia, where adoption by same sex couples has been recently approved by legislative reform). However, many choose to pursue adoption through an independent facilitator, who can search for a birth mother willing to have her child adopted by a same sex couple.

The second stage of eligibility screening is the home study. This involves a series of home visits and meetings with the adoptive parent or parents, performed by a government or private agency. A private home study usually costs between $2000 and $5000. A home study performed by a government agency (usually a children's aid society) is free, but waiting lists are as long as five years. There is no guarantee that the result of the home study will be positive, or that it will be based on unbiased criteria. If it is positive, the provincial director of children's services will authorize the placement of a child with the adoptive parent(s). Even then, there is no guarantee that an adoption will occur.

Before an adoption is finalized, the biological mother must consent to the placement of her child with a particular parent or parents. Before making her decision, she may review extensive personal information about the individuals. Because of the limited supply of children, biological mothers can be very picky about adoptive parents. Many potential parents who are older, financially insecure, or gay or lesbian have difficulty finding a birth mother who will choose them from all the other potential parents.

If a child does become available for adoption after the adoptive parents have completed all the preliminary procedures, the child is placed with the new family temporarily. Within this statutory period (usually thirty days) the birth mother can change her mind at any time. Depending on the province, if the mother doesn't change her mind after six months or more, the adoptive parents may file a court application for a formal adoption, assisted by the agency or a private facilitator.

Same sex couples must obtain an adoption order in the name of one spouse only, and can then consider stepparent adoption so the other spouse can become a parent. (Stepparent adoption is discussed later in this chapter.) The only exception to this is in British Columbia, where recent legislative reform gives same sex couples equal rights to adoption.

An adoption order creates parental rights and responsibilities on behalf of the adoptive parents and terminates the parental rights and responsibilities of the biological parents. Once granted, it cannot be appealed or overturned. All provinces have procedures for amending a child's original birth certificate after adoption, so that the records show the adoptive parents as if they were the natural parents.

International Adoption

Many couples choose foreign adoption because there are more children available, more quickly, with less selective standards for parents than domestic adoptions. The cost of international adoption usually exceeds the cost of conventional adoption, but for many adoptive parents the benefits outweigh this disadvantage. In fact, current figures indicate that two-thirds of all children who have been adopted by Canadians have come from foreign countries.

The recent Hague Convention on International Adoption establishes guidelines for cooperation between countries, sets standards to curtail child trafficking, and gives legal recognition to adoptions that take place under the Convention. The Convention was agreed upon quite recently, on December 3, 1996, so it is hard to predict how it will change the process of international adoption. What we do know is that procedures should be more streamlined and reciprocal as time goes on.

The first step in international adoption is to identify the countries that have children available and that have arrangements with Canada to facilitate the process. The best way to start is by contacting the adoptive parents' association in your city, which will provide information, contacts and names of people who have adopted children from other countries.

FYI

The Adoption Council of Canada in Ottawa (613-235-1566) can point you to your nearest local association. Other good contacts are the North American Council on Adoptive Children (612-644-3036) and the National Adoption Information Clearinghouse (202-842-1919).

The National Adoption Desk, a Canadian federal service, has adoption programs with other countries and provides services to potential parents. Most provinces have agencies within their departments of community or social services to assist parents with international adoptions. Foreign adoptions that are arranged by cooperating governments involve the same application procedures, screening—and red tape—as local adoptions.

Intermediaries that regularly arrange foreign adoptions are also widely available. They may be associations that operate for profit or not for profit. Some are individual lawyers or experienced social workers. If you go the intermediary route, you should be sure that the intermediary is properly accredited, has a good reputation and complies with the country's adoption laws, and you should conduct careful, independent research before you retain anyone. You can also arrange an international adoption privately by contacting foreign countries directly, but this is a complicated process that is not recommended.

Each country has its own application requirements. Most have age restrictions, marital status requirements, and financial standards. Usually, you must complete about fifteen different forms and provide other documentation such as photographs, income tax returns, health and police certificates, reference letters, and marriage certificates if the country requires that the parents be married. The waiting period for a child ranges from six months to five years, depending on the country. Once the adoption procedure begins, you usually have to wait four to six months to bring the child to Canada. Fees differ from country to country. Some countries also require follow-up reports or further payments after the adoption is completed. In most programs, the new parents go to the country, arrange for visas, complete other documentation, and bring the child home.

All provinces require an international home study performed by an accredited agency or social worker. Some provinces recognize home studies only if they're conducted by a provincial government authority.

The legal adoption process may be completed in the foreign country or at home. Adopting at home involves the same provincial procedures as a regular adoption, including a director's certificate and court application. Adopting in the foreign country is easier and therefore more popular. The foreign adoption is recognized as valid in all provinces but Quebec, where a court application is required to complete the process. If you adopt the child in the foreign country, you must then comply with immigration regulations to bring the child home. This is done by completing forms with a Canada Immigration Centre and forwarding them to the Canadian embassy for processing. Provincial authorities must then authorize the immigration application. Inoculations will be required before a child can be brought to Canada from certain countries. You should leave plenty of time to resolve immigration issues, although immigration officials usually give priority to adoptions if you're in a rush.

Stepparent and Family Adoption

In most provinces, adoption procedures are less complicated for a person who:

- is married to or cohabiting with the parent of the child, or
- is a relative of the child by blood, marriage or adoption.

In such cases, the person seeking the adoption applies to the court, with or without the parent of the child joining in the application. If the applicant is a stepparent, notification must be sent to the non-custodial parent, or the non-custodial parent must consent to the adoption. In the case of adoption by relatives, both of the child's natural parents must receive notice or give their consent. The only exceptions to these notice requirements arise if the non-custodial parent is dead, missing or has abandoned the child.

An adoption order extinguishes any parental rights of the biological parent who doesn't join in the adoption. If a mother and her new spouse adopt her child of a previous marriage, the natural father loses his parental rights; if a woman's parents adopt her child, the woman loses her parental rights.

Under some provincial statutes governing stepparent and family adoptions, all parents who do not join in the application lose their rights as parents. If one parent wants to retain parental rights, he or she must apply for adoption jointly with the the adopting parent. With this serious result in mind, you should retain a lawyer if you're considering a stepparent or family adoption, if only to confirm that your proposed adoption does not create this or other unanticipated problems. The process is informal and relatively straightforward, so the lawyer's fee for assisting with the application and attending the hearing is usually relatively inexpensive.

If consent is given or is not required, the court will grant the adoption order in most cases after a brief hearing. If the non-custodial parent refuses to consent, however, the court will hold an informal hearing, often in private, to determine if the adoption is in the child's best interests. Once the court grants an adoption order, it is final and cannot be appealed.

FYI

In Re K., a recent landmark case in Ontario, the court granted stepparent adoption orders to four lesbian women respecting their partners' children who were conceived through alternative fertilization. Several similar orders have now been made in Ontario following Re K., and another claim is underway in Calgary. In British Columbia, recent legislative reform has granted adoption rights, including stepparent adoption, to same sex couples. In other provinces, adoption legislation still excludes same sex partners from adopting each other's children.

ALTERNATIVE FERTILIZATION

Some single women, lesbians, and women with infertile male partners choose to become pregnant through alternative methods of fertilization. This section addresses legal aspects of such situations. It does not address procedures for treating infertility, since these are regulated by the medical profession. Over the last twenty years, reproductive technology has evolved swiftly, and the law has failed to keep pace. As individuals take further advantage of reproductive technologies, we can expect to see wide-sweeping legislative and judicial response. In the meantime, if you are considering modern reproduction, you should remember that you're walking on untested legal ground.

Sperm Banks and Fertility Clinics

The future of sperm banks in Canada is unknown at this time. At the time that this book goes to print, a federal bill is in the works that would make it illegal to pay sperm donors. If the bill becomes law, the number of donors may decline substantially.

All sperm banks screen donors for genetic and sexually transmitted diseases, including AIDS. The tests are done at the time of donation. The sperm is then frozen and released six months later, only after the donor has passed a second HIV test. Most sperm banks also provide profiles of the donors so that potential mothers can select a donor with specific characteristics. Most doctors who assist with fertilization charge an initial fee of about $1000 and a smaller fee for each cycle of fertilization procedures.

Many Canadian infertility clinics will not assist single or lesbian women to conceive. This is clearly discriminatory, but no one has formally challenged these rules. Many sperm banks are affiliated with clinics and provide sperm only to the clinic's patients, thus increasing the difficulties that single women and lesbians face in the area of alternative fertilization. If you run up against such barriers, your choices are to demand equal treatment, to attempt to find a friendly clinic through a lesbian mothers' group, or to try self insemination.

FYI

A Toronto company, ReproMed, will provide sperm to qualified medical personnel across Canada, without screening recipients' marital status or sexual orientation. ReproMed can be reached at 416-233-1212.

Self Insemination

An increasing number of women, especially lesbians, are choosing to inseminate themselves with sperm from a known or unknown donor. Both methods require planning and research. You can find contacts and background information through fertility clinics and lesbian organizations.

Sperm from a known donor provides slightly more security from genetic and sexually transmitted diseases, since you can insist on tests and determine for yourself whether the person is taking health risks. However, since HIV may become apparent only after an incubation period of weeks or months, using fresh sperm may not provide certain protection against HIV and AIDS, even if the sperm has been tested.

Some people prefer to use known donors because it allows them to identify personal characteristics that the child might inherit. The difficulties with known donors are finding a donor who will agree to become involved, and the risk that the donor might later assert parental rights to custody or access.

If you choose to inseminate yourself with sperm from an unknown donor, you usually have to work with a runner, who finds donors, screens them for HIV and other diseases, and delivers fresh sperm. You can find a runner and more information through reproductive technology groups and lesbian parenting organizations.

Some sperm banks and private associations in the United States provide women with frozen sperm. I am told that many lesbians in Canada are undergoing self insemination with American sperm rather than using known donors or local runners. If you choose this route, you should make sure donors are screened for genetic and sexually transmitted diseases, that appropriate measures have been taken for collection and storage of the sperm, and that you are not breaching some federal or provincial regulation in the process. Again, reproductive technology groups and lesbian parenting organizations can help you.

Sperm obtained through a sperm bank usually comes from a donor who has already relinquished his legal rights. But women obtaining sperm privately from known or unknown donors often ask the donor to sign a contract that establishes clear rules for both parties. Under such contracts, the woman agrees to relinquish all claims to child support, while the donor relinquishes parental rights to custody or access.

Unfortunately, donor contracts present many legal challenges. They have not been tested in the courts, and are probably unenforceable. In several recent cases in the U.S., courts have disregarded the agreements, deciding that a donor was the child's father and giving the donor access or custody. This could happen in all provinces and territories in Canada except Newfoundland and the Yukon, where family law statutes say specifically that a sperm donor is not the father of a child unless he is married to or living with the mother. Quebec's Civil Code contains a similar provision but it also expressly prohibits donor contracts. Further, it is illegal to purchase human tissue, and some lawyers believe that purchasing sperm or paying a runner to obtain sperm violates this law. If the proposed federal bill on the subject becomes law, both activities will be offences punishable by fine or imprisonment.

With these potential risks in mind, other disadvantages appear. Donor contracts specify the identity of the man donating the sperm and could provide evidence of paternity if a court set aside the contract. The contract could also provide evidence of an illegal activity if payment was exchanged between the donor and the recipient. For lesbians, donor contracts may also provide proof of their sexual orientation, which might be used against them in a claim for custody or access. Given the untested nature of donor contracts and the risk of custody or access claims, many lesbians say that they would never use sperm from a known donor. Donor contracts are also discussed in Chapter 12, "Domestic Contracts."

FYI

In debates over same sex equality, traditionalists lament the change in "our concept of the family." Others argue, however, that the law and the opinions of some lag behind the family's considerable evolution. The traditional family, with one working man, one homemaker woman and two children is no longer the norm—if ever it was. And family values differ from one family to the next. This is reality, and as Madam Justice L'Heureux-Dubé of Canada's Supreme Court has said, "It is not anti-family to support alternative family forms." This seems especially true considering that in all forms of family the opportunity to preserve the traditional family's valuable qualities—support, interdependencies, loyalty, values, welfare and love—inherently exists.

SURROGACY

A surrogate mother bears a child for someone else. The surrogate mother may be genetically related to the child or to the person to whom she gives the child after birth, or she may be unrelated to the child or its intended parent.

Most surrogacy arrangements involve an agreement between the surrogate mother and the soon-to-be social parents. Under the agreement, the surrogate mother may consent to bear the child, surrender the child to the social parents after birth, and agree to the adoption of the child by the social parents. In return, the social parents may agree to pay for the surrogate mother's medical and other expenses. However, surrogacy agreements present two major problems. First, it is illegal to make any payment in exchange for the adoption of a child and if the proposed federal bill on reproductive technology is passed, it will be illegal to pay or procure a surrogate. Second, these agreements may not be enforceable. They are not recognized by statute in any province except Quebec, where they are void. In other provinces, under common law, any agreement about the transfer of custody of a child is void. Given these legal uncertainties, if the surrogate mother changes her mind and refuses to surrender the child or consent to the adoption, the social parents have no recourse—it doesn't matter that they have an agreement or have paid some of the mother's expenses during her pregnancy.

After registering the birth of a child born to a surrogate mother, as discussed earlier in this chapter under Birth Registration, parents may proceed with adoption. If the social father is also the sperm donor and is recorded as the father at the time of birth, stepparent adoption applies. Otherwise, private adoption applies.

FOSTER CHILDREN

Foster parents provide short-term care for a child who lacks a permanent home. The child may be the subject of child protection proceedings or may be an orphan who has not been adopted by a family. Foster parents must be licensed by provincial child welfare authorities. Foster parents have parental rights and responsibilities during the period of foster care, but have no rights or obligations with respect to the foster children thereafter.

Many child welfare authorities try to place a gay or lesbian teenager with a gay or lesbian couple, and I am told that this kind of arrangement has been a successful parenting method for many gay men in Canada. If you're interested in becoming a foster parent, contact your province's child welfare office about the process, and talk to other foster parents about their experiences.

STEPCHILDREN

If you marry, and you or your spouse bring children to the relationship, the non-biological parent becomes a stepparent. If you cohabit, and either of you bring children to the relationship, you may not have the formal title, but you'll have the same rights and responsibilities as a stepparent. Stepparents have obligations to support any child to whom they show a settled intention to treat as their own. Stepparents also have the right to claim custody of or access to a child.

ABORTION

In 1988, the Supreme Court of Canada heard the *Morgentaler* case, a challenge to the Criminal Code provision that prohibited abortion unless the woman's health was endangered by the pregnancy. A majority of the court struck down the provision because it violated the Charter guarantee of security of the person. Although there is no legislation in place that regulates abortion, the abolishment of the Criminal Code provision gives every woman freedom of choice.

A woman's right to control when and if she becomes a mother was confirmed in a 1989 decision of the Supreme Court of Canada known as *Daigle*. In that case, Chantal Daigle's former boyfriend had obtained an injunction preventing her from having an abortion. Although she disregarded the injunction and went to the U.S. to have an abortion before the appeal was heard, Daigle was successful in the end. The Supreme Court of Canada concluded that there is no fetal or parental right to stop a woman from having an abortion.

On a practical basis, a woman's freedom to choose is restricted by her access to abortion services. Fewer than a third of hospitals in Canada perform abortions. There are no abortion services in PEI, and only two doctors perform them in Newfoundland. Some provinces do not provide medical funding for abortions. Access to abortions is also hindered by anti-choice protesters, except in Alberta, British Columbia and Ontario, where "bubble zones" are imposed around clinics and doctors' offices to prevent protesting and interference with or intimidation of patients and workers around the clinics.

FYI

If you have any questions about access to or coverage of abortions in your province, call the Canadian Abortion Rights Action League (CARAL) at 416-961-1507.

NAME CHANGES

Changing Your Name

If you're over the age of 16 in Ontario, 19 in the Territories, and 18 in all other provinces, and if you've lived in a province for more than three months and can legally live in Canada, you can change your name, for any reason, by applying to the Director of Vital Statistics in your province. You must provide a fee, surrender your old birth certificate, and complete a form, available with other details from the vital statistics office. In most cases, you'll receive a new birth certificate reflecting your new name within six to eight weeks. You can then use the new birth certificate to obtain other documents, such as your passport and driver's licence.

Changing Your Name After Marriage

A legal name change after marriage proceeds in the same way as other adult name changes, except that you also include a copy of your marriage certificate with your application to the vital statistics office. You must surrender your old birth certificate before the office will issue a new one. You can then use the new birth certificate to obtain other identifying documents.

Many women never change their surname legally after marriage. Instead, they adopt their spouse's surname when signing documents and agreements such as banking and credit card documents and even land registration documents. This is called a common law name change. You can effect such a name change by providing your bank or financial institution with a copy of your marriage certificate and asking them to amend their records. However, you should consider three things if you take this approach:

- Be sure to change your passport. You may be prevented from crossing a border if your passport carries your maiden name and your airline ticket carries your married name. You can change your name on your passport by taking your birth certificate and your marriage certificate to your local passport office and paying a $5 fee;
- If you move to another province, the new province may not recognize your common law name change, although this may have little or no

practical effect on your life;
- If you ever remarry, you should use your legal rather than your common law name on the marriage licence.

Changing Your Name After Divorce

If you legally changed your name on marriage by applying to the vital statistics office, you may apply again to reassume your maiden name by including a copy of your divorce judgment with your application. If you make your application within ninety days after the divorce, you pay no fee for the name change. You are not, however, *required* to change your name back, regardless of what anyone says.

If you adopted a common law name change after you were married, you can revert to your maiden name after divorce by providing the relevant institutions with copies of your divorce certificate. If your passport reflects your common law name change, you can change it again by bringing your old passport, your birth certificate, and your certificate of divorce to the passport office and paying another $5 fee. As long as you did not apply legally to change your name after marriage, your maiden name will still be recorded with the vital statistics office.

Changing Your Child's Name

A child's name can be changed by applying to the court under the relevant provincial legislation or by ordinary usage. Every parent who has right of access to a child must consent to, or at least receive notice of, a request for any name change of a child. If the child is twelve years of age or older the child must also consent in writing to the change, but does not have to attend the hearing after providing the consent.

If both parents consent to the change, the court will order the name change and it will then be registered with vital statistics. The vital statistics office in your province will answer procedural questions and send you the required forms.

If one parent does not agree to the change, the person seeking the name change must prove in court that the change is in the child's best interests. Such contested cases tend to favour keeping the current name over a change, unless the opposing parent has no contact at all with the child. Courts usually consider the amount of contact and the emotional and symbolic ties between the child and the opposing parent when refusing to allow a name change. Sometimes courts don't allow name changes even when they are sought to avoid confusion between siblings or the inconvenience of a difficult name. On the other hand, courts frequently grant name changes despite strong opposition from one parent.

If you assume a new surname for your child through ordinary usage, without application to a court, your former spouse may apply to the court to prevent you from using the new name. Courts decide each case individually, although they tend to favour keeping the child's current name. If the applicant is successful, the court may award costs to be paid by the other parent.

Many separation agreements prohibit changing the children's names. These clauses are totally enforceable and should be included in every separation agreement.

If you are separated and are considering changing your child's name, you should examine your separation agreement to confirm that you can proceed. A lawyer or a paralegal can advise you in less than an hour about the procedures involved in applying for a child's name change in your province.

CHAPTER TWO

How Anyone Can Settle a Family Law Case (or Almost) and How to Save Thousands in Legal Fees If You Can't

IN THIS CHAPTER: Appreciating Emotional Barriers to Settlement, Why You Should Do Everything You Can to Settle, Settlement by Nature Involves Compromise, Tax Implications of Settlement, Order of Issues to be Resolved; Children's Issues: Custody and Access, Property, The Matrimonial Home, Child Support, Spousal Support, Other Claims, Separation Agreements, The Divorce

THIS CHAPTER IS FOUND BEFORE A DISCUSSION OF THE LAW RELATING TO SEPARATION TO REMIND YOU THAT TWO REASONABLE PEOPLE WHO WISH TO AVOID CONFLICT *CAN* RESOLVE MATTERS ARISING FROM THE BREAKDOWN OF THEIR RELATIONSHIP, IF THEY SET THEIR MINDS TO IT. IT ALSO OCCURS AT THIS POINT IN THE BOOK BECAUSE THERE'S A LOGICAL ORDER IN WHICH ISSUES SHOULD BE ADDRESSED IN SETTLEMENT CONSIDERATIONS, AND THIS BOOK FOLLOWS THAT ORDER. THIS CHAPTER IS THEREFORE INTENDED TO PROVIDE BOTH A FOCUS FOR YOUR SETTLEMENT DISCUSSIONS AND AN OUTLINE FOR THE SEPARATION SECTION OF THIS BOOK.

APPRECIATING EMOTIONAL BARRIERS TO SETTLEMENT

The process of emotional recovery following separation is comparable to mourning the death of a loved one. The process follows several stages: denial, anger, sadness, loss, acceptance and resolution. Therapists agree that the loss of separation compares closely to grief and that recovery usually proceeds through these stages. But many therapists also believe that separation is actually more emotionally complicated than bereavement, since it can involve rejection, disillusionment, jealousy and unrequited love.

If your partner shows any of these signs to an extreme degree, you should try to appreciate the stage in the recovery cycle that he or she has reached. If separation has just occurred, or if your partner seems stuck in a stage of denial, anger or sadness, you may find it difficult to have reasonable discussions about settlement. Your partner may behave irrationally, change attitudes or positions daily, or simply refuse to be reasonable. In such cases, you may be better off trying to resolve matters on an interim basis, leaving the larger, more final issues for resolution at a later date. If you have children, you will have to address as soon as possible after separation the issue of who will reside with the children and who will move out, and devise a short-term plan for sharing your duties as parents. You should then leave the other issues until both of you have recovered your emotional equilibrium. Pushing ahead in these circumstances may simply waste money on legal fees and aggravate your own emotional stress. In some cases, complete emotional recovery takes years. One spouse may be incapable of reasonable behaviour, while the other feels caught in limbo, without much hope of resolution. So, although it's often advisable to wait until your spouse is emotionally ready for resolution, it's not always possible, or beneficial to either spouse, to wait forever.

WHY YOU SHOULD DO EVERYTHING YOU CAN TO SETTLE

There are many reasons to avoid litigation. Some are obvious: it is costly, it can take months or even years, and it can consume your life and fill you with negative energy. Other reasons to avoid litigation are less obvious but even more important: it fuels hostilities, solidifies resentment and reinforces a pattern of interaction between you and your spouse that can become chronic and harmful. Many couples never forget the negative comments they've exchanged in the course of ligitation.

Who wins in all of this? Is it you, after winning, consumed by anger and financially strapped? Perhaps you think fighting the best fight will provide financial security for you or your children. If you manage to litigate in a cost-effective way—a rare occurrence indeed—you might be right. But in the long run, you'll probably be sacrificing a lot for that security. Any litigation is emotionally stressful, but litigation in the family creates its own set of stresses. The most notable of the risks to emotional health posed by family battles is the risk of irreparable harm to children who witness their parents' ongoing hostility and conflict. Even if you protect your children from direct conflict, which is rarely possible in litigating families, angry spouses make distracted, insensitive parents. So, the message from this lecture is clear: Go forth and settle!

SETTLEMENT BY NATURE INVOLVES COMPROMISE

Settlement involves finding a middle ground. It involves delineating the issues, estimating the differences between positions, evaluating legal costs, and compromising. Sometimes a compromise is easier if it is based on principles like *quid pro quo*: you give a little on the business value, your partner gives a little on support. Other times it's simpler to split the difference between each spouse's position. You can construct a useful framework for settlement by exchanging written offers that address all of the issues. You can make an offer that takes the legal fees and risks of litigation into account and hope that your partner accepts it or makes a counter-offer that brings you closer together. Both parties have to give a little—and sometimes a lot—to settle.

Litigation is at least fifty percent posturing. Parties to litigation frequently assume unsupportable claims and untenable positions to intimidate the other side, increase the other side's perception of the risk of the action, and generally up the ante. A good example is the inclusion of a claim of $100,000 in damages for breach of duties to shareholders in a family business. The facts may well justify the claim, but it is usually added to maximize recovery—to obtain a larger share of the equity in the matrimonial home, for example. If the claim proceeds to trial, its success will depend on the facts, the presentation at trial of the evidence and the law, and the judge who determines it. But damage awards are usually fairly low even in the most awful cases. If the claimant spends $50,000 in legal fees for a trial, a damage award of $35,000 will not be cost-effective. However, if there are a number of issues that remain unresolved, making a trial unavoidable, the damage claim becomes a potential bonus.

Sometimes these "up-the-ante" positions increase the risks involved in litigation; other times, they're transparent ploys. In settlement discussions, both sides must evaluate all the issues in light of the cost of litigation. You must identify positions that create potential costs and fashion a compromise. If a claim is totally transparent, you will often succeed by holding firm to that conclusion and refusing to give credit for that particular claim—even while giving in on other issues.

It is important to remember that the results of litigation can never be predicted with certainty. You can predict, however, that neither party will succeed entirely on every issue. Settlement provides both parties with a measure of control over the result and the costs of the dispute. While you may think that you're capitulating by settling various issues before trial, in the big picture you'll often be doing better than you would have if you'd proceeded to trial.

TAX IMPLICATIONS OF SETTLEMENT

Not only does settlement provide control over the process, it also provides real tax advantages in some situations. Courts do not fashion tax-effective settlements. It is not the court's role to be tax-minded; the court must simply resolve the issues according to the province's family law statute and make an appropriate order for payment of money or transfer of property. In a complicated financial situation, especially one in which you or your spouse have complex tax concerns or in which you or your spouse own an interest in a privately held corporation, out-of-court settlement is usually preferable to a court-ordered resolution. In such cases, you should retain an accountant with expertise in family law to advise you. Such an expert can help you in dividing property most efficiently, assistance that's well worth the fees involved.

ORDER OF ISSUES TO BE RESOLVED

There is a necessary, logical order for considering and resolving issues arising from separation. You need to determine custody and access arrangements before you know whether someone will be living in the former home. You need to determine each party's property settlement before you know whether one will be able to afford to buy the other's interest in the home. You need to know the amount of property and child support before you know if spousal support is an issue. The following discussion expands on this logical order and guides you in understanding and resolving each issue along the way.

Children's Issues: Custody and Access

Developing a parenting plan that acknowledges the particular needs of your children is the first step in settling any case. The sooner you do this, the better it is for each child involved. Even if you and your partner stubbornly disagree on every issue, you must deal with child-related issues if you want to avoid total family armageddon. For the cold-hearted, there are tactical reasons for resolving these issues as well: judges and assessors often regard a parent who will not settle children's issues as angry, selfish and unreasonable. Such a moral judgment against you, whether founded or unfounded, will seriously undermine your position on financial issues.

Specific child-related issues are set out in Chapters 3 and 7. If, after reviewing this information and discussing it with your spouse you still cannot resolve matters, you should consider attending mediation or family therapy together before you proceed with separation. When you consider the effects of litigation on children, along with the costs of pursuing custodial issues in the courts, spending a thousand dollars or less on child-focused counselling will always be money well spent.

Property

There are four steps to resolving property issues in every case. Couples should try to follow these steps themselves, without lawyers, to attempt to reach their own resolution. Even if the attempt fails, the information you compile and analyze before you meet with a lawyer will save you thousands of dollars in legal fees. If you've been involved in an unmarried opposite sex or same sex relationship, statutory law does not entitle you to equal division of assets; instead, you must assert trust claims to obtain property interests. (These issues are discussed in Chapter 5, "Property." Issues related to common law and same sex couples are discussed in Chapters 9 and 10.) While the entitlement may differ, the process of resolving the property issues will generally be the same.

Financial Statements

All provinces provide a form for disclosing property information under family law rules, usually referred to as a Financial Statement. In some provinces, there are two types of financial statements: one for married couples and one for unmarried cohabitees. The forms themselves provide guidance on how to complete the statements, while a basic understanding of property laws in your province (as explained in Chapter 5) will provide the necessary background.

You will need to do some research before you can finalize your financial statement. For example, you will need a reliable evaluation of your home (usually provided in writing by a real estate agent), your savings (compiled from recent bank statements), and all other assets and liabilities in your name. You will need to consider whether you should make deductions from these values to reflect taxes and other costs that are inherent in the asset. You may deduct taxes from the value of RRSPs, for instance, if they are likely to be cashed out for immediate needs; and you may deduct real estate commissions and legal fees from the value of your house if you'll have to sell it.

By completing a financial statement and comparing it with your spouse's, you will both gain an understanding of how property should be divided. You can obtain blank financial statements from a family lawyer, family courthouse or some stationery and legal printing companies. A list of the names of these forms in each province is found in Appendix A.

FYI

If you retain a lawyer, either to litigate or negotiate your separation, the completion of a financial statement is always the first step in the process. You can reduce this cost by completing a first draft of your financial statement and compiling all of the documents that prove your figures.

Proving the Figures

Once you've recorded estimated values in your financial statement and exchanged statements with your spouse, you'll need to compile all back-up documents. You may already have obtained some of these documents, while others will be harder to find. If you're entitled to receive credit for assets that you brought to the marriage, you may need to dig out old tax returns or locate old bank statements to back up your figures. A prudent lawyer will insist on a back-up document for every figure in both financial statements. If such a document is not available, lawyers will ask their clients if they will accept the unproved figure. In your own settlement discussions, you may avoid these strict rules by agreeing on values together. For instance, you may remember that the car that your spouse brought to the marriage was sold the next year for $500, or that you used $30,000 of your spouse's savings to buy a home shortly after the marriage. At the end of this stage, you should agree that most, if not all, of the values in each spouse's financial statement have been proved or agreed upon.

Delineating the Legal Issues and Areas of Dispute

In every province, there are hard and fast rules for property division between married couples. This means that there should be few areas left for dispute after your financial statements have been analyzed. If you're unmarried, property issues will centre on asserting or defending a trust claim or claims. In either case, one or two values or issues may remain hotly contested. Outstanding issues may involve debate about whether one spouse should lose credit for bringing a home into the marriage, or whether property should be unequally divided for some reason. Between unmarried spouses they may involve a trust claim over property. All unresolved issues should be identified on your settlement agenda. Defining the issues that remain in dispute is the first step toward resolving them. If you and your spouse can sit down and discuss these matters, you may be able to resolve one or all of them by agreement. If you can't, you'll at least have a list of the few issues that remain outstanding.

Compromise

The final step in property settlement is, of course, resolving the outstanding valuation and legal issues. You may be able to do this by having further discussions with your spouse. You may get some assistance by retaining a lawyer to provide you with a written legal opinion on the unresolved matters. You may benefit from retaining an accountant skilled in family law matters to advise you of the tax issues arising from any settlement. You may find mediation to be the best answer, retaining a lawyer or someone skilled in such matters to discuss the law with you and help you both move toward settlement. You may both retain lawyers and have a four-way meeting with both spouses and both lawyers. All of these options beat litigation and are substantially cheaper in the long run than protracted negotiation, letter-writing, and posturing by lawyers. Legal and accounting opinions, mediation, arbitration and other settlement options are discussed in detail in Chapter 14, "Alternatives to Litigation." In case you fail to settle, the process of litigation is discussed in Chapter 15, "If You Must...The Structure of the Action."

The Matrimonial Home

Once you understand how the property division will shake out, you can address issues involving the matrimonial home. These usually focus on:

- whether one party will buy out the other's interest if both hold title or if a successful trust claim is contemplated;
- whether one party will have possession of the property for some period, usually with any children, before it is bought out or listed for sale; or
- whether the property should or must be sold immediately.

All of these considerations are discussed in detail in Chapter 6, "The Matrimonial Home," which will provide you with the background to discuss these issues and determine how they can be resolved. Again, if you cannot resolve them, the best and most cost-effective methods of reaching a resolution involve retaining a lawyer to give you an opinion; hiring two lawyers to engage in four-way settlement discussions; consulting an accountant experienced in family law (if the issue relates to whether you can afford to keep the home or how to structure a buy-out); or turning to a mediator or arbitrator.

Child Support

Under new child support guidelines, almost anyone can settle this issue. If you have developed a plan for parenting responsibilities, and if you can use a chart and address a few additional issues logically, you can settle child support. If you're considering resolution before May, 1997, some tax considerations may apply to you and may provide incentive to settle the issue quickly. Settlement of child support and its additional issues are considered in detail in Chapter 7.

Spousal Support

You can't decide upon entitlement, amount and duration of spousal support until you've resolved child-related issues, division of property and child support. This is because property settlement and child support will affect a potential recipient's need for spousal support. Equally, a potential payer will not know the extent to which he or she can afford to pay spousal support until these issues have been determined.

Spousal support is a less predictable area of the law than child support. It is not governed by any basic guidelines and usually involves issues such as the sacrifice and economic loss engendered by the relationship, the need for support, the ability to pay, the time required for retraining or becoming self-sufficient, continuing childcare responsibilities, and many other matters.

Chapter 8 should provide enough guidance to enable you to discuss and evaluate spousal support. If you cannot resolve the issue completely, you will at least pinpoint the issues in dispute and develop the background to retain a lawyer (or lawyers), an accountant, a mediator or an arbitrator to steer you toward resolution.

Other Claims

Even after you've resolved all of these matters, some thorny issue may remain unaddressed. It may be a novel or rare claim, such as damages for assault or damages for corporate wrongdoing in a family business. It may involve one spouse's idea of fairness, which may or may not give rise to a tenable legal argument. It might involve mundane issues such as compensation for credit card or mortgage payments made on behalf of the other spouse after separation, or moral ones such as outstanding arrears of child support. If you can identify these concerns, they should form part of your list of issues for discussion and resolution by compromise. If you're not sure that you've covered all the issues, or if you have a nagging feeling that you should be taking some other position, it isn't a bad idea to retain a lawyer for a one-hour consultation. You can then explain what matters are on the table, get some help in resolving them, and discuss other potential claims.

SEPARATION AGREEMENTS

Once you've resolved all of your concerns, you should retain a lawyer to commit your agreement to writing and incorporate all the necessary releases. This process not only provides enforceable and reliable settlement terms, but often raises other minor issues such as providing life insurance for security, additional tax concerns, or releases against the other's estate which you might not have considered if you'd drafted your own agreement.

If you can't stand the thought of retaining a lawyer, you can obtain preprinted separation agreements, which you can modify to your own form, at legal printing companies and some stationery stores. Even if you take this route, you should ask a lawyer to review the final version. It's worth the cost of an hour or two in legal fees to be sure you've covered all the bases. Some general considerations and sample clauses for separation agreements are found in Chapter 12, "Domestic Contracts."

FYI

If you and your partner come to a lawyer with an agreement in principle, you should be able to obtain a final, signed separation agreement for $1000 or less.

THE DIVORCE

If you're resolving matters amicably and in a timely way—and if you're married—the final step will be obtaining a divorce. Your divorce becomes available after you've been separated from your partner for one year—or earlier if you prove mental or physical cruelty or adultery.

Many people also want to know about religious divorce and annulment. The grounds for divorce, incorporation of settlement terms, and religious divorces are discussed in Chapter 13, "Divorce, Religious Divorce and Annulment."

CHAPTER THREE

How Separation Affects Children and How You Can Help

IN THIS CHAPTER: **Infants & Toddlers' Reactions; Preschoolers' Reactions; Six to Eight Year Olds' Reactions; Eight to Twelve Year Olds' Reactions; Adolescents' Reactions; Cooperative Parenting**

As many as half of children of divorce bear the scars for years, and counsellors warn that about one-third suffer from depression even five years after separation. All children feel its effects for one or two years after separation. Because how much they suffer and how they cope with the pain is almost entirely contingent on their parents' behaviour, it is crucial to understand how the issues affect your child, what the major stressors are, and how to help your child cope. If you are careful and sensitive, and if you focus on strengthening your capacity to parent, your child will adjust to the divorce after a year or two without any long-term effects. In fact, research shows that the few children whose parents have adopted child-focused approaches are actually more independent, more outgoing and more mature than children whose families have remained intact. This glimmer of hope should become the sole motivator in your separation and the sole determining factor as you and your spouse attempt to resolve custodial issues. If you truly appreciate the serious risk that even the smoothest divorce poses to children, you will understand that no other issue arising from separation is more important than ensuring an easy transition for your children.

Unfortunately, up to half of children of divorce witness ongoing conflict between their parents and almost all are subjected to loyalty conflicts at some point after separation. The following summary of the effects of parental separation includes both external stressors and developmental-based internal stressors. Each category continues with a brief discussion of how you can reduce stress and help your child deal with the emotional issues of separation. These are guidelines only that are aimed at helping you understand and communicate with your child. If they don't help, or if signs of distress persist in your child for longer than a few months, see a child psychologist. The potential long-term risks to your child make this mandatory.

The age categories in this chapter contain generalized discussions of how children think, understand and behave at different stages. You should remember as you review them that each individual child's development is unique, and so your child may exhibit behaviour that crosses over between categories. I have alternated gender references between the masculine and the feminine in order to achieve some gender-neutrality. Either reference means "he or she" or "his or her." References to divorce are intended to include separation of unmarried common law couples and same sex couples. References to parents and children are intended to include stepparents and stepchildren.

FYI

Children benefit from any custody and access arrangement that provides them with warm and responsive parenting, by a psychologically healthy parent, in a stable or predictable environment with support from extended family and other loving adults. In high-conflict situations, children benefit from arrangements that minimize the potential for conflict and reduce the number of transitions between parents.

INFANTS AND TODDLERS' REACTIONS

Children from infancy to age three show the following behaviour when their parents break up:

Confusion

The young child's limited cognitive abilities make a family breakup confusing. A toddler cannot understand what divorce means, why mommy and daddy live apart, where daddy's new house is, or when daddy will visit again. Life becomes unpredictable and frightening.

Reflection

Toddlers absorb their caregiver's emotional mood. If parents are angry, frightened, or sad, the toddler senses it and feels the same emotions.

Conflict

Toddlers who witness their parents' fighting do not understand what is going on. They do, however, sense that something is wrong. Their response is not consistent—they may withdraw, they may act out, they may cry or run about wildly—but in all cases they are extremely sensitive and upset.

Disruption

Routine is everything to children of this age. All changes in routine—from minor scheduling changes or one parent's absence at bedtime, to major adjustments such as a new caregiver—can cause substantial distress.

Separation Anxiety

All toddlers panic at times of separation because they depend so much on their parents in all aspects of their lives. This natural tendency is exacerbated when one parent moves out, or they begin to spend more time with a caregiver. Longer visits with the non-residential parent create fear and anxiety because the child cannot tolerate separation from the primary caregiver.

Loss of One Parent

A toddler who infrequently sees one parent loses an internal concept of her relationship with that parent and thus loses attachment. She becomes reluctant to visit the other parent, or is detached and quiet when visiting. These problems are often misunderstood by the non-residential parent and result in his or her withdrawal from the regular access to the child, or increased animosity toward the former spouse.

Reversion

Children may revert to crawling, return to the bottle or reject favourite foods, or show other physical markers of emotional distress.

Emotional Signs of Stress

A loss of emotional control is common among distressed children. They may suddenly violently detest bathtime, or lose their tempers and fly into uncharacteristic rages. Other indicators of stress are outright expressions of anger and fearfulness, and quiet withdrawal.

How You Can Help

Establish Consistency

The absolute answer to many of the stresses of separation on toddlers is consistency. The entire daily schedule should be rigidly set and reliable. Most importantly, the primary caregiver should be the same affectionate, attentive person each day. Timing of pick-up and drop-off with the caregiver and with the access parent should be regular.

Eliminate Conflict

Don't reduce interparental conflict or signs of sadness in front of the child, *eliminate them*. The child's best interest is served by regular, frequent contact with the non-residential parent. But this is completely undermined if the visit involves even the most minor conflict between the parents. Individual psychotherapy is recommended if anger, sadness or depression persists for more than six months after separation.

Custody and Access

Consistency dictates that the child's primary residence should be with the parent who was the primary caregiver before separation. In order to address the child's need to maintain an emotional bond with the other parent, the non-residential parent should have daily contact with the child for short visits and a parenting plan should be implemented immediately on separation. Because of the stress associated with separation, overnights are not usually recommended until the child is three years old. If both parents have been equal caregivers, sharing daytime caretaking is a possibility, but the child should sleep in the same home every night.

Watch for Signs of Distress

If you can recognize the signs that your child is having trouble, you are more than halfway toward fixing it. Most often, toddlers are in distress because a need is not being met. If you cannot determine what that need is, you should seek the advice of a child psychologist.

PRESCHOOLERS' REACTIONS

Children from three to five usually go through the following when their parents break up:

Self-Blame

Preschoolers see themselves as the centre of the world, and see events as arising from their own actions. Almost all preschoolers believe that they are the cause of their parents' divorce. Most counsellors advise parents that children will believe that they are at fault no matter how many times their parents tell them otherwise.

Misconception/Fantasy

Consistent with the tendency to blame themselves for the breakup and the cognitive development of preschoolers, such children develop theories about the breakup or its meaning, believing that it all happened because they had a tantrum in the candy store or that they could have prevented the separation by being more lovable. When they witness conflict, they see themselves as the cause. They also develop fantasies about reconciliation and fears of abandonment. Another fantasy that a surprising number of children of this age express to clinicians is a fear that there will not be enough food, that they will starve to death or that some other basic need will not be met.

Conflict

Preschoolers worry and wonder about the things that they hear their parents saying ("Did mommy really 'throw' daddy out? Is daddy really leaving us in poverty?"). They try to solve the problem, and when they find that they cannot solve it, they are filled with doubt, mistrust, insecurity and confusion. They may become angry at one or both of their parents, and are frightened by that anger. They may adopt their parents' model of interaction and act aggressively with others. Children of this age who are exposed to long-term interparental conflict suffer from aggression, anxiety, insecurity and social withdrawal.

Transitions

Transitions from one parent to the other for access are among the most stressful and confusing events for preschoolers, who will exhibit a broad range of symptoms of stress at these times. They may be happy and excited about the visit, and then cling and cry when the visiting parent arrives. They may be apprehensive about a visit, or have somatic complaints as the time approaches. Parents are sensitive to these symptoms, and often perceive them as reflecting a problem with the other parent, ignoring the separation anxiety and other feelings that the child brings to the situation. Conflict often arises from these transitions, with one parent citing the child's stress as a reason to limit visits, or blaming the other for inducing the child to behave badly.

Disruption

Routine in all things is as important for a preschooler as it is for a toddler, and is especially critical in caregiving for the preschooler. Changes in schedules and social interaction create insecurity, unpredictability and distress.

Changes in Parenting Styles and Quality

Experts say that nearly every parent of divorce shows signs of diminished capacity to parent. Children don't understand that diminished parenting arises from the loss and necessary adjustments of separation. They see these changes as reflecting the parent's view toward them: the parent must be angry or displeased with them, or must not love or care about them anymore.

Reversion

A loss of developmental achievements is also a normal sign of distress in preschoolers. It is similar in all respects to reversion suffered by toddlers, usually involving a loss of the most recent achievements.

Emotional Signs of Distress

Emotional fluctuations and overreaction, and the more obvious expressions of anger, sadness and fear are reflections of undue distress. These are normal reactions to growing up, but it is their intensity and frequency that are remarkable.

How You Can Help

Break the News Calmly

Many parents feel frightened and confused at separation and later admit to having postponed the talk with their children longer than they should have. They are afraid of reliving the anger and pain, of their children's reactions, and of losing control. Experts agree that these fears must be confronted and overcome. Both parents should sit down with the children about two weeks before the actual physical separation and tell them that their parents are getting a divorce. Explain exactly what that means in specific terms: who is moving, where that parent will live, how often they will see each other, and what changes the child should expect. Although many preschoolers do not need to know the details of why the separation is occurring, they do require a basic explanation, such as "Mommy and Daddy aren't happy anymore and need to live apart." The two most important messages should be that divorce is an adult event that has nothing to do with the child, and that both parents love the child. The talk should be brief—five minutes or so, and the main message should be repeated over the following days and weeks.

Communicate

When your young child is grappling with anger, fear and fantasy, you can relieve this stress by accepting that it is happening and talking about it. Therapists recommend communicating with all children by engaging in objective discussions, rather than asking direct questions. An objective discussion can work by using phrases such as "most children whose parents are divorced are afraid and angry," drawing pictures of a girl who lives in two houses, or by acting out the interaction between two dolls or stuffed animals. This type of objective communication can be used to address all signs of distress, and if it goes well, should result in the child sharing his fears or concerns with you. Your role is to advise the child that fear/anger/aggression/fantasy is normal, to provide alternate ways of dealing with the issue, to soothe the child, and to correct any misconceptions.

Eliminate Conflict

Avoiding conflict is much easier than resolving the concerns and fears that arise from having your child witness it. Counsellors advise that many parents will believe that they are doing well, that they are not fighting in front of the children or enmeshing them in the dispute, but that the same children will report screaming matches at access time and overt denigration of the other parent. Any comment that is negative or promotes loyalty conflicts should be avoided.

Establish Consistency

Avoid changing the child's primary residence and routine; if major changes in scheduling and caregiving are necessary, soothe the transition by staying with the child and introducing him to the caregiver or the new environment over several short visits.

Promote Independence

Don't turn to your preschooler for emotional support, or share your worries with her. Don't rely on your child for social support by spending all of your free time with him. Encourage play time with peers. Vigourously promote independence.

Custody and Access

At the beginning, preschool children should spend the same amount of time each day with each parent as they did before separation. If one parent is the primary caregiver, the other parent should spend an hour or two with the child each evening, at the home or elsewhere. If the primary caregiver is not working, this age is especially suited to arrangements in which that parent provides daytime care (either by coming to the home or having the child dropped off each day) and the other provides evening care. Whatever the arrangement, overnights should be gradually introduced, beginning with one per week and increasing to as many as three per week by about age four.

SIX TO EIGHT YEAR OLDS' REACTIONS

Children from six to eight usually suffer from the following when their parents break up:

Self-Blame

Children of this age are as prone to believe that they are the cause of their parents' divorce as preschoolers are. The result is the same: guilt, anxiety, and various other signs of distress.

Misconception/Fantasy

Theories about the reasons for the separation and frightening fantasies about abandonment, starvation and injury abound in children at this age. These concerns burden the children emotionally, creating anger, fear and resentment.

Feeling Caught in the Middle

Children of this age are frequently manipulated and encouraged by their parents to become embroiled in the dispute. Although they do not want to be so completely in the middle, these children lack the assertiveness and skills to refuse to become involved. Cognitively, they have trouble being objective or holding two opposing viewpoints at the same time. They either oscillate between views depending on whom they are with, or if they are capable of forming a view, are prone to telling each parent what he or she wants to hear. They may exaggerate negative stories about the time that they spend with each parent, thinking that each parent will be pleased to hear these reports. Often parents do not appreciate that the child is struggling, and the mistrust and conflict between the parents increases. Children need permission to love both parents, and criticism of one parent denies them that permission and causes extreme emotional pain.

Conflict

Children of this age are acutely distressed by witnessing conflict and become very frightened if the conflict escalates to any form of violence. Some children become debilitated, while others will try to intervene to stop the fighting. Misconceptions about their role in the dispute, fantasies about parents dying or killing the child during an argument, and over-whelming sadness are frequent reactions.

Changes in Parenting Styles

Children of all ages run into this source of stress, because it is a natural by-product of the adjustment to separation that is seen in varying degrees in all parents. See the discussion under this heading for preschoolers.

Loss of the Family

Six to eight year olds find their identity, pride, happiness and security in their newly-developed concept of family. Loss of this sense of family, in all of its components, is the most common source of distress in early school age children grappling with divorce. If not recognized and addressed by parents, such sadness can develop into severe depression.

Loss of a Parent

The child's growing ability to see the big picture that is reflected in sadness at the loss of the family also contributes to a different sense of loss of a parent. It is the overall loss that hurts the six to eight year old: the constant and seemingly insignificant daily contact in the mornings, at the dinner table and at bedtime. This can be eased by access visits, provided that they are frequent, but even then the child is aware that something is different and feels a sense of loss.

Issues Arising from New Partners

These children feel jealous, displaced, replaced, or demoted from a position of power when a parent's new mate moves into their home. As many as sixty percent of children of all ages feel emotionally excluded by a parent's remarriage. They may be angry at that parent for dashing their reconciliation fantasies. They may feel protective of the other parent who is perceived to be rejected. They may be fearful that the new relationship will fail like the last one did.

How You Can Help

Break the News Calmly

The basics for telling all children about separation are described under this topic for toddlers. The six to eight year old may have more need to understand why the separation is occurring than a younger child. Broad language explaining that the parents are unhappy and are arguing frequently, and that they cannot live together anymore is appropriate. The focus of the talk should be on reinforcing that the parents love the children and that this is an adult problem that the children did not cause. Repeat the first talk and provide repeated reassurances several times over the next weeks.

Communicate

Objective communication is discussed under this heading for toddlers. It should have the following goals: to relieve the child by recognizing that her feelings are normal; to provide room for exchange and venting; to give ideas for coping; to provide reassurance that things will get better; and to clear up misconceptions and help the child refocus on the positive.

Focus on Parenting

Remember that all parents suffer from diminished parenting capacity on separation. Try to be patient, and give your child as much time as—if not more than—you did before the separation. Adopt consistent routines and rules.

Be Sensitive to New-Spouse Issues

Tread carefully, and make time for your child. Give her lots of time to become accustomed to the new family actor. Have the new spouse tread carefully as well, as a sense of rushing or surprise can lead to disaster. Most children of this age warm to a stepparent if the new person is gradually integrated.

Custody and Access

Therapists do not agree on what caregiving schedules are best at this age. This reminds us to pay special attention to the child's individual needs. Some need the stability of one primary residence, while others thrive in alternating-residence arrangements. All children need a parenting plan that is established immediately on separation.

NINE TO TWELVE YEAR OLDS' REACTIONS

Children from nine to twelve usually suffer from the following when their parents break up:

Loyalty Conflicts

The level of internal conflict arising from divorce peaks at this age. Cognitively, these children are more developed in abstract thinking than they were a few years earlier. They can understand their parents' emotions. However, although they are developing their ability to be objective, they still have trouble holding two opposing viewpoints or reconciling their parents' differing views. Their inability to stand completely outside of the situation and their sensitivity to contradiction creates painful internal struggles.

As many as half of children of this age cope with loyalty conflicts by forming an unhealthy alignment. The child becomes judgmental of one parent or protective of the other, and finds relief from the conflict in a strong alliance with one parent and corresponding rejection of the other. These alignments can continue well into the child's life if they are not addressed. Most separated parents whose ten or eleven year old is showing signs of alignment with one parent blame that parent, ignoring what the child brings to the situation. While directly influencing the child does create alignments, it is more common that any influence is indirect, and that the alignment is the child's way of coping with loyalty conflicts. An alternative coping mechanism is withdrawal: retreating from both parents, coupled with general ambivalence.

Anger

Intense anger is unique to this age group, and is the most common form of defence mechanism. The child at this age feels anger that is directed at one or both parents, although the primary caregiver is the easiest target.

Loss of the Family

Like younger children, nine to twelve year olds suffer from a loss of the feeling of family. They remember family history and happier times. Often, however, they perceive the loss of the family with less sadness than younger children, and instead feel shame, anger and insecurity.

Witnessing Conflict

Witnessing ongoing conflict between the parents contradicts the child's view of how parents should behave and how problems should be solved. Hearing constant criticism of the other parent makes the child feel that he should agree, either openly or by silence. Demands that the child take sides and the reactions that the child's involvement invokes in each parent create an all-powerful child and reinforce the child's fear that he is the cause of the separation. Feelings of guilt, shame and disloyalty fuel the child's anger toward both parents, contradicting his love for his parents. Venting the anger on peers and siblings provides relief, but creates new conflict. Resentment toward parents has the same positive and negative results.

Being a Little Diplomat

Some children of this age, especially girls, cope by pushing sadness and fear to the back of their mind, focusing on the logic of separation and converting negative feelings to positive ones. They are helpful and loving to both parents, and gain praise from their parents and teachers. These defences often work well and allow many children to become well-adjusted. However, the unseen and longer-term risks are suppressed anxiety, a delay in dealing with the anger and other negative feelings, and a pattern of diffidence.

Becoming a Little Adult

Parents often transform their children of this age into little adults by enlisting their help in the household or engaging them in discussions about the parental conflict, the hurt feelings, and the pressures of separation. Whether they recognize it or not, children are burdened by these roles. They become distracted from normal childhood concerns and lose independence.

Issues Arising from New Partners

All concerns of six to eight year olds over new spouses remain concerns for the nine to twelve year old. These issues contribute to inner conflicts in nine to twelve year olds.

How You Can Help

Breaking the News

Do this in the same way that is described under this heading for six to eight year olds. Keep it brief and repeat the central messages several times throughout the following weeks and months.

Eliminate Stressors

These include interparental conflict, insults and denigration of the other parent, embroiling the child, making the child a messenger or critic, and making the child a little adult. Remain focused on your children and give them plenty of your time. Be sensitive to their concerns regarding a new mate as discussed in younger age categories.

Watch for Loyalty Conflicts

If you see signs of alignment or loyalty conflicts, you can address them by reducing all sources of conflict and telling the child that some kids feel that they must take sides, but that both parents are good people and are important in the child's life. If signs of alignment continue, see a child therapist.

Communicate

The objective communication methods described in the preceding age categories are equally effective for nine to twelve year olds, even if the child denies having the feelings of conflict or provides little feedback. Each defence mechanism should be addressed by such discussions. Seek professional help if your efforts don't seem to be working. Many children of this age are very receptive to counselling.

Focus on Parenting

Remember that on separation most parents suffer from a diminished capacity to parent, and try to be giving, patient and open. Cooperative parenting is discussed briefly at the end of this chapter.

Custody and Access

One primary residence with a specific, predictable access schedule may work well. Alternating residence arrangements may be divided by chunks of three days, alternating weeks, or up to two weeks at a time in each household. Alternating residences will only work if the rest of the child's life—school, friends, and activities—remains the same regardless of where the child is living. A custody and access plan should be implemented immediately on separation.

ADOLESCENTS' REACTIONS

Children from thirteen to seventeen usually suffer from the following when their parents break up:

Internal Conflict

If the adolescent is angry, shocked, disappointed or sad about the separation, the result can be a negative view of parents, which creates internal conflict and anxiety. Another source of conflict is the discrepancy between the adolescent's view of herself as independent, and the insecure feelings that arise from concerns over losing the family support system that she knows is necessary during this confusing time in her life. Still another source of conflict is a desire to be involved in the decision about where she will live, combined with loyalty conflicts and a sense of having too much power.

Feeling Caught in the Middle

Studies show that many parents involve adolescents in the dispute by asking them to take sides or listen to a litany of complaints. Adolescents suffer like all kids from being placed in this position: they feel anger, guilt and depression. Unlike younger children, however, most teenagers eventually eliminate the stress by disengaging themselves from the battle and withdrawing from negative discussions.

Issues of Anger and Morality

The teenager often reacts to separation with an acute sense of judgment, betrayal and anger. The anger may be a coping mechanism for feelings of fear, loss, and confusion, and it may be quite intense. Strong feelings of shame and embarassment also arise from the teenager's moral views and self-conscious tendencies, and result in considerable rage directed at one or both parents. All kids disengage from their parents during the teenage years, and realize that their parents are real people with good and bad characteristics, but divorce may accelerate the process of objective perception of the parents and exaggerate the conclusions. The teenager may feel disappointment, disillusionment, and a loss of self-esteem.

Distancing

A common teenage coping style is withdrawal and distancing, which often does not worry parents, because it seems that the child is unaffected by the separation. This cool stance and self-centred behaviour should be recognized and discussed, but it is not necessarily alarming, since it saves the teenager from anger and upset. In fact, the teenagers who do best in the long run are those who are detached in the period following separation.

Issues Arising from New Partners

The heightened awareness that her parents are sexual beings is particularly acute with the adolescent. Some teenagers who are suffering from anxiety arising from this realization in the context of a new mate express moral indignation or refuse access.

Expressions of Distress

Anger and depression are often expressed by adolescents in dangerous or frightening ways. These include alcohol and drug abuse, troubles at school, inappropriate sexual behaviour, physical fighting, destruction of property, trouble with the law, chronic hostility, and running away.

How You Can Help

Breaking the News

Teenagers need to hear that the divorce will not represent any major changes in their lives. The timing of the first talk should be early—as much as two to four weeks before the separation. If other children are much younger or older than the adolescent, the adolescent should be told separately. These two steps allow her to feel that she can trust her parents and that her maturity is appreciated. Try to keep the talk brief, and repeat the central messages over the next weeks.

Communicate

Combine objective and direct communication about emotional concerns and problems. Be patient and understanding of the teenager's inner conflicts. It is difficult for adolescents to accept help from their parents because they are angry with their parents, they sense that the parents failed at solving their own problems, and because they have a strong independent nature. Talking about how the teenager's behaviour makes you feel is a good starting point. Compromising in levels of discipline and in dealing with emotional outbursts makes the adolescent feel that you respect her autonomy.

Custody and Access

As with all children, an individual approach to solving issues of custody and access is necessary for teenagers. Some want to be part of the decision-making process; some do not want to be forced to take sides. Developmentally, a teenager can handle any type of alternating residence arrangement, provided it is not perceived as a massive upheaval of her current lifestyle. Studies show that adolescents do particularly well in alternating residence arrangements, provided there is no interparental conflict.

COOPERATIVE PARENTING

Emotional recovery is a process that takes time—for all family members. While you are struggling with it, you should look forward to emotional resolution and forgiveness. Trying to get to forgiveness is essential, because it liberates you from the past. In the meantime—and forever after—you must remember these essential facts: your children need permission to love both parents, they have a right to spend time with both parents, and each parent needs to have reliable, comfortable time with the children in order to heal old wounds and build a future. If you accept these essential facts, you can then adjust your attitudes toward the parenting plan and deal with the other spouse on a logical, businesslike level. You are no longer living together, and you no longer will be discussing the intimate details of your lives, but you are still both in the business of raising healthy kids. If you change your interaction with your spouse to reflect an objective, emotionally-neutral attitude that focuses on these premises, you will find that you can co-parent children in a positive and cooperative way.

Respect is essential. You've got to respect your spouse's right to have time with the kids, and respect his or her right to a reliable schedule. You shouldn't impose unilateral changes to the schedule or act as if you're doing the other parent a favour by granting access. You should avoid negotiating with the other parent on the child's behalf or allowing the child to manipulate the two of you by pitting you against each other. Consider the other parent's reputation with the kids as a crucial gem that you have been charged with protecting, and avoid passing judgment. Discuss your criticisms of the other parent with a good friend or counsellor, rather than imposing those views on your kids. In any case, your own critical evaluation of the other parent should be tempered by acceptance of the fact that all parents have different parenting styles and that you cannot control what happens during your spouse's time with the kids. As much as you may disapprove of your spouse's new life, your kids won't die from eating too much pizza, living in a mess or meeting a "new friend." If things like that are bugging you, try focusing on the other parent's good qualities and strong parenting skills, or have a calm discussion out of the children's hearing. Remember that kids are entitled to know both of their parents, and that a child-focused approach to separation will foster mature, independent and resilient children, who are, in the long run, often better off for the experience.

CHAPTER FOUR

Custody

IN THIS CHAPTER: **Who Can Apply for Custody, Custody and Access Defined;** *Interim Custody, Sole Custody, Joint Custody, Split Custody, "Involve and Consult" Custody,* **Access/Residential Schedules;** *Supervised Access,* **Other Custodial Issues, Mobility Rights, Travel Considerations;** *Passports, Written Permission to Travel, Unaccompanied Travel, Child Abduction,* **The Custody Trial, Assessments, Being the Perfect Parent, Child Representation, Variations of Custody**

THE APPROPRIATE CUSTODY ARRANGEMENT FOR CHILDREN OF ANY AGE IS THE ONE THAT MEETS ALL THEIR EMOTIONAL NEEDS. IF YOU AND YOUR SPOUSE ARE MENTALLY CAPABLE OF BEING LOVING, SUPPORTIVE AND COMMUNICATIVE PARENTS, YOU SHOULD BOTH FOCUS ON ESTABLISHING A WORKABLE RESIDENTIAL SCHEDULE IMMEDIATELY UPON SEPARATION. DETAILS OF FORMAL CUSTODY RIGHTS SHOULD BE A SECOND PRIORITY.

However, many situations arise on separation that require spouses to address custody and access in a more formal, detached way. Abusive relationships and those marked by alcohol and drug abuse often require legal intervention. A spouse may be afraid to separate without a restraining order or may be afraid to move out of the home without first obtaining interim custody. If you're involved in a relationship from which you cannot separate without exposing yourself or your children to danger you should likely initiate immediate custody proceedings. If, however, you feel that you should not have to continue to involve your soon-to-be-former spouse in decisions about your children, or that your children will do better without the spouse, think again. Your children need both parents, and there's nothing worse for a child's emotional well-being than a custody battle.

This chapter summarizes different types of custody arrangements. The court has only a limited capability to structure custody and access. Because of the number of children who pass through the courts, judges usually apply basic, general principles of custody and access on an interim basis. You may pursue a custody arrangement more tailored to your needs through a full-blown custody trial. But in the process, the potential harm to your children will often eliminate whatever benefit you might gain from the outcome.

WHO CAN APPLY FOR CUSTODY

Provincial statutes governing child custody focus explicitly on the child's best interests. They make no restrictions about who may apply for custody of a child. Between two biological parents who have separated, both have an equal right to custody. All provinces also allow custody claims by grandparents, other relatives, stepparents by marriage, common law and same sex spouses. Under most statutes "any parent or other person" may pursue a custody claim. Some statutes require the non-parent to have "sufficient interest" or be "responsible" or have "shown a settled intention to treat the child as a family member."

FYI

If you're bringing children to a new relationship, entering a relationship with a person who has children, or caring for a child on behalf of a family member, you should keep in mind that provincial statutes make no restrictions about who may apply for custody of a child. A non-biological "parent" of any description has standing to claim custody.

CUSTODY AND ACCESS DEFINED

"Custody" is the right to make all major decisions about and for a child. Sometimes, the term is also connected to having the child live with the person who "has custody," but this is not automatic under our laws. Both parents have an equal right to spend time with and care for the child. "Access" is the "right of time" that may include visits of a certain number of hours or consecutive days and nights. One parent may be given interim custody, and the other may be given more or equal interim access or residential time with the child.

Interim Custody

If litigation follows immediately after separation you will have to consider interim relief. An interim motion is a court attendance at which you request that a judge consider the short-term issues. These usually include interim support, interim child support, interim custody and interim access.

In order to put all of the evidence before the court, you will be required to swear a financial statement setting out your income, expenses, assets and liabilities, and an affidavit describing the nature of your relationship breakdown and your reasons for turning to the court for assistance. Within a week or so, you and your lawyer can prepare the necessary documents. You will then attend court and ask a judge to consider the short-term issues arising from your separation.

There are several main themes to interim custody and access:

- If violence or mental health are not concerns, you are better off to nego-tiate interim custody and access issues, since only you know what is best for your kids. Going to court is a bit like being processed like another piece of the bureaucracy, and cannot yield individual results.

- If you do go to court regarding interim custody and access, the guiding principle of all custody decisions is the "best interests of the child." However, in most cases, the results will be predictable.

- Both parents have an equal right to interim custody, but if one parent has been the primary caregiver to the child, a judge will usually give that parent interim custody. In such cases, the "usual" companion order gives the other parent interim access once a week and on alternate weekends.

- Judges rarely move children from one home to the other on an interim basis. If one parent has moved out of the home and left the children with the other, the court assumes that the parents know that this is best for the children, and will seldom change the arrangement. If the parents have separated already, "possession" of the children—called *de facto* cus-tody—almost always determines interim custody.

- Early in any custody dispute, the court will appoint a child psychologist to assess the needs of the children. Until the psychologist completes the assessment, judges will usually preserve the status quo custodial arrange-ment. Once again, the idea is to protect the children from the confusion of having their primary residence changed until the outcome of the case.

- Unfortunately for many couples, there is a negative side effect to this good principle of saving the children from disruption. This is why many lawyers advise their clients not to move out until custody is settled. Many parents continue to cohabit, often in extreme conflict, while cus-tody is at issue, because neither wants to give the other the advantage in the custody battle. Interparental conflict at some level is unavoidable.

- Judges will not usually order a parent to move out of the home unless there is conclusive evidence that continued cohabitation will harm the children or the spouse. (More detailed discussions of exclusive possession of the matrimonial home appear later in this chapter, and again in Chapter 6.) In the average case, parents have to agree together who will move out.

- Most children benefit from spending as much time as possible with both parents. Toddlers and preschoolers do best with short, daily visits with the non-residential parent. Many older children benefit by alternating residences. In general, however, judges don't impose an alternating residential schedule on an interim basis, even though most experts agree that it's the best arrangement for many children.

- An interim custody and access order lasts until you settle your case or there is a trial, which may be as long as two years. Sometimes, interim custody and access orders are varied, but usually the judge won't want to move the kids back and forth while custody is in dispute.

A review of these themes in interim custody and access makes many parents wonder what to do. Do you live together in conflict because you cannot agree on custody and access? Do you take advantage of the rule that "possession" often dictates custody and access decisions and run away with the child? Is the court really able to deal with these issues effectively? The answer to all of these questions is a resounding "No." You must first try to resolve the issues together. If that fails or is impossible, you have to face the music of the courtroom—and try to control the process.

If you've been the primary caregiver for your children, the best answer is to provide the court with all the options that would be acceptable to you. You can also ask the court for permission to move with the children to another residence. You should provide the court with as much detail as possible about your concerns, including verified examples of why continued cohabitation is difficult. You should also submit a plan for your intended living arrangements. Or you can serve your spouse with a claim for interim custody and move out with the children on the same day. You can advise the court that you're afraid to expose yourself and the children to a hostile environment by being at home when your spouse receives this material, and you can stress that you are seeking the first available date to obtain the court's approval of the move. Many lawyers will tell you that they don't recommend moving out with the children without court approval, and I agree with this general statement. However, I have found that requesting either interim custody at home *or* permission to move out *or* approval of a very recent move is often successful, since judges recognize the practical problems with continued cohabitation.

If you are not the primary caregiver, you should ask yourself whether a custody battle is really in your children's best interests. You should consider reaching an agreement with your spouse about custody and establishing a residential schedule that will meet your children's needs. You can then move to a new residence and save your children from the extreme distress that comes from living in a battle zone. You can do so feeling assured that you and your children will have a defined and continuing relationship, from which all family members will benefit. If you and your spouse can't deal rationally with each other, you should do everything in your power to obtain professional assistance to help you reach an agreement so that you both can handle the issue calmly and with sensitivity to the children's needs.

If you and your spouse have really been equal caregivers but you can't agree on a parenting plan, and if you feel that your children would benefit from access beyond the standard court-ordered schedule, you should instruct your lawyer to present the court with substantial evidence of the children's needs, including academic articles and expert reports. Ask the court directly for an alternating residential schedule, but be ready to answer this question: "If you're really capable of being cooperative parents, then what are you doing in this courtroom?"

Sole Custody

Sole custody, or full custody, is the legal right to make all decisions relating to the child without the involvement of the other parent. It does not include the right to control access by the other parent. When a court grants sole custody to one parent, it deals with access at the same time. Although many interim motions concerning custody and access proceed in cookie-cutter fashion—granting custody to one parent, for example, and access to the other parent on Wednesday evenings and on alternate weekends—sole custody does not necessarily mean that the access parent must spend less time with the child than the custodial parent. In fact, many custody trials are resolved by the judge giving one parent the decision-making capacity and both about equal time with the children.

Some parents who can agree on a residential schedule without going to court still feel that they will not be able to agree upon any major decisions regarding the children. In such cases, the court may give one parent the title of sole custodial parent, while granting considerable access to the non-residential parent.

Joint Custody

Under a joint custody arrangement, both parents must agree upon and are equally responsible for all major decisions regarding their children. Major decisions usually relate to health (except in emergencies, when one parent can take sole responsibility), education, daycare arrangements, religion, camp, extracurricular activities, and the need for a tutor or educational testing.

Joint custody is a term many parents are familiar with. It has been a popular arrangement, especially in the American courts, for many years. However, our courts have become increasingly realistic about the demands of joint decision-making. The Canadian rule, from which there is almost no deviation, is that joint custody cannot and will not be imposed on an unwilling parent. Cooperation and communication are necessary. If parents are required to agree on all major decisions, and are unable to put their feelings or self-centred views aside, decision-making is impossible. What guests should attend the bat mitzvah party or which doctor should perform the tonsillectomy can become sources of intense conflict and the subject of court intervention or mediation. Parents find themselves in endless deadlocks. It is now the practice for judges to dismiss claims for joint custody out-of-hand if it is a contested issue in litigation, except in rare cases.

Regardless of the law's strict position on joint custody, parents can always agree to joint custody by a separation agreement. Despite the power struggles that may arise, joint custody arrangements offer several benefits. They require parents to put their conflicts aside and to focus on their children. Each parent stands on an equal footing, so that neither has power over the other and neither is the sole disciplinarian or sole bearer of gifts. Under the best of circumstances, it takes substantial effort, selflessness, cooperation and communication between parents to help children adjust to a separation. While the responsibilities of joint decision-making pale in comparison to these goals, the equality that joint custody creates may actually help separated couples attain them.

Split Custody

Under a split custody arrangement, one parent has custody of one or more children and the other has custody of the remaining children. Since separation of the children often compounds the emotional trauma of the parents' separation, split custody is rarely granted. Split custody usually arises when one parent cannot care for all of the children at once, when the children are of very different ages, or when there are severe problems between siblings.

FYI

The person who has custody is entitled to make decisions about the child. Joint custody means joint decision-making. Sole custody means that one parent has ultimate decision-making authority. While custody may involve providing day-to-day care for the child, the difference between joint and sole custody really comes down to decision-making, since both parents will care for the child to some degree. Access is the right to spend time with the child, either for a visit of a few hours or a few days, and the term "residential schedule" is often used when children live in two households.

"Involve and Consult" Custody

A creature of compromise, this negotiated provision in a parenting plan or separation agreement requires parents to involve and consult each other respecting major decisions, to discuss all such issues fully and well in advance, to consider each other's views, and to attempt to reach a consensus. If no consensus is possible, then one parent will have the right to make the final decision. This type of custody arrangement is a good compromise. Most non-residential parents simply want to have a say in decisions and be told about major issues, and take comfort in the requirement that the other parent must "attempt to reach a consensus with them." Equally, most residential parents have no difficulty with the idea of consulting with the other parent—in fact they usually continue to respect the other's views—and have only resisted joint custody because they are afraid of power struggles. This is another example of the benefits of settling custodial issues, since judges will usually choose between the parents rather than make this type of win–win order.

A similar decision-making compromise requires parents to attend mediation if they can't reach a decision. Sometimes either parent can invoke mediation, which both parents must attend. After the matter in question is resolved, the mediator can be empowered to determine if one parent was acting unreasonably and, if so, whether that parent should pay the costs of the mediation. This kind of mediation clause provides a financial incentive to be reasonable, but it presents two potential disadvantages:

- mediation is costly. Often neither spouse can afford to pay for it every time there is a disagreement; and
- parents involved in high-conflict relationships may abuse the mediation requirement or use it to perpetuate power imbalances and conflict in their relationship.

ACCESS/RESIDENTIAL SCHEDULES

Access is visitation time between the non-residential parent and the child. If one parent has interim sole custody, the court will often order interim access for the non-residential parent of one evening per week, either for a few hours or overnight, and on alternate weekends from Friday to Sunday evenings. If custody is disputed, the trial may not occur for as long as two years. In the meantime, the access schedule will become entrenched, and the court, not wishing to disrupt the children's schedule, will often adopt the interim access order on a permanent basis.

Most children benefit from spending as much time as possible with both parents. Toddlers and preschoolers benefit from short, daily visits with the non-residential parent. Older children benefit by alternating residences with each parent. In general, however, judges don't impose an alternating residential schedule on an interim basis, even though experts agree that it's the best arrangement for children.

Turning to the courts for access scheduling should accordingly be a last resort. Almost all parents can negotiate a suitable interim parenting plan by focusing on the children's needs. To provide predictability for the children and protection for the parents, such an agreement should specify dates and times for access.

FYI

The parent who has access has the right to have the child visit or live with him or her; if children live in two households, they will follow a residential schedule. Even if one parent has sole custody, the children may have a residential schedule that gives them equal time with each parent. Any combination of custody and residential schedule is possible, depending on the parents' abilities and the children's needs.

Supervised Access

Under a supervised access arrangement, the non-residential parent visits the child in the presence of a third person to ensure the child's safety. Our laws and judges are so pro-access that they favour granting access in almost every imaginable situation, based on a child's right to know the parent. Supervised access is therefore ordered only in rare cases. Sometimes I am approached by a parent whose spouse was so uninvolved with the children that there is a real concern about their basic ability to care for a child, and the issue of supervised access is raised. The answer is that supervised access is a strong restriction on parental rights that is only imposed if there is a serious concern for a child's safety. It is usually ordered if the non-residential parent has a history of family violence or criminal activity, a problem controlling his or her temper, mental illness, or an addiction to drugs or alcohol. The court may also order supervised access if a child shows signs of alignment with one parent by refusing to visit the other or if the custodial parent refuses access, if there has been no access for an extended period, or if there's a risk that a child will be abducted. In such situations, courts prefer supervised access to terminating access altogether.

The court may order either temporary or permanent supervised access. The court will make a temporary order in cases where there is a disputed allegation that the child will be harmed by unsupervised access, or in order to ease the transition into unsupervised access in cases where there has been no access for some time. In fact, if a claim is made for supervised access and there is some evidence of something that might be dangerous to the child, access is usually ordered to be supervised pending proof or disproof of the allegations. Although courts strongly favour access, they err on the side of caution in the interim stage. As discussed above, permanent supervised access is ordered in the rare cases where a trial has shown that unsupervised access poses potential danger to the child.

The person appointed to supervise access is usually a responsible family member, a friend who consents to the role, or a community facility established for that function. Most cities have supervised access centres that may or may not charge a fee for the services provided. If a fee is payable, the cost should be addressed by the court when it issues the order. If you are looking for an access facility, call a family lawyer or your family court for advice. If you have any concern that supervised access is necessary in your child's situation, you should address the issue with a lawyer. If you are just separating and you have this concern, you should get some advice before any access arrangements begin.

FYI

Most cities have supervised access centres that may or may not charge a fee. If a fee is payable, the costs of supervised access should be addressed by the court when it issues the order.

OTHER CUSTODIAL ISSUES

While you should put parenting plans and access schedules into effect immediately upon separation, you must also keep your eye on the future. Parenting plans, court-ordered interim access and permanent access schedules following a trial should address special events, extraordinary visits and vacations. Otherwise, disputes may arise later that require parents to return to court. Most parenting plans include references to:

- Long weekends such as Thanksgiving, Easter, Victoria Day, Canada Day, or Labour Day.
- Christmas holidays. Most arrangements give parents equal time with their children while they're on vacation from school.
- Rosh Hashanah and Yom Kippur.

- March break.
- Summer holidays. These are divided according to the parenting plan and the age of the children.
- Other special events. Most parents agree that the mother will have the children on Mother's Day and her birthday; the father will have the children on Father's Day and his birthday; the children's birthdays are best celebrated with the parents together if it can be done without conflict; and
- Babysitting or childcare needs. Separation agreements or parenting plans devised by parents with young children sometimes require one parent to ask the other to babysit the children whenever a babysitter is needed, before the parent engages a sitter. This "right of first refusal" for childcare is workable only when parents cooperate.

FYI

In the 1970s and 1980s, society developed an obsession with joint residential care, on the theory that children deal best with divorce when they live for equal amounts of time with both parents. Since then, research has convincingly indicated that children cope equally well in alternating residence, sole-mother and sole-father custody arrangements. Their ability to cope depends much more on other factors, such as communication, continuity, sensitivity and reduction of conflict than it does on the intricacies of their residential schedules.

MOBILITY RIGHTS

Mobility provisions address whether one parent has the right to move with the children to a location away from the other parent. The move may mean a drive of an hour or so, or it may require a trip across the province or country. One parent's desire to move with the children usually arises a few years after separation, although it can happen much sooner.

When the spectre of mobility rights is raised, all custodial issues are opened to reconsideration by the court, which will continue to focus on the best interests of the children. Both parents must show why the move is—or is not—in the best interests of the children.

In deciding a mobility case, a judge will consider:
- existing custody and access arrangements;
- the relationship between the children and each parent;
- the desirability of maximum contact between the children and both parents;
- the views of the children;
- the reasons for the move if they are relevant to the parent's ability to meet the children's needs;
- disruption to the children that will arise from a change of custody; and
- disruption to the children arising from removal from friends, family, school and the community.

In general, the court weighs the importance of having the child continue to live with the residential parent against the importance of having continuing contact with the non-custodial parent and other family, friends and community.

Although the courts determine mobility issues on a case-by-case basis, some common factors often affect the result:
- The court will give great weight to the views of the custodial parent, who is with the children every day. It is a right of custody to determine where the custodial parent and children will live. The court assumes that the sole custodial parent has decided to move with the children's best interests in mind;
- The advantage of the sole custodial parent must be balanced against the benefit that the children receive from access with the non-residential parent. The closer the relationship between the children and the non-residential parent, and the more dependent the children are on the parent for emotional well-being and development, the more likely the court will find that the children may suffer from the proposed move;
- If the parents have joint custody, one parent will have more difficulty moving away with the children, since joint parenting is in the children's best interests. The same holds true if the children spend equal or near-equal time with both parents;
- If there are economic reasons for the move, or if the court identifies another good reason—and if all other factors are neutral—the court will usually allow the move.

If you are contemplating a move, or discussing the possibility with your former spouse, make sure to consider alternative access arrangements as well as the costs of travel. If the move makes the current visitation schedule unworkable, an acceptable alternative usually involves visits for all long weekends, most school holidays, and most of the summer. Most parents will also agree to reduce child support by the cost of the travel. It remains unclear exactly how Canada's new child support guidelines (see Chapter 7) will consider access costs in determining child support. It is prudent to agree to share access costs equally or to determine child support separately from these costs. If you're applying to the court for permission to move, the court may look favourably on your offer to reduce child support by, or make a direct contribution to, the costs of travel.

FYI

If you're negotiating a separation agreement, it's a good idea to address mobility issues at the outset. Most agreements provide that neither party will move more than a certain distance (e.g., sixty kilometres from city hall, out of a township or district, or out of a province) without the consent of the other party or a court order approving the move. Some agreements require mediation as a first step to avoid a court action when dealing with a proposed move.

TRAVEL CONSIDERATIONS

Passports

Children under the age of sixteen may hold their own passport or be added to the passport of a parent. If one parent has sole custody, that parent may apply for a child's passport or to have the child added to an existing passport. Before issuing the passport, the passport office will require the acknowledgment or consent of the non-custodial parent. If it does not receive such an acknowledgment, the passport office will require court authorization. If the parents have joint custody, both must sign the application.

Separation agreements should refer to passport arrangements, including who will apply for the passport, where it will be kept, and under what circumstances it may be released to either parent.

Written Permission to Travel

You should check the entry requirements of the country that you plan to visit to see if you require your spouse's consent to travel there with your children. If parents have joint custody, written permission from one parent is almost always necessary. If one parent has sole custody, the permission of the other parent is not usually necessary, but you should carry the court order or agreement giving you sole custody on any trip abroad. Many countries require a sworn declaration of permission rather than a signed note from the other parent. In fact, the Department of Foreign Affairs suggests that parents use a statutory declaration in all cases to avoid problems. The permission must be specific to the trip, including references to dates of departure and return. Most countries will not accept a blanket permission to travel.

Separation agreements should contain a provision that both parties must cooperate with the other's requests for travel permission and passports whenever necessary. If you have such an agreement in place and a spouse is not cooperative, you'll have to apply to the court, but the uncooperative spouse will likely have to pay the costs of the application.

Unaccompanied Travel

Children between five and eleven years of age may travel unaccompanied by a parent, with the assistance of an airline representative. This is usually a complimentary service that begins when the parent turns the children over to a representative at the gate to the aircraft. At the end of the trip, the adult picking up the children must produce identification and sign some documentation. Unaccompanied travel is a substantially cheaper alternative to having the custodial parent travel with the children, and can allow for more frequent access for parents and children who live far apart.

Child Abduction

It is an offence to disregard a custody or access order and withhold children from the other parent or remove them from the jurisdiction in which a custody order applies. It is equally inadvisable to remove children from the jurisdiction at the time of separation, even before legal proceedings have begun. Remarkably, many parents believe that they can run away to another province or country with their children and still succeed in getting custody in a later custody dispute. This is almost never the case. On a practical basis, you can't access the justice system in another province. Only the court in the district where the children ordinarily reside has jurisdiction to make a custody order, and a quick move doesn't change the children's ordinary residence. Courts in other provinces will usually refuse a request to take jurisdiction, especially if the request comes from a parent who has moved from another province without the other parent's consent. And there are credibility issues to be considered as well. Even if there is a serious risk of violence, many judges will still look upon flight as foul play. Where there is no violence, you face a kidnapping charge.

FYI

Always obtain the address to which the travelling parent plans to take your children. If there's a serious risk of abduction, either because of past conduct, threats or the nature of the country being visited, you can ask a court to require the travelling spouse to post a bond or other security to ensure the return of your children.

FYI

One of my clients received bad advice from a lawyer who suggested that she should take her infant to her hometown in the U.S. and start a custody proceeding there. Her husband succeeded in getting an order requiring that she return the baby to Ontario, and the wife lost on a later custody motion. When I took over the file, I found that she continued to suffer from a real credibility problem on all issues in the lawsuit, because no judge could get past the allegation (misplaced, in my view) that she had kidnapped her child.

Canada and each of its provinces participate in a reciprocal arrangement with over forty other countries in accordance with the Hague Convention on the Civil Aspects of International Child Abduction. The Hague Convention will operate to require the return of a child who has been taken from Canada to another country or vice versa. This is a complicated procedure, and it must be followed with precision to avoid hassles. You must also act quickly, because the odds of finding an abductor decrease dramatically over time, especially once the offending spouse has arrived in a new country. If such an issue arises, you will need immediate and experienced assistance.

FYI

The Federal Orders and Agreements Enforcement Assistance Unit (1-800-267-7777) and Justice Legal Services, in the Canadian Department of Foreign Affairs (613-992-6302), will provide emergency assistance and lawyer referrals to parents trying to trace their children in other countries. Your local police will also give you immediate assistance and guidance.

THE CUSTODY TRIAL

Many parents become entrenched in their positions on custody and insist that their only inspiration is to protect the children. If you speak to a family therapist or mediator, you will be told that ninety-nine percent of custody disputes involve the agendas of the parents themselves. And make no mistake about it, the fighting does hang over the children's heads. Many children whose parents are in the midst of custody litigation are pressured by parents and family to take positions or express their wishes. They spend uncountable hours with various counsellors discussing the issues. They describe themselves as the central figure in their parents' fighting, like a rope being pulled on from both ends. Many can see no end to the problems, and believe that the fighting will never stop—some may even feel that it would better if they were dead.

If you are in the one percent of custody battles that legitimately involve a focus on the child's needs, and if there is absolutely no room for compromise, you may find yourself in the unenviable position of being a custody litigant. The following discussion should give you an idea of how the process will work, and how you can manage it and feel in control.

A custody trial works like any other trial. First, all parties attend a meeting with the judge before the trial is scheduled. This is called a pretrial, and its purpose is to make the parents settle the case. If that doesn't work, the judge will set a trial date. At that time, the person who initiated the action will give evidence, be cross-examined, and call any appropriate witnesses, including friends, family members, teachers and caregivers. The judge will have appointed a child assessor, who will also give evidence at the trial. The other spouse may also call witnesses and other experts, if there are any. When the evidence is all in, the lawyers make legal arguments, and the judge gives a decision and his or her reasons for it. Or, the judge may reserve judgment until a later date.

Under most provincial statutes, the conduct of the parents involved is irrelevant in determining custody unless it affects their abilities as a parent. Some provinces do not allow allegations about a person's past behaviour, and restrict such conduct allegations to the question of whether the conduct occurs in the present or might occur in future. In any case, the court is concerned solely with determining which of the two parents can better provide for the children's best interests. The court will usually refuse to entertain discussions about who had an extramarital affair, who instigated the breakdown of the relationship, or who is a better cook.

Often the best strategy in a custody dispute is to acknowledge the other parent's abilities as a parent without appearing critical or antagonistic, while simultaneously giving evidence about why you're the better parent. By avoiding adversarial positions, you can only help yourself, since the court will also be considering your ability to facilitate access by the other parent. If you're still full of rage or looking for revenge, a court will question your abilities as a parent.

FYI

In custody trials, more than any others, you must take reasonable positions and watch your step throughout the proceeding. The spouse who wins a custody dispute usually is perceived by the court to be the closest thing to a perfect parent.

ASSESSMENTS

As the first step in custody litigation, the court appoints a child psychologist, psychiatrist or social worker to report on the best interests of the children. Because assessments are ordered in the vast majority of cases, you can save time and legal fees if you agree to an assessment and choose an assessor. If you can't agree, you should bring a motion requesting the appointment of an assessor as soon as possible after the action begins, because nothing will be resolved until the report is complete. Assessment reports can cost between $1000 and $6000, and may be billed on a flat rate or hourly rate basis. Parents usually share the cost of the assessment, but if one parent has no income or no control over the assets the other parent usually has to pay the initial fee, subject to adjustment in the final settlement. In most provinces, a provincial body can conduct the assessment at reduced rates—or no cost, if the court makes such an order or if the parents show financial need. You should consult with a lawyer or the appropriate provincial authority (usually the Children's Lawyer or the Official Guardian) to see if such programs are available. Reports usually take between six to twelve weeks or sometimes longer. Most assessors estimate that the process will take about thirty hours of their time to complete.

Theoretically, the judge—not the assessor—makes the final decision in a custody case. However, unless the report is inconclusive or lacks impartiality, a judge gives great weight to the assessor's opinion. In fact, most lawyers and judges would agree that ninety percent of all custody trials are decided on the basis of the assessment report. It is therefore important to choose your assessor carefully. Most family lawyers deal frequently with three or four assessors. You should make sure the expert you select is sensitive to your particular situation. Some have experience dealing with spouses in abusive relationships, for example; others have experience with alcohol and drug abuse, eating disorders, religious issues, special-needs children, and angry, depressed or violent children. You should also determine whether the proposed assessor has any biases—some always suggest joint custody, others are very mother-minded, still others firmly believe in giving fathers a fair result. Unless you feel you'll benefit from the bias, you should avoid such assessors.

When you have agreed upon an assessor and paid the retainer, the assessment can begin. It usually starts with an initial meeting of the parents and their lawyers. The assessor then meets individually with all family members, often including extended family, and then meets with different combinations of the parents and children. Some meetings take place in each parent's home, but most are usually held at the assessor's office. The assessor also reviews reports from schools, doctors and other sources, and may perform psychological testing. The assessor focuses on understanding the family dynamics, how the separation is affecting the children, how the parents are each dealing with the separation and with the children, and which parent, in all of the circumstances, is best able and most willing to meet the children's needs. The assessor also considers the attachment of the children to each parent, parenting ability, plans for care, permanence of the family unit, relationship by blood, and the children's views and preferences. You should ensure that the assessor spends adequate time with all parties and with anyone else you feel is appropriate. The final report will summarize the meetings and present objective judgments of the parents. A thorough report will make specific recommendations on custody, access and a parenting plan.

Once the assessor submits the report, most lawyers recommend resolving the custody issues on the basis of the recommendations made in it. Given the weight that courts usually give to these reports, you should seriously consider this advice. If you object strongly to the report and can determine that the assessor took a one-sided approach, followed a specific bias or overlooked some pertinent issues, your lawyer should cross-examine the expert to highlight these concerns and analyze the expert's techniques. In rare cases, the court may order a new report. If the assessor has ignored relevant facts—such as the wishes of the child—you can argue that the court should reject the assessment, without calling another expert. You can also retain your own expert witness to provide a second opinion or to oppose the court-appointed expert at trial. Besides the obvious financial costs of such a step, beware of the emotional cost to your children resulting from another set of visits to a clinician's office, and worse, further delays in resolving custody.

BEING THE PERFECT PARENT

If you're involved in a custody dispute, your every word and deed comes under scrutiny. You should consider the following suggestions to show the court that you're fair, reasonable and child-focused.

Eliminate Conflict

This is mandatory for your children's welfare. Not taking steps to do so undermines your credibility. A good opposing lawyer will raise every instance of your negative, antagonistic conduct at the trial, no matter how minor. Do nothing that makes you appear unreasonable. Don't engage in conversation with your spouse at pick-up and drop-off times. If necessary, establish neutral ground for such interaction. Don't have antagonistic phone calls. If you can't put your anger aside for the children's sake, do it for tactical reasons.

I was involved in a custody trial in which the wife's counsel introduced at least ten transcripts of angry telephone calls made in the child's presence and twenty letters written by the husband to the wife after separation, a few of which were written during the trial. They contained such statements as "I am going to replace you as a mother for our child" and "[The child] knows that you abandoned us." This evidence directly contradicted the husband's position that he was shielding the child from conflict, and the implications on his credibility did not escape the judge.

Don't Discuss Issues with the Child

Don't tell the children any more than you have to. Don't try to involve the children or influence the result of the assessment by prompting them to take sides. Don't denigrate the other parent in the presence of the children. Such inappropriate discussions with the children will come back to haunt you in the assessment report or at the trial. More important, they will injure the children indelibly. The fact that the custody battle is raging will not escape your children, but spare them the grisly details.

Resolve Other Issues

If the children are really your focus, make the trial a custody trial and nothing else. Settle all property issues. Pay appropriate child and spousal support. If you're the recipient of support, do everything you can to settle it, even if that means compromising. Don't take any aggressive positions in the action unless they deal with custody. Ask your lawyer to ensure that the legal position you take on every issue is completely reasonable and represents true compromise.

Resolve Interim Custodial Issues

Be sure that the court knows that you are child-minded. If you are the interim custodial parent, give the other parent appropriate, if not generous, access. If you and your spouse can't agree on who should be the interim custodial parent, compromise by at least establishing visitation schedules that are sensitive to your children's particular needs. If neither you nor your spouse wants to move out of the matrimonial home, consider moving out yourself to reduce conflict and entering into a "without prejudice" interim agreement to document your decision. A judge will not fault you for moving out if you explain that you were trying to shield the children from conflict and if you still maintain regular contact with them after the move.

FYI

In all custody disputes, you're better off to resist litigation and pay an expert such as a psychologist, psychiatrist or social worker to mediate your separation and child-related concerns. It is positive, and sets the stage for moving on. Mediation is discussed in Chapter 14, "Alternatives to Litigation."

CHILD REPRESENTATION

In all provinces, courts can appoint an official guardian or a lawyer to represent children in custody disputes. Even if this power is limited by statute, courts will not hesitate to appoint counsel for a child in appropriate cases under their power to look after the best interests of children, called the *parens patriae* jurisdiction.

A child's lawyer must treat the child like any other client, and therefore must act on the child's instructions. The lawyer cannot make submissions arbitrarily about the child's best interests or contradict the child's instructions. This can present problems if the child's wishes contradict their own best interests or if the child is involved in a pathological relationship with one parent. Some judges believe that children are incapable of forming objective views; others believe that children's wishes should determine the outcome of a custody dispute; others sit somewhere in the middle, depending on the child's age and individual capacities. If the judge is inclined to consider a child's wishes, you should consider hiring a lawyer to represent your children, because some judges will interview children in their chambers or allow you or your spouse to call children as witnesses in the case.

It can be extremely damaging for children to express their views about custody or, many say, even be called upon to express their views at all. Doing it in open court can be devastating. I endorse child representation in custody disputes for the same reason that I hate the custody trial: because the children should be shielded. In the real world, hostilities can overcome protectiveness. If the wishes or wills of children are at issue in a custody battle, child representation may be a good idea. If you know that your spouse intends to call children as witnesses, you should retain a good lawyer. The lawyer will shield the children from involvement and give them a voice without, in most cases, asking them to testify.

I was once appointed by the court to act for an 11-year-old girl who refused to see her mother. The mother felt that the custodial father was influencing the child and claimed custody. The process was extremely expensive for the father, my appointment was hotly contested by the mother, and the child had very firm views about what she wanted. Although my involvement in the trial was an unpleasant experience that I wouldn't wish on anybody, it did ensure that the court heard the child's wishes. In the end, the court respected her views and did not move her from her father's residence. The court also ordered counselling to redevelop the girl's relationship with her mother.

The court appoints a child's lawyer on a motion either before the trial or at its commencement. The Official Guardian and the Children's Lawyer in each province have their own rules about the custody issues in which they will become involved. If the provincial authority refuses to act or has a long waiting list that will delay the proceedings, the court can appoint a lawyer to act for the child. Legal aid will sometimes pay for an independent lawyer for the child. Failing that, one parent will have to foot the bill. This can be quite costly, since it means that the parent must pay for two lawyers to participate in the custody trial.

VARIATIONS OF CUSTODY

Courts have an overriding power to look out for the best interests of the children. If a "material change of circumstances" occurs at a later date, all custody arrangements, whether agreed upon by the parents or ordered by the court, are subject to variation. Unlike variations of financial agreements, courts take a more lenient attitude toward variations involving kids. The practical question is really whether there has been any change at all that affects the child's best interests. This is a pretty loose standard, and so any request for variation is essentially a new custody trial. Procedurally, a variation will take the same form as an original custody trial.

Some parents feel insecure knowing that no custodial arrangement is ever really permanent. But considering that the focus is on the child's needs, the variability is understandable. It should give some comfort to couples who agree upon their own parenting plan or who are having difficulty with court-ordered custodial arrangements: you will not be stuck with the current arrangement if it really isn't working. The technical aspects of variation proceedings are discussed in Chapter 15, "If You Must...The Structure of the Action."

CHAPTER FIVE

Property

IN THIS CHAPTER: **Conduct is Almost Always Irrelevant, Property-Sharing Rules in Canada;** *Alberta, Ontario, Prince Edward Island & Saskatchewan; British Columbia, Manitoba, Newfoundland & Nova Scotia; New Brunswick, Quebec & Yukon Territory; Northwest Territories,* **Canada Pension Plan, Resulting and Constructive Trust Claims, Adjustments to Property Division, Advances on Property Division, Interest on Property Awards**

BEFORE THE LATE 1970S, CANADA WAS CAUGHT UP IN UNFAIR PROPER-
TY RULES THAT WERE BASED LARGELY ON THE ARCHAIC NOTION THAT
MARRIED WOMEN DID NOT HAVE THE POWER TO HOLD PROPERTY IN
THEIR OWN RIGHT. THE FIRST MATRIMONIAL PROPERTY RULES
REFLECTED THIS PRINCIPLE AND GAVE HUSBANDS FINANCIAL ADVAN-
TAGES ON MARRIAGE BREAKDOWN; THEY POSSESSED THE INCOME AND
ASSETS AND, IN MOST CASES, BENEFITED INEQUITABLY COMPARED TO
THEIR WIVES UPON SEPARATION. IN 1975, THE *MURDOCH* DECISION OF
THE SUPREME COURT OF CANADA SHOWED THE UNFAIRNESS OF THESE
PROPERTY RULES AND ATTITUDES.

The parties had acquired a cattle ranch during their marriage, but title
was registered in the husband's name alone, and Mrs. Murdoch was not
entitled to share in its value under matrimonial property law. Although
she made no direct financial contribution to the operation, she performed substantial labour on the property and assisted her husband with
every facet of the business. Mrs. Murdoch was unsuccessful in her claim
for an equal share of the ranch both at trial and on appeal. She also lost
in the Supreme Court of Canada, where one judge described her fifteen
years of labour as the "work done by any ranch wife." The decision
sparked a public outcry. Mrs. Murdoch was identified as a victim of the
unfair matrimonial property system. In response, legislation reflecting the
idea that marriage is a partnership and recognizing direct, indirect, financial and non-financial contributions to matrimonial property was enacted across the country. The current laws of matrimonial property, which
have changed in minor ways in most provinces, continue to generally
reflect the initial wave of law reform that followed the *Murdoch* decision.

CONDUCT IS ALMOST ALWAYS IRRELEVANT

The right of married spouses to share in property is generally an absolute
right that has nothing to do with personal conduct. In all but very rare
cases, it makes no difference to the division of property if one spouse
caused the marriage breakdown or had an affair or was an alcoholic.

Many people think that proving some kind of misconduct will help them in the property division, or are angry that they still have to give their spouse half of everything when that spouse was entirely responsible for the breakup. These beliefs, apart from being quite normal reactions, are probably reminiscent of the old days when you couldn't get a divorce without proving adultery or cruelty and when the deviant spouse often suffered financially as a result of the misconduct. Those days are gone. In most cases, a judge won't even entertain discussions of spousal conduct.

There are three exceptions:

- Most provinces provide specific protection to spouses whose partners have recklessly depleted the family asset pool or made false gifts of assets to other people to avoid their matrimonial property obligations. The usual remedy is to act as if the money hadn't been depleted or given away and to adjust the payment accordingly;
- All provinces allow the court to adjust the property division if the normal division would be inequitable or unconscionable. Such considerations allow for some discussion of blatant misconduct, although, as discussed later in this chapter, unequal division is rarely ordered; and
- In provinces in which business assets are not necessarily shared, conduct may be considered in deciding whether the business asset will be excluded. Such cases focus on whether the spouse contributed to the business, either directly (financially or by working in the business) or indirectly (by working in the home or saving money). Conduct that is sometimes relevant to this issue includes alcoholism or drug addiction, spousal abuse, irresponsible spending habits, or some refusal to assist or cooperate with a family business venture. Extramarital affairs or other matters between the spouses will not be relevant.

Conduct may be relevant to custody, but only as it affects an individual's capabilities as a parent. Again, extramarital affairs and other matters— such as who caused the breakup—are irrelevant. Conduct may also be relevant in determining spousal support. But only the most egregious and shocking conduct will persuade a court not to order spousal support to a spouse who otherwise shows entitlement and need. For more information, see Chapter 4, "Custody," and Chapter 8, "Spousal Support."

PROPERTY-SHARING RULES IN CANADA

The family law statutes of each province provide for the sharing of matrimonial property. They also establish a method of calculating the amount of money (or, in British Columbia, the amount of property) that one spouse owes to the other, although the exact nature of the formula differs from province to province. All provinces and territories (except for the Northwest Territories, which has no such formula) recognize three different classes of property:

i.   property that is automatically subject to sharing or division;
ii. property that may be shared depending on various considerations; and
iii. property that is excluded from sharing.

The most notable difference between these groups is the treatment of business assets. In some provinces, businesses and investments are automatically shared. In some they are not technically shared but, in practice, are almost always shared. And, in others, they are not usually shared at all. Most but not all provinces give credit to spouses for their net worths at the date of marriage.

   The following generalizations about property division are arranged by groups of provinces that have similar property regimes. To determine the precise nature of the property-sharing formula in your province and to see how it applies to your particular situation, you should refer to the standard form financial statement required in court proceedings in your province. Descriptions of these forms appear in Appendix A. Most provinces also produce forms under the family law rules that include both spouses' property positions and show the method of calculating a settlement. (In Ontario, for instance, such forms are called Net Family Property Statements.) You can obtain copies of these forms by contacting the court directly or by calling a family lawyer and requesting them. Legal printing companies produce them, and some of the larger stationery stores sell do-it-yourself packages that include financial statements and property statements. Note that legislated division of property applies only to married couples. Unmarried and same sex couples can only assert constructive and resulting trust claims to obtain an interest in property. (These claims are discussed in detail in this chapter following the description of statutory division for married couples, and for common law and same sex couples in Chapters 9 and 10 respectively.) Some general suggestions on negotiating and resolving property issues are found in Chapter 2, "How Anyone Can Settle a Family Law Case (or Almost)."

FYI

Legislated division of property applies only to married couples. Unmarried opposite sex and same sex couples can only assert constructive and resulting trust claims to obtain an interest in property.

Alberta, Ontario, Prince Edward Island & Saskatchewan

In these four provinces, all property acquired during the marriage is shared equally, with only a few exceptions. All property owned by each married spouse at the date of separation is shown as an asset on the financial statement of the spouse who is on title to or otherwise owns the property. No distinctions are drawn between family and business assets. Liabilities on the date of separation, again according to who actually owes the debt, are deducted from the value of the assets owned on the date of separation. Property that was received by gift or inheritance during the marriage and damages received for personal injury are shown as assets and then deducted as excluded property so that they are not eligible for sharing. All property brought to the marriage is also deducted from the net asset position at the date of the marriage, and liabilities brought to the marriage are added back on, so that both parties get a credit or deduction for their financial position at the date of marriage.

In Ontario, Prince Edward Island and Saskatchewan, matrimonial homes receive special treatment. In Ontario and PEI, a matrimonial home brought to the marriage cannot be deducted as an asset at the date of marriage; the same rule applies in Saskatchewan, whose statute also provides that the matrimonial home or its value should be distributed equally unless it would be unfair to do so. The result of these calculations is a total property value for each spouse. The spouse whose property value is greater will owe the other a payment representing one-half of the difference between their totals. The court may order property to be transferred to satisfy the amount owing.

Courts are entitled to disregard or adjust the amounts found to be owing under each province's property division formula. The test for unequal division is cast in strict terms: whether the payment would result in "unconscionable" circumstances (Ontario and PEI) or "unfair and inequitable" circumstances (Alberta and Saskatchewan). A list of matters that might create unconscionable circumstances is included in each statute. The courts' discretion to vary the payment is not taken lightly, and is only exercised in very rare cases.

The sample case on the following page is an example of property division in Alberta, Ontario, PEI and Saskatchewan.

Several things should be noted about this calculation. The most important is that all property division calculations start by considering who actually owns or owes what. Assets and liabilities are shown according to whose name is on the title or loan document. This example presumes that the home and the bank account are in joint names, so one-half of their value is shown on each spouse's side. The husband shows his pension on his side. Although the line of credit may be considered a debt to both parties, it's shown according to whose name is on the loan—in this example, the husband's, increasing his debts by $15,000.

Pensions are a delicate issue in family law. They're considered to be property at the date of separation and are usually included in the calculation, but there's no real cash available until retirement to fund a payment that may have to be made because the pension is included. A spouse who owns a pension may have to pay half of the future value of the pension out of his or her other assets. If this isn't possible, there are other options available, such as long-term payment plans or the more risky alternative of waiting until the actual benefits become payable and sharing them equally.

The valuation of pensions is a business in itself. If either spouse has a pension that you believe is valuable, you should get some advice on evaluating it from an actuary, an accountant or a family lawyer. Many family lawyers use a computer program to estimate pension values. Unfortunately, two evaluations of the same pension may differ by hundreds of thousands of dollars. If your pension is substantial, you can bet that your spouse will contest the evaluation you provide. In such cases, you'll need legal and actuarial assistance to sort out the assumptions on which the values are based and lead you toward settlement. You can save

NET FAMILY PROPERTY STATEMENT
Summary Page - Husband / Wife

1. VALUE OF ASSETS OWNED ON VALUATION DATE	HUSBAND	WIFE
(a) LAND Jointly-Owned Matrimonial Home (half value shown for each)	$100,000.00	$100,000.00
(b) VEHICLES: Husband's 95 Volvo, Wife's 96 Caravan	$12,000.00	$25,000.00
(c) SAVINGS: Joint Account (half value shown for each)	$2,500.00	$2,500.00
(d) SECURITIES	$25,000.00	$5,000.00
(e) PENSIONS	$80,000.00	
(f) INHERITED PROPERTY		$10,000.00
TOTAL VALUE OF ASSETS OWNED ON VALUATION DATE	$219,500.00	$142,500.00

2. VALUE OF DEBTS & OTHER LIABILITIES ON VALUATION DATE	$65,000.00	$50,000.00

3. NET VALUE OF PROPERTY, OTHER THAN A MATRIMONIAL HOME, OWNED ON DATE OF MARRIAGE	$1,000.00	($1,000.00)

4. VALUE OF PROPERTY EXCLUDED UNDER SUBS. 4(2) OF THE "FAMILY LAW ACT"		$10,000.00

5. NET FAMILY PROPERTY	HUSBAND	WIFE
TOTALS of 1 minus TOTALS 2, 3, 4	$153,500.00	$83,500.00

6. EQUALIZATION PAYMENTS	Husband Pays To Wife	Wife Pays To Husband
	$35,000.00	

Wife Buys Husbands Interest in Matrimonial Home, less Equalization, for $15,000
Husband Buys Wife's Interest in Matrimonial Home, plus Equalization, for $85,000

yourself some time and money by compiling all the necessary information yourself before you retain an expert. This usually involves contacting the employer who holds the pension, advising them of the date of marriage and the date of separation, and asking them for a breakdown of the contributions made to the pension during the marriage and its value at both dates. This initial information will give you an idea of the pension's value. If you have any doubts whatsoever, see a family lawyer. A potentially sizable pension is not an asset you should overlook, even if it's your own, since settlements can be set aside because of material non-disclosure.

In the area of excluded property, note that inherited stocks go into the calculation at the date of separation and come out as a deduction, so that their value is not shared. The only requirement here is that the gift or inheritance be owned on separation or be shown by a paper trail to have been invested in another asset. If excluded property has been invested in jointly owned assets, it loses its identity as excluded property and will be shareable. Equally, if it has been spent and there's nothing to show for it, no deduction will be available.

On the marriage date deductions, note that the husband gets credit for the fact that he brought his $1000 car to the marriage, provided he can prove this value or the parties agree upon it. The wife is, in theory, penalized for the fact that she brought a debt to the marriage in the form of her student loan, and this liability is a negative deduction that results in adding $1000 to her net family property figure.

For the sake of simplicity, this example doesn't include any costs of disposition. Deductions could be made from both spouses' figures to represent the taxes that will be payable if the RRSPs are cashed in or to represent the mortgage penalties and real estate fees that have to be paid on the sale of the home. The general rule on costs of disposition is that they're deductible from the value of the asset if they're likely to be incurred. If you're going to sell the house, the associated costs should be deducted from its value; if you're not going to cash in the RRSPs until you're sixty-five, they should be shown without tax deductions.

The example also doesn't include any values for household contents. The usual practice is for spouses not to include values for these figures, but to actually divide them up equally. Each spouse is entitled to share equally in all household contents accumulated during the marriage.

Those contents that were brought by one spouse to the marriage or received as gifts or inheritances are usually retained by that spouse. Contents can be a sticky issue, but you should avoid the temptation to include them in contested matters, since the value of that favourite couch will likely be consumed by one or two telephone calls with a lawyer. I usually tell clients that I won't deal with household contents. If they can't agree to walk around the house marking down items that each will take on separation, I suggest that they create two lists representing equal halves of the contents. Then I ask each spouse to choose one list. Usually, with a little calm discussion and some compromise, people can divide household contents themselves.

FYI

There's an exception to the general practice of dividing household contents equally, without contesting their value. It occurs if one spouse is keeping the home and all the contents. In that case, that spouse should include the market value of the contents on his or her side of the calculation. Market value means the value if you tried to sell them today—think garage sale prices.

The end result in our example is that the husband owes the wife a payment of $35,000. Each retains all the assets in his or her name, such as cars and RRSPs, as shown on the chart. Each is also responsible for the liabilities that are shown in his or her name on the chart. Because the home is jointly owned, each continues to own half the equity in the matrimonial home, and this must be considered in settlement. Either the property must be listed and sold and the proceeds divided equally, or one party can buy out the other's interest. In this case, if the wife wanted to stay in the home, she could buy the husband's equity for $50,000 minus some costs of disposition. Since the husband otherwise owes her a payment of $35,000, she could resolve all property matters and buy his interest in the home by paying him $15,000. If the buy-out was higher, she could get a mortgage to help her make the payment. (The husband's ongoing guarantee of the mortgage will sometimes be necessary.) Likewise, the husband could buy her interest in the home for $50,000, making her total settlement $85,000. If neither can afford the buy-out, the home will have to be sold and the proceeds divided after the mortgage is paid. The husband would probably want to pay the line of credit out of his share of the proceeds, and the individuals would each pay off his or her share of the credit-card debt out of the proceeds as well. The husband's property payment of $35,000 to the wife would come out of his share.

Not every case is this easy. The most common problem occurs when one party owns a valuable pension but there are no other assets to cover the payment to the other spouse. If one individual owes so many debts that his or her net family property is a negative amount, the spouse will be stuck with all the debt. If both parties have substantial debts, neither will owe the other a property payment, and each will be responsible for the debts in his or her own name.

British Columbia, Manitoba, Newfoundland & Nova Scotia

Calculation of property division in these four provinces and the logistics of settlement are similar to our earlier example. The main difference is the treatment of business assets—in these provinces, they are shared or presumed to be shared, unless the non-titled spouse made no contribution to the business or venture or it would be inequitable to share the asset.

British Columbia includes all personal and business assets in sharing unless the business asset is used "primarily for business purposes" and the spouse who doesn't own the property made no direct or indirect contribution to the acquisition or management of the business. An indirect contribution includes "savings through effective management of household or childrearing responsibilities by the spouse who holds no interest in the property." There are no other exclusions for property brought to the marriage, or gifts, inheritances or damages. The B.C. statute contains specific provisions about how to value and divide pensions. It's also unique in that it actually grants each spouse "an undivided half interest in family property as tenants in common," meaning ownership in family property as opposed to a right to receive a payment on account of property, which is given in all other provinces. The difference is theoretical, since other provinces can order the transfer of property, if necessary, to satisfy a money payment that is owed pursuant to the statutory division.

FYI

Tenancy in common is a form of holding title to property. All tenants-in-common are co-owners and have an equal right to use and enjoy the property. On the death of a tenant-in-common, his or her interest passes in accordance with a will, or if there is no will, by intestacy laws.

Joint tenancy is another form of holding title to property. All joint tenants have an equal interest in the property. If one joint tenant dies, his or her share passes directly to the other joint tenants, without passing through the deceased's estate.

Manitoba gives married spouses a right to equalization of all assets. There are exclusions for property acquired before the marriage (except if it was acquired in contemplation of marriage), gifts or inheritances (unless they were given to both spouses), personal injury damages and personal apparel. The court has the discretion to vary equalization of the "commercial assets" (and therefore protect a business asset from sharing) only if it would be "clearly inequitable" to do otherwise, having regard to a list of factors including the "responsibilities and other circumstances of the marriage." The statute states specifically that the conduct of either spouse is irrelevant to this determination.

Newfoundland excludes business assets from sharing, along with property brought to the marriage, gifts, inheritances, personal injury damages and personal effects. The statute provides that, if one spouse has contributed work or money to a business, the court shall direct the business owner to pay an amount to the other to compensate for the contribution or to give the other an interest in the business asset. The section that allows the court to deviate from an equal division of all included property also requires the court to consider, among many factors, "contributions made by each of the spouses to the welfare of the family," including "looking after the matrimonial home or caring for the family." Spousal conduct is explicitly irrelevant. The statute gives special treatment to matrimonial homes: each spouse has a half interest in the home, regardless of title, and is entitled to receive half the net proceeds of sale.

Nova Scotia's statute is similar to Newfoundland's. It excludes gifts or inheritances (except if they were used for the benefit of both spouses and the children), damages for personal injury and personal effects. But assets acquired before the marriage are not excluded and are shared. Business assets are excluded from sharing, but a separate section provides that, if one spouse has contributed work or money to a business, the court "shall" direct the business owner to pay an amount to the other to compensate for the contribution or give the other an interest in the business asset. The section that allows the court to deviate from an equal division of all included property also requires the court to consider, among many factors, "contributions made by housekeeping, childcare or domestic responsibilities that enabled the other spouse to acquire, manage, maintain, operate or improve a business asset."

Family law statutes in all these provinces allow the court to adjust the payment and order unequal division if the normal division would be "unfair" (British Columbia), "unfair or unconscionable" (Nova Scotia), "grossly unfair or unconscionable" (Manitoba), or "grossly unjust or unconscionable" (Newfoundland). Regardless of the difference in terminology, unequal division is ordered with the same reluctance and rarity in all of these provinces, respecting business assets as discussed above.

New Brunswick, Quebec & Yukon Territory

These provinces divide assets into two categories. Family or matrimonial assets are automatically shared. Business assets, gifted or inherited property, and property brought to the marriage are not automatically shared or included in the calculation.

In New Brunswick, business assets are defined as property owned by one spouse and used primarily in the course of a business. Marital property means property that's ordinarily used by the family—whether acquired before or after marriage—and all other property acquired during the relationship except business assets, gifts or inheritances or property acquired after separation. Unlike some other provinces, New Brunswick does not specifically discuss contributions to business assets, making it more difficult for a spouse to share in business property. However, the courts have the power to divide assets that are not marital property if the result of the division would otherwise be "inequitable," that is, if one spouse had assumed household or childcare responsibilities that assisted the other in acquiring, managing, maintaining, operating or improving the property. Unequal division of marital assets may also be ordered if it would be "inequitable" to do otherwise. A family asset that was acquired before the marriage or as a gift may be excluded from sharing if it would be "unfair and unreasonable to the owner to include the family asset." Matrimonial homes receive similar treatment in New Brunswick as in Newfoundland: each spouse is entitled to receive half of the net proceeds from the sale of a matrimonial home, regardless of actual title. However, in New Brunswick, the court may order an unequal division of the net proceeds if it would be "inequitable" regarding a list of factors.

In Quebec, there is a limited right to divide property on separation. The "family patrimony" includes the residences of the family, furnishings, cars, retirement plans, RRSPs and pensions. Debts related to the family patrimony are deducted, and gifts and inheritances are excluded. The family patrimony is then "equally divided" with the result that one spouse may owe the other a payment. Property may be ordered to be transferred to satisfy the payment. Any other property is considered to be "privately owned" and is not subject to sharing. If a spouse cannot prove private ownership, the property is owned jointly. Quebec's statute makes no reference at all to business assets and gives no statutory power to adjust the payment on equitable grounds. While marriage contracts are recognized by the Quebec Civil Code, spouses are not allowed to contract out of the minimum entitlement to divide family patrimony.

In the Yukon, family assets are defined as property ordinarily used by both spouses or their children for shelter or transportation, or for household, educational, recreational, social or aesthetic purposes. Only family assets are to be divided equally. There is no mention of deductions for property brought to the marriage, gifts or inheritances. Neither are business assets specifically mentioned. Non-family assets may be ordered to be divided if a division of family assets would be "unconscionable" regarding several factors, including an assumption of household or childcare responsibilities that assisted the titled spouse in acquiring, maintaining, managing, operating or improving a non-family asset. Another section specifically allows equitable claims to be made against any property as if the parties were unmarried.

In all provinces but PEI, equity, whether or not it's referred to in the statute, would operate to allow trust claims to be made against business or non-family assets if the claiming spouse contributed to their acquisition, growth or value (by investing money in the business or assisting with its operation, or by saving money for other purposes), or if the claiming spouse assumed primary responsibility for childcare or household management. (See the discussion of Resulting and Constructive Trust Claims below.) Given the availability of trust claims in family law, the end result in the average property dispute in these provinces may still be an equal sharing of business assets, provided that the spouse claiming an interest has made direct or indirect contributions to the assets.

Northwest Territories

The Northwest Territories is the only Canadian jurisdiction that doesn't provide for automatic equal division of property or a formula of property division between spouses. Instead, the judge in each case determines division of property according to fair and reasonable criteria. The judge must consider all contributions made by the spouses, including any non-financial contributions.

CANADA PENSION PLAN

An equal division of Canada Pension Plan credits earned by one or both spouses during the marriage is mandatory, if the divorce became final after January 1, 1987. There is no time limit for the application. The credits will be automatically divided by the CPP office once the required forms are submitted to the government. Spouses are not allowed to contract out of mandatory division. The court will ignore any such provision in a contract unless specific provincial legislation allows such agreements. At the time of writing, only British Columbia and Saskatchewan allow a spouse to enforce an agreement in which the parties have contracted out of a division of CPP credits.

RESULTING AND CONSTRUCTIVE TRUST CLAIMS

A trust claim is a claim for a property interest in an asset that is not reflected on title to the property. Trust claims are available outside of and separate from legislation, pursuant to the jurisdiction of Canadian courts to determine "equity," (i.e., what is fair and equitable). In family law, such claims are usually made:

- to obtain a share of a business or non-family asset that's not included in property division or shared between spouses under the relevant family law statute (except in PEI, where such claims are specifically prohibited);
- to share in the increased value of property that has appreciated since separation in provinces in which there is equal sharing of all assets at the date of separation;
- when no property payment would be owed, in order to obtain a share of some particular property; and
- to enable common law and same sex couples, who have no automatic right to divide property under family law legislation, to obtain a share in the asset at issue.

Trust claims are usually made against homes, real estate and business assets. There are two types of trust claims: resulting trust and constructive trust. A resulting trust interest will be granted when the claimant shows that he or she contributed money to the asset or had an express understanding with the other spouse that the property was jointly owned. Either the contribution or the understanding must be definitively proven. If the claim is based on a financial contribution, evidence must show that the money was given and that it was invested in the asset. If the claim is based on an understanding, something more than a mere statement by the claimant is required. The statement must be substantiated by witnesses to the promise, letters confirming it, or other evidence such as proof that the property was transferred into the other's name to avoid creditors. Because these requirements are strict, resulting trust interests are not granted very often.

A constructive trust interest will be granted when the claimant can show that there has been "unjust enrichment":

- that the person against whom the claim is made has enjoyed an "enrichment" because of the actions or contributions of the claimant;
- that the claimant has suffered a corresponding deprivation;
- that there is no reason in law—such as a contract, an obligation or a gift—for the enrichment.

A host of family law cases have concluded that unpaid childcare and normal household services usually create an enrichment and corresponding deprivation. Financial or non-financial contributions to a business (such as a ranch, as in Mrs. Murdoch's case) are also now usually considered to create enrichment.

Once the court finds unjust enrichment, it has a range of remedies available. The two most common remedies in family law are a monetary award representing the value of the contribution or a constructive trust interest giving a percentage property interest in the asset.

The constructive trust interest will be granted only if:
- a monetary award would be insufficient and a property interest as opposed to a money payment is expected; and
- there is a connection between the contribution and the property interest sought.

Factors that point to an "expectation of receiving property interest" are the actual expectations of the parties, the length of the relationship and the extent of the contributions.

In many cases courts have held that the "connection between the contribution and the property" will be satisfied even if the property was acquired before the relationship. In one case, the successful claimant had assumed responsibility for most of the farm chores while her partner travelled, even though he owned the property when they met. Over time, courts have recognized that more general household contributions to the family enterprise may be "linked" to the property. In the court's view, domestic labour and childcare provide the property owner with the time and energy for other matters, including business development and property concerns.

Trust cases are difficult and litigious. Because there are strict requirements in the law and because each case is entirely fact-driven, you may need to obtain legal advice to determine whether you have a viable trust claim. Often after receiving such advice and ascertaining the cost of litigation for both you and your spouse, settlement becomes possible. In other cases, negotiation is fruitless. If you have a good claim, you should persevere, especially if a trust claim is your only means of recovery. Although the road may be long and hard, the majority of constructive trust claims made in a domestic setting are successful.

ADJUSTMENTS TO PROPERTY DIVISION

Most settlements involve some adjustments to the final property numbers representing other financial issues. The most common adjustment is the payment by one spouse of one-half of the mortgage and other costs that have been paid by the other spouse since separation. Sometimes one spouse has retired debts such as credit card obligations owed by the other spouse. Joint debts for which one spouse takes responsibility after separation—such as a loan owed to a family member or outstanding realty taxes—may be subject to an adjustment of one-half the debt. The tax payable at the end of the year on spousal support and sometimes on child support received since separation is sometimes paid by the payer of support as an adjustment to the property payment.

ADVANCES ON PROPERTY DIVISION

If disagreements over property issues persist, one spouse may need an advance on the spousal entitlement. Such an advance may be made by agreement by the parties or may be requested by a spouse in court on an interim motion. If the individual can show that some minimum amount will have to be paid on account of property, a judge will usually make an order for an advance. This is especially so when one spouse shows a clear financial need for the advance, because support is unavailable or insufficient, because the spouse wishes to acquire a home or another necessary asset, or because the spouse needs money to pay legal and accounting fees for use in the litigation.

INTEREST ON PROPERTY AWARDS

Courts often grant an advance on property division (and spouses often agree to it) because interest usually runs on the property division from the date that an action begins. The interest accumulates at a rate prescribed under court rules, usually comparable to commercial interest rates. Many court decisions about interest on a property payment favour the party who has made an advance payment. Likewise, if a spouse refuses unreasonably to give the other spouse an advance, the court will often award a generous interest payment, reflecting the fact that the party controlling the asset has had the sole use and benefit of it since separation.

CHAPTER SIX

The Matrimonial Home

IN THIS CHAPTER: **Matrimonial Home Defined, Automatic Rights of Ownership, Special Treatment of the Home for Property Division Purposes, Exclusive Possession of the Matrimonial Home;** *Who Can Apply for Exclusive Possession, General Principles of Exclusive Possession, Considering Exclusive Possession on Separation,* **Consent to Sale or Encumbrance, Orders for Sale of the Matrimonial Home**

ALL PROVINCES RECOGNIZE THE SPECIAL NATURE OF THE HOME IN THEIR FAMILY LAW LEGISLATION. HISTORICALLY, ONLY THE WIFE HAD A RIGHT TO REMAIN IN THE HOME, BASED ON HER HUSBAND'S OBLIGATION TO SUPPORT HER. NOW THE HOME IS REGARDED AS A PLACE OF SECURITY FOR SPOUSES AND CHILDREN ALIKE, AND MAY OFTEN BE THE SOLE ASSET OF THE SEPARATING SPOUSES. FOR THIS REASON, SPECIAL PROTECTIONS ARE GIVEN TO SPOUSES DURING THE MARRIAGE, AND RIGHTS OF POSSESSION ON SEPARATION ARE EXHAUSTIVELY CONSIDERED IN FAMILY LAW LEGISLATION ACROSS THE COUNTRY.

MATRIMONIAL HOME DEFINED

Rights respecting matrimonial homes are granted only to married couples. Unmarried common law couples and same sex couples are not subject to or granted the same protections of the matrimonial home, except for a limited right given in some provinces to obtain exclusive possession of the matrimonial home as an incident of spousal support.

The exact definition of a matrimonial home varies from province to province (some provinces use the term "family home" or "marital home") but the basic principles are the same across the country. A matrimonial home is a home that is ordinarily occupied by the parties to a marriage as their family residence at the time of separation. A couple may have more than one matrimonial home: a city home, a cottage, a ski chalet and a condo in Florida can all be matrimonial homes.

A matrimonial home does not have to be owned by the spouses. A court may order that a rented property be subject to an order for possession or that the spouse in possession be treated as the tenant for all purposes. However, protections regarding disposition and ownership of the matrimonial home relate only to owned rather than rented dwellings.

AUTOMATIC RIGHTS OF OWNERSHIP

Many people believe that the term "matrimonial home" means that both spouses own the home. This is true only in Newfoundland and New Brunswick, where family law statutes actually create equal ownership of the matrimonial home regardless of actual title, and where the court will order that both parties receive half of the home. These provisions apply only to married couples.

SPECIAL TREATMENT OF THE HOME FOR PROPERTY DIVISION PURPOSES

In Ontario, Prince Edward Island and Saskatchewan, property-sharing rules do not allow a spouse to receive a deduction for a matrimonial home brought to the marriage. The value of all other property brought by a spouse to the marriage can be deducted by the spouse before calculating the value of communal property. The special treatment of the matrimonial home in these provinces means that, if the individuals have little other property apart from the home, if they have substantial debts, or if they don't owe each other an equalization payment for other reasons, each will share equally in the home's equity on separation. In the absence of a marriage contract, a person who brings a home to the marriage often ends up giving a gift to the other spouse of one-half of the home's equity.

The Saskatchewan statute goes even further and requires that the court shall equally divide a matrimonial home or its value unless it would be unfair or inequitable to do so. If the matrimonial home is the only asset to be divided, if the spouses have about equal property, or if no property payment is owed for other reasons, the effect of this provision is to require equal sharing of the equity in the matrimonial home.

EXCLUSIVE POSSESSION OF THE MATRIMONIAL HOME

In all provinces, both spouses have an equal right to possess—that is, to live in—the matrimonial home during the marriage or on separation, regardless of who holds title to the property. Many people misunderstand this fundamental right, believing that it grants equal ownership in the home. But with the exception of the provinces mentioned earlier, family law does not automatically assign ownership rights to the matrimonial home. A "right of possession" merely ensures that, unless a court or the spouses provide otherwise, neither spouse can change the locks or require the other to move.

Spouses can agree in writing, or a court can make an order on an interim or permanent basis, that one spouse shall have exclusive possession of the matrimonial home. Through exclusive possession, one spouse has the sole right to live in the home, to the exclusion of the other. It may include exclusive access to household contents. The spouse in possession may change the locks and, in extreme cases, may contact the police to force the other spouse to vacate the premises. It is an offence, punishable by fine or imprisonment, to breach an exclusive possession order.

Claims for exclusive possession have been refused in the following cases:

- when the wife operated a small business out of the home;
- when there was insufficient evidence that school-age children should stay in the home until they finished Grade 8, given that a change of residence is more the rule than the exception;
- when the only evidence supporting the claim was that the children had suffered trauma as a result of the separation;
- when upkeep costs were so high that they placed too great a burden on one spouse; and
- when it would have been unfair to tie up the husband's equity.

Who Can Apply for Exclusive Possession

Protection of the matrimonial home relating to sale or encumbrance is available to married couples only. But exclusive possession of the home may be granted as "an incident of spousal support" to opposite sex or common law couples as well, since a common law spouse may receive the right to use a home as a supplement to spousal support. These rights are given to common law spouses in British Columbia, Newfoundland, New Brunswick, Ontario, Prince Edward Island and the Yukon. However, if a common law spouse has no need for spousal support, the remedy of exclusive possession may not be available. In provinces where these protections are not available by statute, other arguments could be made in support of a claim for exclusive possession, such as the argument that it's unconstitutional to deny common law couples the rights that are given to married couples. This potential for law reform and other arguments that might be made to obtain exclusive possession are discussed in Chapter 9, "Common Law Couples."

Some recent Charter decisions on the subject of same sex rights indicate that same sex and common law couples should be given equal treatment under the law, and specifically that same sex couples may be entitled to spousal support. If the spousal-support decision is upheld on appeal, exclusive possession may be available as an incident of support to same sex couples in provinces that give the right to opposite sex couples. This potential for law reform and other arguments that a same sex spouse might make to obtain exclusive possession are discussed in Chapter 10, "Same Sex Couples."

General Principles of Exclusive Possession

Because our law grants both spouses an equal right of possession, judges often refuse to grant exclusive possession unless there are very strong reasons to believe that it would be harmful to your emotional health and the health of your children for the family to continue to cohabit. An exclusive possession order is assured only in dramatic cases in which there is a history of physical violence, extreme emotional and verbal abuse, alcoholism or drug addiction, or mental illness. Every order is granted at the discretion of the judge, so other facts may suffice—such as a pattern of strange behaviour, inconsistent parental behaviour, or behaviour that causes some concern to the court. Of course, what is sufficient to one judge may be insufficient to another. It's clear, however, that it's not enough to say that you just can't handle the stress of cohabitation anymore, although that may well be the case.

Considering Exclusive Possession on Separation

Once a couple knows that they're separating, the first practical issue is usually whether one spouse will move out of the home. Many considerations should be evaluated at this time, the most important of which are domestic harmony, emotional stress, and the effect on any children if physical separation does not occur and conflict continues. If one spouse is violent, the issue of exclusive possession becomes urgent, and negotiation will probably not be fruitful or even safe. (This matter is discussed in detail in Chapter 11, "Violence in the Family.") If custody is an issue, the general theory is that your chances of obtaining custody are seriously compromised if you move out and leave the children behind. If you have children, it is usually recommended that the news of the separation precede the physical separation by a week or more to allow the children to absorb the reality. If financial considerations require the immediate listing and sale of the home, you might be reluctant to move out if you wish to control the listing and sale. If you and your spouse are financially strapped, it may be difficult to afford two residences until the home is sold. These are the basic issues, and every situation will be different. In any case, your emotional health and the stress on the kids from witnessing continuing conflict should not take a back seat to tactical concerns unless those concerns are truly pressing and substantial.

Most separating spouses recognize that it's difficult and unhealthy to continue to cohabit after they've made the decision to split. In such cases, an interim agreement can often be negotiated that provides that one spouse will remain in the home, with or without the children. This is also an opportunity to resolve a number of issues, at least on an interim basis. It's essential to agree upon the allocation of financial responsibilities respecting the home, and interim arrangements can often be made with respect to child and spousal support, custody and access.

If you and your spouse can't agree to possession on an interim basis, there are three obvious options: you can wait until other matters are resolved, you can move out, or you can commence an action against your former spouse and ask a court to deal with the matter on an interim motion.

If there are no children and no other motivating concerns, the answer will be to move out yourself. If it appears necessary to ask a court for exclusive possession because of custody issues, you should ask for interim exclusive possession. You should also ask for interim resolution of the ancillary matters such as custody and support, while submitting an alternative claim for interim custody and financial relief that would allow you to move out with the children. In this way, even if your facts are insufficient to require your spouse to move out, you will probably obtain the right to move with the kids.

Exclusive possession can be a frustrating and immediate issue on separation. If you can't resolve it amicably, you should get some legal advice. Be prepared to provide your lawyer with all the facts relating to your current financial situation and show why continued cohabitation is intolerable. The better prepared you are, the more you'll save in legal fees. Comprehensive notes about your spouse's current conduct, including dates and times, exact quotations, and other exhaustive details are essential. For example, a parent who insists on a young child sleeping with him or her after separation, who puts the child in the middle of the conflict, who contradicts the other's attempts at discipline or denigrates the other in the presence of the child may appear to be wholly unreasonable and even emotionally dangerous in the eyes of a child-minded judge. Don't worry that your examples of household difficulties are insignificant: a long list of otherwise insignificant problems may often be sufficient evidence in the big picture. Your lawyer will sort out the compelling facts, and you'll have to swear an affidavit containing all of this evidence. (See Chapter 15, "If You Must...The Structure of the Action.") If the matter is urgent, you'll be pleased that you came prepared and, when you see your own notes transformed into the affidavit, you'll know that you saved yourself time and legal fees.

FYI

Courts often deal with exclusive possession and interim sale at the same time, since they involve many of the same criteria. In response to either claim, the best defence is a good offence. A motion for exclusive possession is usually answered by a cross-motion for interim sale, and vice versa.

CONSENT TO SALE OR ENCUMBRANCE

Family law statutes in all provinces require that both spouses consent to the sale or encumbrance of a matrimonial home, even if only one spouse has actual titled ownership. Any transaction that purports to sell a matrimonial home or encumber it without the consent of both spouses can be set aside by a court. An encumbrance is normally defined as a mortgage or guarantee that is actually registered against the home, but recent Ontario cases have defined an encumbrance more broadly to include any debt-incurring instrument that will likely result in seizure of the home on default. This protection applies during the marriage and after separation unless the parties have released all rights by a separation agreement.

The provision protects both spouses from losing what is often the only asset in a marriage. It was originally aimed specifically at protecting wives, who in earlier times did not always know about their husband's business dealings, from a surprise seizure or sale of the home.

Sometimes it's necessary to ask a court to dispense with one spouse's consent to the sale of the home, or their involvement in the sale process. If a reasonable offer is on the table and your spouse refuses to deal with it appropriately, you should seek an extension from the purchaser and bring an immediate motion before the court asking for approval of the sale or the removal of your spouse from the process. You will have to satisfy the court that the offer reflects market value, with supporting evidence from a real estate agent or appraiser. If one spouse is in possession of the property, with or without children, the court may entertain arguments from that spouse about why the property should not be sold at this time. There is no guarantee of success on motions to dispense with consent; much depends on the evidence presented and the judge's view of what is fair in light of all of the facts.

ORDERS FOR SALE OF THE MATRIMONIAL HOME

As a general rule, a sale of the matrimonial home will not be ordered before spouses have settled all issues between them, except in extraordinary circumstances. However, courts and negotiating spouses always deal with specific facts, ignoring general principles when the practicality of the matter is considered. If you want to get the matrimonial home sold, you need to answer a few important questions before you proceed with a request for sale, either through negotiation or by court application.

Who has title to the property?

If you're the sole owner of the property you have a right to request its sale, either from your spouse or from the court. If you and your spouse are both on title, either as joint tenants or tenants in common, you have a right to request partition and sale. If you're not a titled owner, you will be entitled to request a sale of the property only in limited circumstances.

Who is in possession of the property?

If you're in possession without some reasonable defence from your spouse, and assuming you're entitled to seek a sale, you have a right to request it. If your spouse is in possession, and especially if your spouse and a child or children are in possession, your spouse may raise legitimate reasons why the house should not be sold immediately. If the issue goes before a judge, the judge will consider the availability of alternative accommodation, the cost of carrying the property, and the best interests of any children who are living in the home.

Why do you want the property sold?

If, individually or together, you and your spouse can't afford to continue paying the carrying costs of the property, you'll usually be able to negotiate or obtain a court order for a sale. If you want to free up your capital so that you can purchase alternative accommodation, the odds are about equal that you'll be entitled to a sale, depending on other considerations. If you want the property sold for emotional reasons or because it seems unfair that only one spouse has possession, don't count on it. Unless there are other motivating factors, such considerations are not usually sufficient to obtain a sale of the matrimonial home.

Is the entitlement to equity in dispute?

Payments on account of equalization of property or other property division are often satisfied with the equity from the matrimonial home. So you'll need to have some idea of whether a payment will be owed from one spouse to the other, who will owe it, and from what source it will be made. (See Chapter 5, "Property.") If the matrimonial home is jointly owned and there is little other property, there will sometimes be no dispute about entitlement to the proceeds of sale; each spouse will be entitled to half the net proceeds. In such cases, unless there are other valid considerations, sale of the home will be assured. Even when there's a dispute about the property division, if all other considerations point to the sale of a home the sale will usually proceed as long as some or all of the net proceeds are held in trust as security for the property division. The exact amount held in trust will depend on an estimate of the amount that will be owed or is in dispute.

Logic usually dictates the result of a request for an interim sale. If it's truly necessary for financial reasons, reasonable spouses or their lawyers can usually come to an agreement. If property issues remain unresolved for a long period, and you have a real need for your capital, most judges will be sympathetic provided there are no other more pressing concerns, and provided security for property division is held in trust or paid into court.

The following claims have been used to attempt to avert an order for sale:
- when a wife defended a sale motion by claiming that her friends and family lived in the area and that the family dog would have to be given up upon the sale, she was unsuccessful and the sale was ordered;
- the same result was found for a wife who said that her 23-year-old child required the residence to complete a ski management course;
- where there was insufficient evidence about the children's best interests, a motion for sale was found to be "premature"; and
- when the sale of the matrimonial home "would only compound the emotional devastation of the children" and financial resources were suffi- cient to allow the husband to purchase another home, the wife was suc- cessful in defending a motion for sale and was given three years of exclusive possession.

Given the speculative nature of court applications in this area, especially when children are involved, you should seek legal advice if you feel that the property should be sold. In most cases, the claim should be made in conjunction with other interim relief, so that you get the most for your legal buck. Or you should forgo the interim motion and spend your legal fees on negotiating a comprehensive settlement. Any such settle- ment should, of course, include specific provisions that govern the listing and sale of the matrimonial home, so that you don't have to undergo yet another proceeding to enforce the agreement.

CHAPTER SEVEN

Child Support

IN THIS CHAPTER: **Child Support Guidelines, Federal Guidelines Apply to Married Parents Only, Agreements or Orders Made Before May 1, 1997;** *Grandfathering, Automatic Right of Variation, Negotiations Before May 1, 1997, Arrears Before May 1, 1997,* **Determining Child Support Under the Guidelines;** *Selecting the Provincial Chart, Calculating Income, Number of Children of the Marriage, Plugging Into the Chart, Add-Ons,* **When the Guidelines Do Not Apply;** *Undue Hardship, Household Standard of Living, Considering Undue Hardship for Negotiation Purposes,* **Split Custody, Shared Custody,**

Disclosure Requirements; *Applications and Variations, Annual Disclosure,* **Lump Sum Awards and Security, Variation of Child Support, Enforcement of Child Support;** *Provincial Enforcement Agencies, Garnishment, Monitoring of Payments, Opting Out, Suspension and Refusal of Passports and Licences, Contempt Motions, Enforcement Proceedings*

CHILD SUPPORT IN CANADA IS ABOUT TO UNDERGO REVOLUTIONARY CHANGE. THE FEDERAL GOVERNMENT HAS PASSED ITS FEDERAL CHILD SUPPORT GUIDELINES AND DRAFT REGULATIONS THAT ESTABLISH NEW RULES FOR THE CALCULATION, TAX TREATMENT, VARIATION AND ENFORCEMENT OF CHILD SUPPORT UNDER THE DIVORCE ACT. THIS CHAPTER EXAMINES SOME OF THE CHANGES THAT WILL RESULT.

CHILD SUPPORT GUIDELINES

The basic changes in the new guidelines are that:
- For income tax purposes, the government will no longer allow payers of child support to deduct support payments from their income, nor will it require recipients of child support to include payments in their income;
- The amount of child support will be calculated according to the income of the payer and the number of children, based on the prescribed formula established by each province. With very few exceptions, everyone will have to follow these prescribed calculations;
- To punish debtors and encourage compliance with child support orders, the government has put into effect new and stricter enforcement measures.

The new guidelines make it easier to predict with some certainty the size of child support awards and to encourage settlement of child support. In the average case the guidelines work, since the child support award is taken straight off a chart. However, many arguments can be made about whether the guidelines should apply and whether the amount should be less or more than the guidelines provide. When these arguments arise, the guidelines become complicated and the analysis is confusing. After you review this chapter, you'll probably want to get legal advice—if only for a brief consultation—to be sure that you've reached an appropriate child support figure and considered all the relevant criteria.

FEDERAL GUIDELINES APPLY TO MARRIED PARENTS ONLY

The federal guidelines are passed under the *Divorce Act* and therefore apply to married couples only. Natural parents, common law parents, same sex parents, and others who stand in a parental relationship to a child are often liable to pay child support, but at this point the guidelines apply only to married parents.

Claims for child support by unmarried parents or others are governed by the children's legislation or support legislation in each province. The provinces have to pass their own guidelines that will apply to such claims.

All provinces except Quebec (which has already introduced draft guidelines that consider both parents' incomes) have signed off on the federal guidelines and are expected either to adopt the same guidelines for provincial purposes or to draft their own. The federal government has promised that its guidelines will become effective on May 1, 1997, and has said that its provincial counterparts will also be in place at that date.

It remains to be seen whether this schedule will be met. At the time of writing, the guidelines bill has received Royal Assent, but it remains to be seen what the individual provinces will do. It's possible that different provincial guidelines will be passed, thus creating two different regimes of child support depending on whether the parents are married—this is constitutionally questionable and, if it occurs at all, will probably not survive the scrutiny of our Charter. It's more likely that the provinces will adopt the federal guidelines. If no provincial guidelines are passed, judges will likely determine all child support by looking at the federal guidelines, regardless of who is making the claim.

FYI

If you have any questions about the new provisions, you can call the federal government directly at 1-800-343-8282. You can obtain a copy of the most recent version of the guidelines over the Internet at canada.justice.gc.ca. You can also get a summary of current child support information at www.mcbinch.com/family/childsupport/, the family law website of the law firm of McMillan Binch. Other useful sources are the provincial enforcement agencies, law societies (listed in Appendix C) and the Children's Lawyer.

AGREEMENTS OR ORDERS MADE BEFORE MAY 1, 1997

Grandfathering

The new child support rules will not apply to any agreement or order respecting child support made before May 1, 1997. Old orders or agreements will continue to be in force in the same amount, and the amounts will continue to be deductible from the payer's income and includable to the payee for income tax purposes. Such orders or agreements will be "grandfathered" and will thus retain their validity and tax status until they're varied or terminated. New orders, however, will automatically be subject to the new tax rules.

Automatic Right of Variation

If you're currently paying or receiving child support, you should note that the mere passage of the new rules will entitle all payers and payees to request a variation based on the guidelines. All variations will be subject to the new tax treatment. If you believe that you'll be entitled to a variation because the child support you're currently paying or receiving is more or less than the new guidelines, you should consider negotiating variation before May 1, 1997, to change the amount but stay under the old tax rules.

The guideline amounts are not extremely generous. But there is an assumption that certain add-ons will be shared on a *pro rata* basis in addition to the guideline amounts. This will commonly result in increased child support payments, especially for families with high annual daycare or nanny expenses, since all such expenses are add-ons. In most cases, the guidelines will lead to increased support.

Negotiations Before May 1, 1997

Payers and recipients have good incentive to negotiate child support before May 1, 1997. In almost every case, both parents can benefit, because the payer can retain the tax deductibility and the recipient can increase the amount of the payment based on the guidelines. To reach this win-win situation, you start with the non-taxable guideline amount, plus any add-ons. (Calculating the guideline amounts is discussed later in this chapter.) This amount is then grossed-up for taxes, and the net cost and net benefit to each of the parents is compared. A new computer program called VARYmate (designed by DIVORCEmate Software Inc.) performs this task once the basic income and tax information is provided.

The following example compares the old and new tax treatments. Let's say the husband earns $58,000 and is currently paying $1100 per month, taxable, as child support for two children. The wife earns $15,000 working part-time. The guideline amount of support is $772, non-taxable. The wife pays $4800 annually for daycare, which is an add-on paid on an income-ratio basis (the husband pays 77% of the total cost). The total support payable by the husband under the guidelines is $1039 non-taxable.

AMOUNT OF SUPPORT	TAXABLE?	ACTUAL COST TO HUSBAND	AFTER TAX BENEFIT TO WIFE
$1100 (current)	Yes	$ 664	$ 867
$1039 (guideline am't)	No	$1039	$1039
$1300	Yes	$ 785	$1016
$1500	Yes	$ 906	$1164

Note that the change in tax treatment from taxable to the non-taxable guideline amount means an increased cost to the husband in our example of $375 a month once the guidelines come into effect. However, if the husband pays $1500 a month, and stays under the old tax system, the wife receives $1164 after taxes, and the payment actually costs the husband $906 after the deduction. Both do better than they would under the guidelines. Every case that's negotiated before the enactment of the guidelines will have potential for this kind of win-win situation. The VARYmate calculation that determines the appropriate amount of support and performs these comparisons is excerpted later in this chapter.

It's not easy to perform this kind of comparison without a computer program. If you're trying to determine whether you'll benefit from the new guidelines, you can compare your current amount to the guideline amount by first calculating the guideline amount and then grossing it up for tax purposes. The appropriate gross-up is your average rate of tax— the total amount of income from last year divided by the total amount of tax paid. You'll then have two taxable figures and some idea of whether the guidelines will entitle you to more support than you're receiving. Note that you may be entitled to more or less than the straight guideline amount. (See the Add-Ons and Undue Hardship sections of this chapter.)

If you conclude that you should negotiate an agreement before the guidelines are enacted, go for it. But get some legal advice first (you won't require more than a brief consultation). At a minimum, get your hands on the VARYmate program or a similar product that compares the two tax regimes. If you reach an agreement, state specifically that the agreement contemplates the guidelines, and set out child and spousal support as separate amounts.

In rare cases, the new tax regime will provide better results. If spouses have about equal incomes, there will have been no benefit to the old tax treatment. Some people may simply wish to have non-taxable support to save them the trouble of keeping money for taxes every year. If you decide that the new tax regime is more beneficial to you, you should apply for a variation after May 1, 1997. Be sure to consider whether the difference between the old payment and the guideline amount is sufficient to make the variation process, including legal fees, worth the effort. You'll probably need a brief consultation with a lawyer to ensure that this is the case. Also, most provinces will likely establish special administration programs to assist people in obtaining variances under the new guidelines, which may dramatically reduce or eliminate the cost of proceeding with variation. Contact your law society or provincial enforcement agency to see if such a program has been established in your province.

FYI

The federal government has promised to give the provinces funding to assist with putting the new guidelines into effect, so special variation committees may be set up to help you. The DIVORCEmate software may be installed at family courts, law societies, legal aid offices and community legal clinics. Call your provincial law society, the Federal Child Support Information Line (1-800-343-8282) or DIVORCEmate directly (905-709-7322) for information on locations of the VARYmate program.

Another possibility for settlement after the guidelines are in force is to divide up spousal and child support in a different way to take full advantage of the deductibility/includability of the spousal support. Spousal support has not been affected by the changes to child support: it continues to be deductible/includable. It could also be possible to structure child support entirely as spousal support in a separation agreement. However, such schemes have been unsuccessful in the United States, and it has been suggested that Revenue Canada will see through these arrangements. Courts may also be reluctant to grant a divorce if there is no child support in place. (See Chapter 13, "Divorce, Religious Divorce and Annulment.") You should obtain some tax advice before agreeing to any of these more-creative provisions. Be sure that any such agreement contains a provision that allows for the other spouse to pay any taxes and for variation in the event that Revenue Canada decides that the payments are not deductible/includable.

Arrears before May 1, 1997

Another incentive to negotiate provided by the change in tax treatment of child support is that unpaid arrears may no longer be deductible to the payer if they're paid after the guidelines come into force. Under the old tax regime, late payments continued to be deductible. It seems from the guidelines (although it is not completely clear) that they no longer will be. This change could effectively double the amount of arrears that a payer owes at the time that the guidelines are enacted.

DETERMINING CHILD SUPPORT UNDER THE GUIDELINES

Selecting the Provincial Chart

The appropriate chart is the one for the province in which the payer resides at the time that the child support application is made. If the payer lives outside Canada, then the appropriate chart is the one for the province in which the recipient resides. (See the FYI on page 105.)

Calculating Income

To use the guidelines, you need to know the income of the payer. Income is specifically defined in the guidelines so that a figure can be determined in even the most complicated of cases. If the payer in your case earns simple employment income, his or her current gross salary is the only number you need to apply the guidelines.

If the payer's income is earned through self-employment, from investments, from a privately owned business, or is complicated for other reasons, the final guidelines will contain special provisions for calculating income. The basic idea is that the payer's real income will be considered. So, for example, capital gains and dividend payments will be considered in the actual amount received, rather than the amount shown on the tax return. The starting point will be line 150 of the T1 Tax Return; then specific adjustments will be made. At the time of publication of this book, the final version of income calculation had not been released. The final regulations will be widely available when the guidelines are enacted.

If the amount of income from the tax return or business still doesn't reflect the actual amount of money available for support, the court has broad powers to:

- consider all or part of a business's pre-tax income as the payer's income, or estimate an income that reflects the amount that the payer should be paid for the services performed for the corporation;
- look at the payer's income over the last three years and deduct any amount that is considered to be non-recurring;
- look at the most recent year's income if income has increased or decreased in all of the last three years;
- average out the income received over the last three years, or choose another income that the court considers fair; or
- determine a reasonable income or impute income to a payer if the payer is intentionally unemployed or under-employed (except if this is required by the needs of a child or health reasons), has intentionally reduced income to avoid child support, is not using assets reasonably to generate income, has failed to provide adequate disclosure, unreasonably deducts expenses from income, or lives in a country with lower taxes.

....

FYI

In 1993, Suzanne Thibaudeau sued the federal government, claiming that being taxed on child support offended her right to equal treatment. The government argued that benefits accrued to the family unit from the tax scheme. Thibaudeau lost at trial, won in the Federal Court of Appeal, and lost in the Supreme Court. A year after the final judgment, the government announced that it would change the tax rules of child support. In press releases and speeches, the government adopted all of Thibaudeau's arguments in favour of the change. Our analysis here shows that, in most cases, the government was right; the tax treatment did make more money available for child support. While the government's position in the case may have been principled, this only highlights that the change can be seen as a tax grab.

....

Number of Children of the Marriage

There are separate charts in the guidelines depending on the number of children of the marriage. "Children of the marriage" has been redefined in amendments to the *Divorce Act* to include:

- any natural or adoptive child of the parties;
- a child who is under the age of majority and who has not been withdrawn from parental control, with whom the payer stands in the position of a parent;
- a child who is the age of majority or older and is pursuing "reasonable education" or is unable to withdraw from parental control or be self-supporting because of disability or other cause.

All children who are under the age of eighteen—whether they are the natural, adoptive or stepchildren of the spouse—are entitled to child support. Children over the age of majority as defined above are also entitled to continuing child support. Disabled or mentally ill people or those who for other reasons can't obtain the necessities of life will continue to be children of the marriage after the age of eighteen. However, in the case of children over the age of majority, the court has the discretion to set an amount of child support different than the guidelines, in an amount that the court considers appropriate regarding the financial ability of both parents and the means of the child. This makes both parents' incomes relevant, and will continue the old body of case law that required adult children to make some contribution toward their expenses. In the average case of an adult child who is enrolled in school, the provision may make little difference to the guidelines, but there's room for discretion in some cases to reflect the fact that a child may have an income source or that both parents should be sharing some of the costs.

Plugging Into the Chart

The amount of support is determined by choosing the provincial chart that corresponds to your number of children, and going down the chart until you reach the appropriate income range payable. You will then have to calculate the exact amount of support for the specific income. This amount is the basic guideline amount of non-deductible/non-taxable child support. It may be subject to increase based on add-ons or decrease based on undue hardship or your particular custody arrangement.

Add-Ons

Either parent may be ordered to pay for certain special or extraordinary expenses for a child. Usually, add-ons will be claimed by the recipient, but there may be cases where the payer will ask to have the recipient contribute to an extraordinary expense.

Add-ons are limited to:
- childcare expenses, including daycare or nanny costs;
- extraordinary medical or health-related expenses;
- extraordinary private school expenses or other educational programs that meet the child's needs;
- expenses for post-secondary education; and
- extraordinary expenses for extracurricular activities.

In determining whether to make an order for an add-on, the court will take into account the necessity of an expense in relation to the child's best interests, the reasonableness of the expense having regard to the means of the parents and the child, and the family's pattern of spending before the breakdown of the marriage. The federal government has stated that daycare and nanny costs should be added on in every case in which they're a cost to the family.

The payment of any add-on is to be "in proportion to the parents' incomes," which involves a calculation of the ratio of one parent's income to the other's income. Exactly how this will be interpreted and whether other support payments may be considered remains unclear. The total amount to be apportioned should be reduced by tax deductions that will be available (such as childcare or tuition deductions).

The court can specify a dollar amount or a percentage of the expense to be paid; either by adding or subtracting from child support otherwise payable, in a single annual payment, or directly to the institution.

The chart is an excerpt from the VARYmate computer program. The first page shows the calculations of the guideline amounts and finds the ratio of the parents' incomes for add-on purposes. The second page is the comparison of current support obligations to the guideline amounts and various other taxable and non-taxable support payments. This is useful for calculating an appropriate amount of taxable support if you're negotiating a taxable award before the guidelines are enacted.

VARYmate Variation Optimizer (Page 3)
Federal Child Support Guidelines and
Special or Extraordinary Expenses Calculations
(Complete or amend all shaded areas as applicable)

Federal Child Support Guidelines Payment Schedule Calculation

Number of children of the marriage   2

	Monthly	Annual
Total Payor's Income *(includes actual amount of dividends from Canadian corporations and employment expenses)*		$58,000.00
Adjustments *(if applicable)*		
Plus:		
Actual amount of capital gains in excess of actual capital losses		
Applicable "non-arm's length" payments *(including salaries, wages, management fees or other payments)*		
Other income as determined		
Less:		
Applicable deductible carrying charges		
Other as determined		
Total Payor's income for guideline purposes		**$58,000.00**
Guidelines payment schedule amount (A)	**$772.00**	

Special or Extraordinary Expenses

	Monthly	Annual
Child care	$400.00	$4,800.00
Extraordinary medical and health related (for children only)	$0.00	$0.00
Extraordinary primary, secondary education or to meet child's needs	$0.00	$0.00
Post secondary education (for children only)	$0.00	$0.00
Extraordinary extracurricular activities	$0.00	$0.00
Less:		
Value of $400.00/mth child care deduction, $0.00/mth medical and $0.00/mth educational credits	$51.70	$620.40
Value of applicable subsidies or benefits	$0.00	$0.00
Total Special or Extraordinary Expenses	**$348.30**	
Payor's proportion according to family means *(from "C" below)* X	76.78%	
Total: Payor's portion of special or extraordinary expenses (B)	**$267.42**	
Plus:		
Guidelines payment schedule amount *(from "A" above)*	$772.00	
Total: Guideline + Special or Extraordinary Expenses	**$1,039.42** (A) + (B)	

Calculation of Payor's Proportion of Family Means

Recipient's total means		$17,542.10
Payor's proportion of family means and Payor's total means (C)	76.78%	$58,000.00
Total family means		$75,542.10

D'MORC Emate Software Inc.

DMORC Emate Software Inc.	Comparison of:					Page 4
	(A) Current Support Obligations.					
	(B) Federal Child Support Guidelines + Special/Extraordinary Expenses and					
	Various Other Levels of Taxable and Non Taxable Support Payments					
	1997 - Ontario					
	Monthly Amounts					

Payor: James Example

	Gross Income	Non Taxable Child Support	Deductible Support Payment	Income Tax	Net Disposable Income	Net Cost of Paying Support
A.	$4,833	$0	$1,100	$789	$2,351	$664
B.	4,833	1,039	0	1,225	1,976	1,039
1	4,833	0	1,300	710	2,230	785
2	4,833	0	1,500	631	2,109	906
3	4,833	0	1,700	552	1,988	1,027

Current and Guideline Support Amount Information	
A. Today's Taxable **Child** Support Obligation	$1,100
B. Guideline + Special Expenses entitlement after April 30, 1997	$1,039
Taxable **Spousal** Support Obligation *(if applicable)*	$0

Recipient: Jane Example

	Gross Income	Non Taxable Child Support	Taxable Support Payment	Income Tax	Net Disposable Income	Net Benefit of Receiving Support
A.	$1,250	$0	$1,100	$233	$2,306	$867
B.	1,250	1,039	0	0	2,478	1,039
1	1,250	0	1,300	284	2,454	1,016
2	1,250	0	1,500	336	2,602	1,164
3	1,250	0	1,700	399	2,739	1,301

Payor's Net Disposable Income = Gross Income - Taxable and Non Taxable Support Payments
- Income Tax - RRSP contribution ($417/mon) - RPP contribution ($0/mon)
- CPP ($71/mon) + Child Tax Benefit ($0/mon)
- UIC ($106/mon) + GST Credit ($0/mon) - Deductions at source and taxable benefits ($0/mon)

Recipient's Net Disposable Income = Gross Income + Taxable and Non Taxable Support Payments
- Income Tax - RRSP contribution ($0/mon) - RPP contribution ($0/mon)
- CPP ($26/mon) + Child Tax Benefit ($212/mon)
- UIC ($38/mon) + GST Credit ($40/mon) - Deductions at source and taxable benefits ($0/mon)

When the Guidelines Do Not Apply

The strict guideline amount will not apply, or will be subject to scrutiny, in the following situations:
* in cases of "undue hardship";
* when one spouse earns more than $150,000 a year;
* in cases of shared custody; and
* when the child for whom the support is paid is over the age of majority.

All of these situations are discussed in this chapter. If one of them exists, or a claim is made in respect to one of them, the income of the recipient will be relevant and mutual financial disclosure will be required. (See the Disclosure Requirements section later in this chapter.) Remember that the federal guidelines will apply only to married, separating spouses. Unmarried parents, same sex parents and non-parents claiming child support will be governed by provincial rules.

Undue Hardship

Support may be increased or decreased from the guideline amount in cases of undue hardship. Because of the add-on provisions, it's unlikely that undue hardship will be claimed in support of increases, although this is a possibility.

Are there factors that create undue hardship? The first step in considering undue hardship is to ask yourself this question. The guidelines provide some circumstances that may cause undue hardship, but the list is not exhaustive and courts will no doubt consider other factors as well. The list indicates that the following may create undue hardship:
* when the spouse is paying "unusually high levels of debt" that were incurred to earn a living or before separation;
* when the spouse has "unusually high" access expenses (if a child lives in another province or country);
* when the spouse has a support obligation to any person under a court order or separation agreement (in which case the amount deducted from the guideline amount shall not exceed what is paid annually after considering tax deductions); or

- when the spouse has a duty to support a child who is not a child of the marriage (usually this would be a child of a new relationship).

One of these facts, or some other fact that strikes the court as creating undue hardship, must exist before the guideline amount is adjusted. You must also know the amount of this hardship expense, since the amount will be inserted into the household standard of living test.

Household Standard of Living

The person claiming undue hardship must show that payment of child support under the guidelines will result in his or her household having a lower standard of living than the household of the other parent. The household standard of living may be determined according to the complicated calculation set out in the draft guidelines, which takes the incomes of all household members, deducts only certain undue-hardship expenses (for example, any extraordinary access costs or debt payments), and adjusts for a basic low-income amount.

The end result of the calculation is a ratio based on each party's household standard of living. Only the spouse whose household standard of living is lower can claim undue hardship. It will be very difficult to satisfy the household standard of living test to get over the undue hardship threshold. The following excerpts from the SOLmate program (produced by DIVORCEmate Software Inc.) illustrate the point. The husband from the example discussed earlier in this chapter will still have a higher standard of living than the wife if he pays the guideline amounts and another $24,000 in debts annually (note that the undue hardship expense of these debts is deducted when considering his standard of living). If he has another $6000 in access expenses annually, these will make his household standard of living lower than his wife's and may invoke the undue hardship provisions. Note also that if he has a new spouse who earns $20,000 gross annually, his household standard of living will be higher than his wife's even if he has the extra $30,000 in allowable undue hardship expenses to pay on top of the guideline amounts.

SOLmate – Comparison of Household Standards of Living Test (Page 1) SCHEDULE II (*Subsection 5(4)*) Adjusted Household Income Ratio Comparison *(Complete or amend all shaded areas as applicable)*		
Total Adjusted Household Income	Payor Annual	Recipient Annual
Family Name(s) **James Example**		
Total Income:		
Employment income	$58,000	$15,000
Self-employed (net)		
Rental (net)		
Dividends (actual $Cdn amount received)		
Other taxable income		
Social Assistance & other non taxable income		
Child Tax Benefit		$2,542
Other Income		
Totals	$58,000	$17,542
Adjustments *(if applicable)*		
Plus:		
Actual amount of capital gains in excess of actual capital losses		
Applicable "non-arm's length" payments *(including salaries, wages, management fees or other payments)*		
Income *(including adjustments)* of any other person(s) in the household		
Other income as determined		
Less:		
Applicable deductible carrying charges		
Other as determined		
Total Household Income	$58,000	$17,542
Less:		
Sch II, 2a)(i) Circumstances that may cause undue hardship:		
5.(2)(a) Unusually high level of debts reasonably incurred to support the spouses and their children prior to the breakdown of the marriage or to earn a living	$24,000	
5.(2)(b) Unusually high access costs and expenses		
5.(2)(c) Legal duty under any court order or separation agreement to support any person		
Sch II, 2a)(ii) Guideline + Special Expenses amount paid	$12,473	
Sch II, 2a)(iii) Cost to the Payor of any other support obligation		
Other as determined		
Plus:		
Sch II, 2b)(i) Guideline + Special Expenses amount received		$12,473
Sch II, 2b)(ii) Benefit to Recipient of any other child support received		
Other as determined		
Total Adjusted Household Income (A)	$21,527	$30,015

Household Configuration and Low Income Measures Amount		
	Payor	Recipient
Number of children in household		2
Number of adults in household	1	1
Applicable Low Income Measures Amount (B)	$12,299	$20,908

| **Adjusted Household Income Ratio (A)/(B)** | 1.7503 | 1.4356 |

© MORC Emate Software Inc.

SOLmate - Comparison of Household Standards of Living Test (Page 1) SCHEDULE II (*Subsection 5(4)*) Adjusted Household Income Ratio Comparison *(Complete or amend all shaded areas as applicable)*		
Total Adjusted Household Income	Payor Annual	Recipient Annual
Family Name(s) :James Example		
Total Income:		
Employment income	$58,000	$15,000
Self-employed (net)		
Rental (net)		
Dividends (actual $Cdn amount received)		
Other taxable income		
Social Assistance & other non taxable income		
Child Tax Benefit		$2,542
Other Income		
Totals	$58,000	$17,542
Adjustments *(if applicable)*		
Plus:		
Actual amount of capital gains in excess of actual capital losses		
Applicable "non-arm's length" payments *(including salaries, wages, management fees or other payments)*		
Income *(including adjustments)* of any other person(s) in the household		
Other income as determined		
Less:		
Applicable deductible carrying charges		
Other as determined		
Total Household Income	$58,000	$17,542
Less:		
Sch II, 2a)(i) Circumstances that may cause undue hardship:		
5.(2)(a) Unusually high level of debts reasonably incurred to support the spouses and their children prior to the breakdown of the marriage or to earn a living	$24,000	
5.(2)(b) Unusually high access costs and expenses	$6,000	
5.(2)(c) Legal duty under any court order or separation agreement to support any person		
Sch II, 2a)(ii) Guideline + Special Expenses amount paid	$12,473	
Sch II, 2a)(iii) Cost to the Payor of any other support obligation		
Other as determined		
Plus:		
Sch II, 2b)(i) Guideline + Special Expenses amount received		$12,473
Sch II, 2b)(ii) Benefit to Recipient of any other child support received		
Other as determined		
Total Adjusted Household Income (A)	$15,527	$30,015

Household Configuration and Low Income Measures Amount	Payor	Recipient
Number of children in household		2
Number of adults in household	1	1
Applicable Low Income Measures Amount (B)	$12,299	$20,908
Adjusted Household Income Ratio (A)/(B)	1.2625	1.4356

D MORC Emate Software Inc.

SOLmate – Comparison of Household Standards of Living Test (Page 1) *SCHEDULE II (Subsection 5(4)* Adjusted Household Income Ratio Comparison *(Complete or amend all shaded areas as applicable)*		
Total Adjusted Household Income	**Payor Annual**	**Recipient Annual**
Family Name(s):**James Example**		
Total Income:		
Employment income	$58,000	$15,000
Self-employed (net)		
Rental (net)		
Dividends (actual $Cdn amount received)		
Other taxable income		
Social Assistance & other non taxable income		
Child Tax Benefit		$2,542
Other Income		
Totals	$58,000	$17,542
Adjustments *(if applicable)*		
Plus:		
Actual amount of capital gains in excess of actual capital losses		
Applicable "non-arm's length" payments *(including salaries, wages, management fees or other payments)*		
Income *(including adjustments)* of any other person(s) in the household	$20,000	
Other income as determined		
Less:		
Applicable deductible carrying charges		
Other as determined		
Total Household Income	$78,000	$17,542
Less:		
Sch II, 2a)(i) Circumstances that **may** cause undue hardship:		
5.(2)(a) Unusually high level of debts reasonably incurred to support the spouses and their children prior to the breakdown of the marriage or to earn a living	$24,000	
5.(2)(b) Unusually high access costs and expenses	$6,000	
5.(2)(c) Legal duty under any court order or separation agreement to support any person		
Sch II, 2a)(ii) Guideline + Special Expenses amount paid	$12,473	
Sch II, 2a)(iii) Cost to the Payor of any other support obligation		
Other as determined		
Plus:		
Sch II, 2b)(i) Guideline + Special Expenses amount received		$12,473
Sch II, 2b)(ii) Benefit to Recipient of any other child support received		
Other as determined		
Total Adjusted Household Income (A)	$35,527	$30,015

Household Configuration and Low Income Measures Amount		
	Payor	Recipient
Number of children in household		2
Number of adults in household	2	1
Applicable Low Income Measures Amount (B)	$17,219	$20,908
Adjusted Household Income Ratio (A)/(B)	2.0632	1.4356

DMORC Emate Software Inc.

SOLmate - Comparison of Household Standards of Living Test (Page 1) SCHEDULE II (*Subsection 5(4)*) Adjusted Household Income Ratio Comparison *(Complete or amend all shaded areas as applicable)*		
Total Adjusted Household Income	Payor Annual	Recipient Annual
Family Name(s) James Example		
Total Income:		
Employment income	$58,000	$15,000
Self-employed (net)		
Rental (net)		
Dividends (actual $Cdn amount received)		
Other taxable income		
Social Assistance & other non taxable income		
Child Tax Benefit		$2,542
Other Income		
Totals	$58,000	$17,542
Adjustments *(if applicable)*		
Plus:		
Actual amount of capital gains in excess of actual capital losses		
Applicable "non-arm's length" payments *(including salaries, wages, management fees or other payments)*		
Income *(including adjustments)* of any other person(s) in the household	$20,000	
Other income as determined		
Less:		
Applicable deductible carrying charges		
Other as determined		
Total Household Income	$78,000	$17,542
Less:		
Sch II, 2a)(i) Circumstances that **may** cause undue hardship:		
5.(2)(a) Unusually high level of debts reasonably incurred to support the spouses and their children prior to the breakdown of the marriage or to earn a living	$24,000	
5.(2)(b) Unusually high access costs and expenses	$12,000	
5.(2)(c) Legal duty under any court order or separation agreement to support any person		
Sch II, 2a)(ii) Guideline + Special Expenses amount paid	$12,473	
Sch II, 2a)(iii) Cost to the Payor of any *other* support obligation		
Other as determined	$7,000	
Plus:		
Sch II, 2b)(i) Guideline + Special Expenses amount received		$12,473
Sch II, 2b)(ii) Benefit to Recipient of any *other child* support received		
Other as determined		
Total Adjusted Household Income (A)	$22,527	$30,015

Household Configuration and Low Income Measures Amount	Payor	Recipient
Number of children in household		2
Number of adults in household	2	1
Applicable Low Income Measures Amount (B)	$17,219	$20,908
Adjusted Household Income Ratio (A)/(B)	1.3083	1.4356

DIVORCEmate Software Inc.

There is room for other evidence to be filed about the comparative standards of living in each home other than by the guideline calculation, because the guidelines say that the court *may* consider that calculation. Some lawyers have suggested that actuaries or accountants could provide other forms of evidence that would support an undue hardship even if the claimant doesn't satisfy the household standard of living test.

Considering Undue Hardship for Negotiation Purposes

If you wonder whether undue hardship will be a factor in considering child support in your case, get a copy of the guidelines and do the math for the lower standard of living test, even if you have to estimate incomes for the other household. If you want to be really sure that your calculations are correct, retain a lawyer who can plug the information into the SOLmate program, or call the contacts referred to earlier in this chapter. In most cases, estimating incomes will give you a reliable idea of whether a court will entertain arguments about undue hardship, which will allow you to consider appropriate amounts of child support for settlement purposes. In some cases, spouses will simply have no clue of the income of the other household. To find out, they'll need to make a claim for variation. If you're considering this before the guidelines come in, you should try to resolve it directly with your former spouse by initiating negotiation, either privately or through lawyers, to achieve a win-win situation.

SPLIT CUSTODY

Where both parents have custody of one or more of the children of the marriage (for example, one lives with one parent and another lives with the other parent), child support will be equal to the difference between the amount each parent would pay to the other under the guidelines. To calculate this amount, you should plug one parent's income into the chart with the number of the children in their care, and then do the same for the other parent. The parent whose guideline amount is greater will pay the difference to the other parent. The net add-ons payment is determined by the same set-off method.

SHARED CUSTODY

Where the parents share custody of one or more kids on an approximate-
ly equal time basis, the guidelines may not apply. The draft version of the
guidelines states that in shared custody arrangements the court will have
broad discretion to take into account the following:

- the amounts set out in the guidelines;
- the increased costs of shared custody arrangements; and
- the conditions, means, needs and other circumstances of each parent and
  of any child for whom support is sought.

The first consideration in the list presumably requires the calculation of
each parent's entitlement to child support under the guidelines, assuming
each had sole custody of the children, and a comparison of those
amounts as prescribed for cases of split custody. However, since the
guideline amounts were reached by assuming that one parent had the
child full-time, they're of little help in considering a shared custody
arrangement in which both parents have about equal costs all of the
time. It seems more appropriate to divide the guideline amounts in half,
to reflect the fact that each parent has the child half the time, and then
compare the two amounts.

The second and third considerations represent the pre-guideline
analysis of child support in alternating residence arrangements. In such
cases, childcare budgets for each parent were studied (considering the
fact that each has costs associated with having the child half the time)
to determine the child's total needs. The parents' incomes in ratio to
each other were then applied to the total amount to determine the
amount that the higher-income parent should pay to subsidize the
other's childcare costs.

This section of the guidelines has been highly criticized for being
vague and the federal government is considering revising it before the
final version is released. If you have an equal-time access arrangement,
you'll need to find out how the final guidelines have treated the issue.
You can do this by contacting the federal government or the other agencies described in this chapter.

For settlement purposes, the practical answer in these cases will be
to look at the childcare costs of both parents, including attributing a
portion of all household expenses to the child and considering any

particular child-related expenses. Taking a ratio of each parent's income to the other is a logical way of equalizing costs. The calculation under the guidelines described for split custody, divided in half, may provide a comparative figure. Consider any add-ons (although they are noticeably absent from the shared custody considerations). Look at what your childcare expenses were when you were together, consider who'll pay each expense now that you're separated and each parent's costs of maintaining the child half the time, and come up with a figure, based on the ratio of your incomes, that will amount to a subsidy of the lower-earning spouse's expenses. Since shared-custody situations require cooperation and communication, most couples in such a position can also agree upon an amount of child support that seems fair and reasonable in all circumstances.

DISCLOSURE REQUIREMENTS

Applications and Variations

The following information comprises the standard disclosure document:
- personal tax returns and notices of assessment for the three previous years;
- if you're an employee, the most recent statement of earnings or a letter from your employer setting out your current rate of annual salary and remuneration;
- if you're self-employed, financial statements from your business for the three previous tax years;
- if you're in a partnership, confirmation of your income including draw from, and capital in, the partnership for the partnership's three previous tax years; and
- if you control a corporation, financial statements of the corporation and its subsidiaries for the three previous tax years.

The following disclosure rules apply under the guidelines:
- If you're an applicant for child support or for variation of child support, the standard disclosure documents must accompany your application;
- If you're served with a claim for child support or for variation of child support, the standard disclosure documents must be served on the claimant within twenty-one days;

- If either parent claims add-ons or undue hardship in a child support application, the parent who would be receiving child support must provide the standard disclosure documents to the other within twenty-one days (presumably only if those documents have not already been provided in the course of the application); and
- If during the course of the child support application or variation it is determined that the parent who will be paying child support earns income of more than $150,000, the other parent must provide the standard disclosure documents within twenty-one days (again, presumably only if those documents have not already been provided in the course of the application).

Note that there's no formal requirement for disclosure of standard documents by non-parties, such as new spouses or other persons with whom the parent cohabits. This information is directly relevant to claims for undue hardship and indirectly relevant to add-ons and shared custody cases. Presumably an adverse inference will be drawn from a failure to provide such information in the case of undue hardship, since it will be impossible for a court to perform the lower standard of living test.

If your spouse or former spouse fails to comply with disclosure requirements, you may take the following steps:

- apply for a hearing or a move for judgment, in which case the court may draw an adverse inference; impute income to a parent; or order costs against a parent who has failed to meet disclosure requirements;
- apply (without notice to the other parent) for an order requiring the disclosure to the court. If the order is disregarded, the court may strike the other parent's pleadings, make a contempt order, draw an adverse inference, or impute income or order costs against a parent who has failed to meet disclosure requirements; or
- instruct your lawyer to examine the other parent for discovery in order to obtain the information.

Annual Disclosure

If an order is made for child support under the guidelines, the payer is required to provide the standard disclosure documents annually to the recipient, at the recipient's request. This is intended to be informal disclosure without court involvement. If disclosure is refused upon request, the court will make an order for disclosure on application and will require the refusing parent to pay all of the applicant's costs.

If an order has been made pursuant to the add-ons, undue hardship provisions, or because one party earned more than $150,000, both parties must provide annual disclosure on request from the other. Presumably, although it is not specifically mentioned, annual mutual disclosure would also be required in split custody and shared custody arrangements.

Annual disclosure means annual potential for variation of child support. Annual disclosure should, over time, allow parents to look at the changes in their positions and agree upon minor adjustments to the child support as needed, rather than engaging in costly litigation each time a change occurs. If deals are made, the court will usually approve the agreement, although it does have a duty to satisfy itself that the consent variation makes reasonable arrangements for the child.

On the face of the guidelines, you can't contract out of annual disclosure. Nevertheless, two methods have been suggested for avoiding the disclosure requirements. Neither is foolproof. First, parties who enter into agreements with terms that are not incorporated into an order or judgment would not be strictly bound by the annual disclosure requirements, since the guidelines refer to court orders. However, in some provinces agreements that are filed with the provincial court become court orders, which would defeat this plan. Even failing this, a child support agreement would probably provide only a few years of peace until it benefited either spouse to request disclosure, at which time a court would order it. The second method of avoiding annual disclosure is by agreeing upon a lump-sum payment of child support, which is discussed below.

The sensible conclusion is that you can't contract out of the annual disclosure requirements in the guidelines. From now on, just think of annual disclosure as one of the realities of life, like death and taxes.

LUMP SUM AWARDS AND SECURITY

Child support is usually to be paid on a monthly basis. There will be some cases in which a lump sum is ordered, as follows:

- If child support is adjusted retroactively, to the date of commencement of the application or some other date, a single lump sum representing the retroactive payments may be ordered in addition to the periodic payments;

- If there's real concern about future enforcement and there's property available to satisfy a lump sum, one may be ordered instead of periodic payments.

Since it may be difficult to calculate an appropriate lump sum under the guidelines, other forms of security for the payment (such as a charge on property) may be preferable if there's a pattern of non-payment or a risk of the payer leaving the jurisdiction.

Another form of security is the common provision in court orders or separation agreements requiring one or both parties to designate an irrevocable life insurance policy with a specified face value and to keep such a policy in place until the child support obligation terminates.

For settlement purposes, there may be cases in which a single lump sum representing child support for the child's life is required by circumstances or preferable because it ends interaction between the parents. As indicated above, a lump sum may also be attractive because it eliminates annual disclosure requirements. All child support settlements have to be approved by a court, so it remains to be determined if courts will continue to approve lump sums or property transfers that are meant to terminate child support obligations.

In the past, it has been held that a parent can't bargain away a child's rights. If the lump sum was entirely spent or turned out to be too low, or if the child was suffering a real need, more child support could be ordered even if the agreement contained a waiver of future child support claims. This tendency to reopen child support cases has resulted in a standard demand by payers of lump sums for the recipient to provide security—usually in the form of a mortgage on property or a personal guarantee—that could be called upon to obtain a refund of the lump sum if the issue was later reopened. This highlights the difficulties for both parties in predicting that a lump sum will meet the child's needs for a long period. Given that the policy behind the guidelines is to regularize support and to ensure that accurate amounts are ordered for all children, courts may be even more willing to disregard agreements than they were in the past, making lump sums even more volatile. Additionally, given that the child support amount may be changed as frequently as once a year and that there could be changes in custody, a single payment is dangerously speculative for both parents.

If you want to determine what an appropriate lump sum of child support would be, calculate the appropriate amount of support under the guidelines, including add-ons, and then estimate how long the child support will be payable. Call a stock broker or insurance agent and find out the present amount required to purchase an annuity that would pay the total amount of support annually, over the estimated number of years. This will be an appropriate lump sum, and the court will likely approve the arrangement given that it is based on the guidelines. Security may or may not be granted to give the payer some remedy if a later claim for support is made. If the estimated number of years doesn't include the years of post-secondary education, you could agree that the parties will share those costs in accordance with the guidelines or on a ratio of their incomes, at the time that they are incurred.

VARIATION OF CHILD SUPPORT

Variation of pre-guideline child support is discussed earlier in the section called Agreements or Orders Made Before May 1, 1997. As indicated, the guidelines will entitle either party to an existing child support arrangement to seek a variation. There may be facilities in your province to short-cut initial variations because such a great number of variations are anticipated. Comparing the guidelines to your current child support and considering the costs of variation are also discussed in that section.

Variation of orders made or negotiated under the guidelines will proceed in the same way as the initial application. Disclosure will be required according to the issues raised. Add-ons and undue hardship will be considered if raised—or reconsidered if they were part of the original package. Annual disclosure requirements are meant to facilitate the frequent analysis of the adequacy of child support, and allow parents to consider the costs and benefits of proceeding with a variation. If the annual disclosure shows that you would be entitled to pay or receive a different amount of child support under the guidelines, a court will vary the amount. This should create incentive for amicable adjustments to the child support as required from year to year.

ENFORCEMENT OF CHILD SUPPORT

Provincial Enforcement Agencies

Governments have become very sensitive to the pervasive problem of non-payment of child support. In the last five years, all provinces have established enforcement agencies to collect child support and assist parents in enforcing agreements without legal representation. The difficulty with many of these agencies is that they are understaffed. In Ontario, for example, ninety-seven caseworkers manage 150,000 current files. They simply can't manage all possible enforcement cases. It may be necessary to inspire the agency to action or to retain your own counsel to take enforcement measures if you have difficulty. (A list of agencies is found at the end of this book.)

The features common to most of the enforcement agencies are: the computerized monitoring of support payments; automatic, province-initiated enforcement proceedings in the event of default; the provision of Crown lawyers to act for recipients in the enforcement process; and legislation to assist in locating absent debtors.

FYI

Provincial governments have set up enforcement agencies to collect child support and assist parents in enforcing agreements without legal representation. Unfortunately, these agencies are understaffed. In Ontario, for example, ninety-seven caseworkers manage 150,000 current files.

Garnishment

Provincial enforcement agencies administer the garnishment of child support directly from the payer's income. Garnishment is automatically ordered when child support is granted in Alberta, Saskatchewan, Manitoba, Ontario, Newfoundland, New Brunswick, the Yukon and the Northwest Territories. In all other provinces, such orders are regularly made on proof that the payer is defaulting regularly. Amazingly, many payers are insulted or angered by garnishment. Given that it's mandatory in many provinces and common in all, payers should stop reacting emotionally and recognize garnishment as a fact of family law designed to protect their children.

Monitoring of Payments

In most provinces, whether or not the support is paid by garnishment, support payments are made directly to the provincial enforcement agency rather than to the other parent. A computerized system keeps track of payments and spits out immediate notices of default. If a garnishment system is in place, the garnishment will be automatically increased in the event of the default to start making up the arrears. If defaults continue, or garnishment is ineffective, the provincial authority will commence an enforcement proceeding, and will represent the recipient at the hearing. (In some cases, the recipient is not even required to attend the hearing.)

When the support begins to be paid through the agency, there is often a lag time of a few months as the administrative issues are handled. It is a good idea to handle the first few payments directly to avoid the hardship that comes from these initial delays. You can always adjust for any overpayment later. Once the payments begin to flow, they usually continue without further delays and arrive on a regular basis.

If you're paying or receiving child support through an enforcement agency, be aware that mix-ups can occur. Because the administrative machine is so complex and the number of cases so large it is sometimes quite a task to sort out the confusion. Your best bet is to visit the enforcement agency first thing in the morning, or fax them until you get a response. Telephone communication is usually more than a little frustrating.

Opting Out

In some provinces, you can opt out of monitoring of payments and/or automatic garnishment by a written agreement or by court order that instructs the agency not to take any enforcement measures unless one party makes a further request. If you or your spouse wants to avoid making payments through the agency or automatic garnishment, call your provincial agency to see if those options are available and, if so, what specific words must be in the agreement or court order. If you're a recipient, you should insist on language in such an agreement that allows you to enforce the agreement in the event of one or more defaults in payment. This will also provide incentive for prompt payment to avoid future enforcement by the provincial agency.

Suspension and Refusal of Passports and Licences

The draft regulations to the guidelines allow for the suspension and refusal of passports and all types of federal licences, including, for example, commercial and private pilot licences, fishing and shipping licences, and federal certificates. Similar legislation is expected to be contained in the provincial guidelines and will likely include drivers' licences. Ontario has already enacted such legislation. Such packages are also expected to include reports of default to credit bureaus, seizure of lottery winnings, registration of defaults against assets to allow the collection of arrears when an asset is sold, and better methods for locating debtors.

The guideline provisions about passports and federal licences require a provincial enforcement agency to complete a prescribed form and swear that the debtor is in "persistent arrears"; that the enforcement agency has made reasonable attempts to enforce the order before making the licence denial application; and that the debtor has received thirty days' notice that a licence denial application will be initiated. Immediately upon receipt of the licence denial application, the appropriate minister is required to suspend the licence, inform the debtor of the suspension, and refuse to issue any further or other licence to the debtor.

There is no appeal from the suspension of a licence, but the provincial agency must immediately stop all action under these provisions when it is satisfied that the debtor is no longer in arrears or is complying with a payment plan that the provincial agency considers reasonable; or is unable to pay the amount in arrears and the licence suspension is deemed unreasonable in the circumstances.

Contempt Motions

Enforcement may also be pursued by a motion for contempt. In most provinces, chronic non-payment of child support amounts to contempt of court, and the contempt is punishable by fine or imprisonment for up to ninety days. Judges have held that contempt is not the first step in enforcement; where garnishment is available, it should be attempted first. These motions are usually countered by claims by the debtor that the child support should be varied because the debtor cannot afford the current amount. Claims to reduce arrears are often made as well. Because of the serious nature of contempt motions, there are specific procedural rules in each province that must be met before the motion can be heard. The most common requirement is that the motion must be served personally on the debtor. If your spouse is chronically in arrears, you should consult with a lawyer and discuss contempt as an option. Courts are often reluctant to order a payer to go to jail until payment is made, because incarceration hinders the ability to earn income. However, in cases of willful refusal to pay or clear ability to do so, an incarceration order usually inspires immediate payment of arrears.

Enforcement Proceedings

As indicated earlier, provincial enforcement agencies will initiate enforcement proceedings against a parent who owes child support. If the arrears are substantial and your agency shows no inclination to commence proceedings, you can attempt to get them going or you can start your own proceeding without their assistance. You do so in the same way as you commence any action, by filing an application and supporting materials with the court and serving the documents on the defaulting parent. Often such proceedings are countered by claims for reduction of the amount of child support and/or reduction of outstanding arrears.

No rule prohibits enforcement of large amounts of arrears. In fact, there are several cases involving orders for payment of more than $100,000 in arrears. But it is a good idea to take enforcement measures early to avoid the accrual of substantial arrears. If the arrears are very high and are thus unmanageable, courts are often sympathetic to debtors and will reduce the total. This seems very unfair to the child in most cases, and the result should be avoided by fast action. Given the current attitudes and procedures with respect to enforcement of child support, such long-term arrears will probably not be allowed to accrue in any event.

Enforcement proceedings are essentially trials, involving live evidence and legal arguments. Even in courts designed just for these purposes and in systems that encourage parties to act on their own behalf, it is still dangerous to do so. On the other hand, it is costly to retain a lawyer—and you may not recover the costs from your former spouse, especially if there are also arrears to collect. This brings us back to the motivation of the legislatures in establishing provincial enforcement agencies. With the new powers of garnishment and licence suspension, along with anticipated provincial measures, it should be possible to avoid taking on enforcement for yourself. If you're considering doing so as a last resort, talk to the provincial agency again or retain a lawyer to pressure the provincial agency to take up your cause.

Chapter Eight

Spousal Support

IN THIS CHAPTER: **Objectives of Spousal Support,
Entitlement;** *Who Can Claim Spousal Support, Establishing
Entitlement,* **Amount of Support, Duration of Support, Tax
Treatment, Lump Sum Support, Interim Support Orders,
Security for Support, Enforcement, Variation of Support**

THE LAW OF SPOUSAL SUPPORT WAS ONCE SO UNPREDICTABLE AND SUBJECT TO SUCH JUDICIAL WHIM THAT MADAM JUSTICE ABELLA DESCRIBED IT AS A RUBIK'S CUBE FOR WHICH THERE WAS NO ANSWER BOOK. THE FEDERAL *DIVORCE ACT* AND PROVINCIAL LEGISLATION GIVE AUTHORITY TO COURTS TO GRANT SPOUSAL SUPPORT, AND THESE STATUTORY PROVISIONS ARE OVERFLOWING WITH LISTS OF PURPOSES AND FACTORS THAT THE COURTS SHOULD CONSIDER. IN 1992, THE SUPREME COURT OF CANADA ISSUED A LANDMARK DECISION IN THE CASE OF *MOGE* V. *MOGE*, WHICH CONSIDERED ALL ASPECTS OF SPOUSAL SUPPORT AND PROVIDED GENERAL PRINCIPLES FOR ALL SUPPORT APPLICATIONS. WHILE SPOUSAL SUPPORT IS ALWAYS BASED ON THE FACTS BETWEEN THE PARTIES, THE *MOGE* DECISION HAS COME A LONG WAY IN PROVIDING US WITH THE ANSWER BOOK FOR SPOUSAL SUPPORT IN CANADA.

Mr. and Mrs. Moge had been married about twenty years, and separated in 1973. Mrs. Moge had a Grade 7 education, and during the marriage she took care of the children and the house, earning money by cleaning offices at night. When they separated, Mr. Moge was ordered to pay spousal support of $150 a month; in 1989, when Mrs. Moge was earning $800 a month from her cleaning job, and Mr. Moge was earning $2200 a month—and remarried to a working spouse—Mr. Moge successfully applied to terminate support. Mrs. Moge appealed, and the Manitoba Court of Appeal reinstated the old amount. Mr. Moge appealed to the Supreme Court of Canada; Mrs. Moge fought the appeal, but didn't contest the support amount. The Supreme Court devoted some twenty pages to a discussion of the feminization of poverty, and provided new guidelines for courts to consider in all support applications.

OBJECTIVES OF SPOUSAL SUPPORT

The primary objective of spousal support is to provide compensation for the economic consequences of marriage or cohabitation. Most often this involves compensating women who have sacrificed employment opportunities because of the assumption of family responsibilities. As a general principle, modern support does not depend on the gender of the spouse and is concerned with providing a remedy for the economic need created by the relationship or its breakdown.

The following are the four primary objectives of spousal support:

i.   to recognize any economic advantages or disadvantages to the spouses arising from the relationship or its breakdown;

ii. to apportion between the spouses any financial consequences arising from the care of any child of the marriage;

iii. to relieve any economic hardship of the spouses arising from the breakdown of the marriage; and

iv. to promote the economic self-sufficiency of each spouse within a reasonable period, as far as is possible.

The following are some of the factors that a judge will consider in hearing a support claim:

- the length of time the spouses cohabited;
- the functions performed by each spouse during cohabitation; including childcare, contribution to the other spouse's business or helping the other spouse obtain a licence, degree or other training;
- any order, agreement or arrangement relating to support of the spouse or any children;
- the economic advantages and disadvantages to both spouses resulting from the relationship or its breakdown, including those arising from assumption of childcare or household responsibilities, loss of future earning power and benefits such as pension plans because of time out of the workforce, and diminished employment opportunities arising from family-centred decisions (such as refusing a transfer or promotion, or moving to another city to accommodate the other spouse's career); and
- the extent to which any of the sacrifices or activities have been addressed in the division of assets.

ENTITLEMENT

Who Can Claim Spousal Support

Any spouse who has been married can apply for spousal support. A spouse who has lived in a common law relationship can claim spousal support in all provinces except Quebec and the Northwest Territories:

- in Manitoba, common law couples can claim support after five years of cohabitation if the applicant has been "substantially dependent," or after one year if there is a child;
- in Ontario, New Brunswick, PEI and Saskatchewan after three years or less if there is a child and the relationship is of "some permanence";
- in British Columbia after two years;
- in Newfoundland and Nova Scotia after one year; and
- in the Yukon after cohabiting in a relationship of some permanence without time requirements.

A recent Alberta case called *Taylor* v. *Rossu* allowed a cohabitee to claim support, although the statute did not give support rights to common law couples. While the decision is under appeal, it remains good law at the time that this book goes to print.

Same sex couples can claim spousal support in Ontario, as a result of a Charter challenge, but the matter is currently under appeal. If the appeal is upheld, same sex couples will eventually be entitled to claim support in all provinces where common law couples can do so.

Establishing Entitlement

The guiding principle of entitlement to spousal support is to remedy the economic consequences of the relationship or its breakdown. In most cases, a spouse's financial need arises either from the distribution of labour within the family or from the dramatic change in standard of living that results from separation. Accordingly, a claim for spousal support is rarely defended, either in negotiation or in court, by a claim that the need arises from factors outside the relationship or its breakdown. In fact, if the parties have cohabited for more than ten years, entitlement is presumed.

There are some difficult cases involving entitlement. Usually they involve illness or disability that is arguably unrelated to the relationship. The modern view of these cases is that the economic need has still arisen as a result of the breakdown of the relationship, and entitlement is still possible. This is especially so in cases involving long-term relationships.

Other difficult entitlement issues arise when one spouse claims that the other is not disadvantaged by the relationship itself, but by a lack of education, a lack of interest in or refusal to pursue employment (especially in childless relationships), or by economic factors such as a recession. Judges usually dismiss these arguments on the grounds that the breakdown of the relationship creates a need, and that "choice" and "conduct" arguments have little or no place in the discussion. Short-term relationships, or ones involving serious breaches of conduct such as alcoholism, spousal abuse or intentional unemployment, are the exceptions to this generalization. In such cases, much depends on the individual facts and the judge's view of choice and conduct arguments.

FYI

*Everyone benefits from the **Moge** decision—except Mrs. Moge. When Mr. and Mrs. Moge separated in 1973, support of $150 a month was ordered. In 1989, Mr. Moge successfully applied to terminate support. Mrs. Moge appealed, and the old amount was reinstated. Mr. Moge went to the Supreme Court; Mrs. Moge fought the appeal, but didn't contest the support amount. The Supreme Court then wrote a discussion of the feminization of poverty and new guidelines for courts to consider in all support applications—but Mrs. Moge didn't benefit from this wisdom. Her failure to cross-appeal for increased support tied the Supreme Court's hands, and although she was successful on appeal, she continues to receive spousal support in the meagre amount of $150 a month.*

AMOUNT OF SUPPORT

The compensatory model of support and the detailed discussion it received in *Moge* provide little guidance on appropriate support amounts. A strict equalization of income is not appropriate except in the longest-term relationships, in which support really involves the division of pension payments and retirement savings. The amount of support is evaluated on the basis of need and ability to pay; an assessment of child and spousal support (with child support taking priority); and a consideration of the effect the property division will have on need.

Typically, spousal support awards represent thirty to fifty percent of the payer's gross income. The most generous awards provide a recipient with as much as sixty-five percent.

Negotiations and court applications considering spousal support begin with a budget of income and expenses and an evaluation of the claimant's total economic need. That need is reduced by any child support payable and is tempered by considerations of the total property package that the claimant will receive on settlement and the income that can be earned on the package. The final factor is the ability of the other spouse to pay support. In addition to gross income, this includes individual issues such as payment of debt incurred during the relationship and any new obligations of the payer (such as a second family, a new business, or other new expenses). If there is limited ability to pay, that will be the ceiling against which reasonable need is measured. If there is no ability to pay, no spousal support will be ordered, unless the claimant can demonstrate that there has been an intentional reduction of income to avoid support obligations. If there is unlimited ability to pay, the earlier considerations will govern. The courts have considered new obligations differently—sometimes they consider a new family or fledgling business to be a valid limitation on ability to pay; sometimes they conclude that a spouse can't avoid the old obligation by knowingly undertaking a new one.

DURATION OF SUPPORT

Courts can order three types of support: long-term support, open-ended support and time-limited support. The greatest contribution of the Supreme Court's decision in *Moge* is the view that promoting self-sufficiency is not an overriding consideration, but only one of the four primary objectives of spousal support. As a result, courts now grant time-limited awards only in exceptional cases. There are still no strict rules governing spousal support, but the following generalizations provide reliable guidelines.

Long-Term Support

Long-term support is usually explicitly stated to be "permanent" or "for life or until remarriage." If there are dramatic changes in either need (including remarriage or cohabitation) or ability to pay (including disability, retirement, or other marked decreases in income), even permanent support remains subject to review. Without strong reasons to the contrary, permanent support is presumed to be appropriate in all relationships that have lasted for more than twenty years or if there's a substantial disparity in the spouses' incomes.

Open-Ended Support

Open-ended support is granted without time limitation but is reviewable. Relationships that have ended after ten years usually inspire open-ended support, again subject to individual considerations.

Time-Limited Support

Time-limited support is ordered to establish an arbitrary limit for the attainment of self-sufficiency. While these arrangements were quite popular before *Moge*, they have all but disappeared in long-term or traditional relationships in which one spouse has been out of the workforce for an extended period. If a relationship has broken down after ten years or less, or if both parties have worked full-time throughout the relationship—making need more reflective of a change in standard of living—time-limited support is usually considered to be appropriate. If sacrifice for childcare has occurred in a shorter-term relationship, or if the claimant worked only part-time throughout the relationship or compromised career potential because of family considerations, courts usually reject time-limited support in favour of an open-ended award.

Settlement options for support are unlimited. If economic recovery or compensation is uncertain in your particular case, open-ended support is probably most appropriate. If self-sufficiency is a goal, and incentive to retrain and enter the workforce is desirable, a schedule of support that declines annually, is reviewable after five or ten years, or terminates at some point is often a workable compromise. Open-ended support agreements can also provide for the automatic mediation or negotiation of the issue at a certain future point (for example, five years after separation or after the kids are in school full-time). However, all support settlements, regardless of their terms, are subject to variation by a court. Because litigation is speculative and costly, people are usually better off to negotiate a schedule of spousal support. Exceptions arise if one spouse is clearly entitled to long-term support—in such cases, spouses should not be pressured into compromising. Since *Moge*, a spouse who holds their ground and insists on long-term support will often succeed before trial, because all reasonable lawyers know that judges generally disapprove of time limits.

TAX TREATMENT

Spousal support is taxable for income-tax purposes in the hands of the receiving spouse, and is deductible from the taxable income of the paying spouse. If there's a disparity between the spouses' incomes, there will be a substantial tax saving because the payer pays the support with pre-tax dollars and the recipient pays tax at a lower rate. This means that—all other things being equal—there's more money available for support. Unlike child support, which may be taxable or not in certain circumstances (see Chapter 7), periodic spousal support is always taxable.

Once the appropriate amount of support is determined, either by a court or in negotiations, that amount will need to be increased to ensure that the recipient receives the appropriate amount on an after-tax basis. The actual amount of the increase depends on the recipient's income from other sources, although it's usually based on the recipient's average tax rate ranging from thirty to fifty-four percent.

If you receive spousal support, taxability of support is a crucial consideration in determining an appropriate amount. Be sure that you're using the correct gross-up so that your support is not eroded by taxes, even if you have to retain an accountant or lawyer to advise you. Once you're receiving support, it's important to get some tax-planning advice so that you don't find yourself with an unmanageable or unexpected tax liability at the end of the year.

If you pay spousal support, remember that the after-tax cost of support is about half of what you actually pay out and that you'll receive a substantial tax refund at the end of each year. If you'd prefer to receive the refund in the form of a reduction in the tax taken from your regular paycheque, you should contact your employer's finance or payroll department and submit the appropriate Revenue Canada forms. If you're self-employed, you can adjust your installments by contacting Revenue Canada directly.

LUMP SUM SUPPORT

The great majority of spousal support is paid on a periodic basis, usually monthly. Periodic support is taxable and deductible for tax purposes; lump sum support is not. Courts have the power to grant lump sum support as an alternative or in addition to periodic support. But lump sum awards are the exception rather than the rule, and there must be a real and immediate need to justify the award.

The most frequent justifications for lump sum support are to allow a spouse to purchase new accommodation or if there's reason to doubt that periodic support will be paid. In both situations, a claim for a lump sum is more compelling if there's only limited property to divide. Sometimes, to avoid continuing contact or long-term obligations, spouses agree to lump sum support as an alternative to periodic support. Courts may also order payment of both a small lump sum and periodic support to allow the recipient to meet a single large expense.

FYI

Periodic support is taxable to the payee and deductible to the payer for tax purposes; lump sum support is not.

INTERIM SUPPORT ORDERS

If you and your spouse have separated and you cannot agree on financial arrangements while you attempt to resolve all issues, a court has the power to make an interim support order, intended to provide immediate financial relief pending trial. Courts evaluate all criteria discussed in this chapter when considering interim support, including entitlement. Interim support is considered to be temporary in nature and therefore doesn't cover entertainment, vacation or other extravagant expenses. In reality, however, the final support figure is often the same as the interim award.

If you're proceeding by court application as opposed to negotiation, it's important to do everything you can to get a reasonable support award on the interim hearing, regardless of whether you're the payer or the recipient. You should be sure that your financial information is detailed and accurate, that your need or ability to pay is described in detail, and that your affidavit materials set out every relevant consideration that will lead to the result you want. Because the interim amount may be payable for one or two years and the interim result often promotes settlement, you should not underestimate its importance.

SECURITY FOR SUPPORT

The *Divorce Act* and most provincial statutes allow courts to grant support recipients some form of security for the payment of support, either to prevent default or to provide a fund from which support can be paid in the event of the death of the payer. While support continues to be an obligation after the death of the payer unless an agreement provides otherwise, there are often limited assets from which an estate can satisfy this obligation. Security for support is most often assured by requiring the payer to irrevocably designate the spouse as beneficiary of a life insurance policy. The face value of the insurance and the length of time that the policy must be in effect vary depending on the facts of each case. Other forms of security include a mortgage or trust interest in property.

If you're the recipient of spousal and/or child support, you should claim life insurance security. Such provisions are commonplace in negotiated separation agreements. If you have children—and especially if you have an alternating residence arrangement—you should consider mutual life insurance requirements.

ENFORCEMENT

In most provinces, all support orders will automatically be filed with the provincial enforcement agency, and support payments will be garnished by the province from the payer's income each month. As a recipient of support, you may or may not be able to opt out of these rules. If you can, you'll still be able to enforce payment, although you'll have to spend some time and effort getting started if the payments go into default. If you can't, you can expect some delays in receiving the first few payments and some other minor problems associated with the fact that your payments are being collected by a bureaucracy.

You can enforce a support order that's in arrears by one of two methods. The easier and cheaper method is to follow the procedures prescribed by your province's agency for support enforcement. These agencies enforce both child and spousal support and are listed in Appendix B. Usually, you have to take your separation agreement or court order to the appropriate provincial office, along with evidence that the payments are in arrears and fill out the necessary forms. Depending on the facts, this may result in garnishment from the payer's income, seizure of property, or an application to the court. If a court attendance is required and you're the recipient, the enforcement agency will act as your lawyer and you will not need any other legal assistance. You can get your own lawyer if you want, but it's not usually necessary unless the enforcement agency is so bogged down that it can't assist you promptly.

The other method of collecting arrears is by simply suing your spouse. You can proceed by Statement of Claim or Application, depending on the facts. These procedural issues are discussed in Chapter 15, "If You Must...The Structure of the Action."

The standard response to enforcement proceedings is a claim for a reduction of the support. This is obvious, and there may be some truth to the claim that the support is too high based on the fact that the payer fell into arrears. But the payer must show more: there must have been a material change since the order was made, as discussed in the next section.

Another common response to enforcement proceedings is a claim to reduce the amount of arrears that are owing. This is really a plea for mercy, usually based on the argument that the arrears are so high that the payer will never be able to pay them. It's hard to predict a court's reaction to such a claim. Some judges say that you shouldn't be able to avoid your obligation just because you neglected it for so long, while others are more sympathetic. The scales are often tipped in favour of sympathy when the recipient waited for a long period before acting or made the payer believe that he or she wouldn't insist on the support. The best way to avoid a claim for reduction of arrears is to take some enforcement measures as soon as the support goes into default.

In general, claims for reduction of support or arrears do not sit well with judges unless the facts clearly support them, since courts are reluctant to award payers for falling into arrears by reducing their obligations. If you're a payer who has fallen into arrears, you're better off initiating your own claim for reduction of support than raising the issue in defence of an enforcement proceeding.

VARIATION OF SUPPORT

Both negotiated and court-ordered support are subject to variation in the form of increased payments, decreased or terminated payments, or extension of time-limited support. If there has been a material change in the recipient's need or the payer's ability to pay since the original order or agreement—which wasn't foreseeable at the time—a court will usually vary the support award. If child support has terminated for one or more children, there's now an automatic right to seek a variation of spousal support contained in the *Divorce Act*. Essentially, the same considerations apply on a variation application as on an original support application. All the objectives of spousal support should be considered. It is clear that economic self-sufficiency is not an absolute obligation, and is not possible in every situation.

Even separation agreements that specifically provide that the support can't be varied may be subject to alteration if the court is satisfied that its refusal would create unconscionable results. Until 1995, the rule was that negotiated support waivers or specific provisions that precluded variation should not be interfered with, but should be respected by courts. This rule has now been rejected as being too inflexible and unrealistic.

FYI

No support order or agreement is ever really final. You have no alternative when negotiating support but to recognize this fact as one of the realities of family law.

CHAPTER NINE

Common Law Couples

IN THIS CHAPTER: **Cohabitation, Support, Exclusive Possession of the Matrimonial Home, Property;** *Trust Claims, Other Creative Property Claims, Evaluating Property Claims,* **Canada Pension Plan, Custody and Access, Child Support, Definition of Spouse for Benefits, Predictions for Law Reform, Planning Your Future and Protecting Your Interests;** *Taking Title Jointly, Renting and Household Contents, Basic Estate Planning, Cohabitation Agreements*

THE TERM COMMON LAW COUPLE REFERS TO TWO PEOPLE OF THE OPPOSITE SEX WHO COHABIT IN AN INTIMATE RELATIONSHIP BUT ARE NOT MARRIED. ALTHOUGH THE RECENT TRENDS OF LAW REFORM AND CONSTITUTIONAL CHALLENGE IN CANADA SUGGEST THAT THERE ARE NO REAL DIFFERENCES BETWEEN MARRIED, COMMON LAW AND SAME SEX COHABITEES, THE THREE GROUPS CONTINUE TO BE TREATED DIFFERENTLY UNDER THE LAW. I HAVE CHOSEN TO USE THE CONVENTIONAL TERM "COMMON LAW" TO DENOTE UNMARRIED OPPOSITE SEX COUPLES.

Living common law means different things for different purposes, and the differing rules for support, property and employment benefits are confusing. The result is that many common law couples don't know when they'll have legal obligations to each other or what those obligations are. This is complicated by the fact that there's a very real possibility that our current family law rules for common law couples may be amended in the near future to eliminate distinctions between married and common law couples. The discussion of common law couples that follows, especially in the areas of property and matrimonial homes, must be read with this understanding. Given this caveat, this chapter will attempt to demystify the rights and obligations of common law couples.

COHABITATION

Because common law couples don't go through a marriage ceremony, the law requires some test to establish when such relationships commence. Since every relationship is different, and since family law aims to provide remedies on the basis of looking fairly at the reality of the situation, the test must be flexible.

Our definition of "cohabit" is based on principles from several family law decisions. Cohabitation is an integrated relationship that will usually have many—though not necessarily all—of the following elements:
• financial interdependence;
• a sexual relationship;
• shared shelter or a common principal residence;
• holding oneself out as a member of the couple;
• shared household responsibilities;

- shared use of assets such as cars, boats, etc.;
- shared responsibilities for raising children;
- shared vacations;
- mutual estate planning; and
- commitment.

A relationship does not need to possess each listed characteristic to qualify as cohabitation. For instance, I was once involved in a trial in which the couple spent almost every night together, but the woman had her own apartment. She rarely slept there, and when she did, she usually slept there with the man. In reality, these parties lived together as we understand the term: they shared expenses, they shared household responsibilities, they took vacations together, and they considered themselves to be partners. The man claimed that they did not cohabit simply because the woman had her own apartment and, accordingly, that he had no obligation to her after their ten-year relationship ended. But the judge looked at the whole situation and concluded that they had indeed cohabited.

SUPPORT

Common law couples have an obligation to pay spousal support to each other on breakdown of the relationship in all parts of Canada except for Quebec and the Northwest Territories. This is the only statutory family law obligation that common law couples have to each other. There are no automatic property sharing requirements for common law couples. I stress this point heavily because almost every member of a common law relationship that I've ever met believes that, at some point, the law considers them to be "officially married" and that obligations flow from this status. The only thing that happens automatically on the breakdown of a common law relationship is a division of Canada Pension Plan credits. Even provinces that allow for spousal support between common law couples provide only the right to make a claim; spousal support is not automatic, but depends on the facts of each case.

In Manitoba, common law couples can claim support after five years of cohabitation if the applicant has been "substantially dependent," or after one year if there's a child; in Ontario, New Brunswick, PEI and Saskatchewan after three years, or less if there is a child and the relationship is "of some permanence"; in British Columbia after two years; in Newfoundland and Nova Scotia after one year; and in the Yukon after cohabiting in a relationship of some permanence without time requirements. A recent case in Alberta indicates that common law couples will have support rights even though they're excluded by the statute, but no time requirement is set by the decision and the matter is under appeal.

A claim for spousal support is evaluated in the same way as a claim made by a married person. The claimant must confirm the relevant years of cohabitation and/or the facts required for a support obligation in the province. The claimant must show that he or she has a need for support that arises from the relationship or its breakdown. This is usually presumed if the spouse establishes entitlement, unless the potential payer makes a strong argument that any dependency has arisen from factors outside the relationship. The claimant must then show financial need for support and prove that the payer can pay the amount claimed. Once an appropriate amount has been determined, it is increased to reflect the fact that it's taxable in the recipient's hands and deductible to the payer. (This analysis and the court's evaluation of spousal support issues are discussed in Chapter 8, "Spousal Support.")

There are other types of spousal support that are available to common law couples, including continuation of spousal employment benefits (if they were available to the couple before separation), life insurance and other forms of security, and indexing the support for inflation. These issues are also discussed in Chapter 8.

EXCLUSIVE POSSESSION OF THE MATRIMONIAL HOME

Protection and rights of possession of the matrimonial home do not apply to unmarried couples in any province in Canada. But exclusive possession may be ordered on a temporary basis as part of an overall spousal support package in British Columbia, Newfoundland, New Brunswick, Ontario, PEI and the Yukon. (This possibility is described in Chapter 6, "The Matrimonial Home.") You should discuss this issue with a lawyer shortly before or after separation to find out whether it applies to you. Generally, if you don't need spousal support, you won't be able to get exclusive possession under this rule. If you're not entitled to make a claim for exclusive possession because you're a common law spouse without need for support, you may still be able to obtain the equivalent relief if your spouse promised you that you could live in the property in the future. This claim would be based on promissory estoppel, licence or proprietary estoppel. They are creative claims that are often recommended in litigation between same sex couples. (They're discussed in detail in Chapter 10, "Same Sex Couples.")

PROPERTY

Unmarried couples have no automatic rights to share in property. No family law statute in Canada includes common law couples in its matrimonial property rules or formulas. This is obviously unfair in many circumstances. Because there are often few if any functional differences between unmarried and married couples, the courts show increasing flexibility when claims are made against property by a common law spouse.

Common law spouses can obtain an interest in property that is owned by the other spouse only by making a claim in "equity," based on the right of Canadian courts to make decisions that reflect fairness and equity. The essence of an equitable claim is that the spouse who holds the property has benefited from the contributions made by the other spouse during the relationship, and that it would be unfair for the titled spouse to retain those benefits.

Trust Claims

There are two types of equitable claims: resulting trust claims, based on an express understanding or promise that the property at issue is shared by the parties or held entirely in trust for the other spouse; and constructive trust, which is a remedy for unjust enrichment. If your situation doesn't amount to a resulting trust, you'll need to consider unjust enrichment to obtain a share in property. (The requirements are discussed in detail in Chapter 5, "Property," under the heading Resulting and Constructive Trust Claims.)

Essentially, unjust enrichment requires proof that:
i.   the titled spouse has benefited from direct or indirect contributions made by the claiming spouse;

ii. the claiming spouse has suffered a corresponding deprivation or disadvantage; and

iii. there is no reason for the enrichment.

As discussed in Chapter 5, the first and second requirements are easily satisfied in a domestic setting. Recent decisions involving property claims by common law couples have concluded that, in most cases, contribution to home or childcare, sharing of finances or contribution in the form of labour on the property will create unjust enrichment, because the spouse who receives these contributions would have had more time and money to spend on business or property concerns. The third requirement (whether there is a reason for the enrichment) may be a sticking point if title has been transferred from the claiming spouse to the other to avoid creditors or to bestow a gift on the spouse. In these situations, courts sometimes conclude that, although there may be unjust enrichment, the claim can be denied because of the rationale for the transfer and the transferor's participation in it.

Once the court finds that unjust enrichment exists, it has a variety of remedies available, which can be summarized as the granting of a proprietary interest—a declaration that the titled spouse holds a percentage interest in the property in trust for the claiming spouse—or a money judgment that is not connected to the property but reflects some value of the contributions made. Courts are reluctant to grant the more powerful relief of a property interest if a money judgment will suffice. The various considerations entertained by courts at this stage are discussed in Chapter 5. When married couples make unjust enrichment claims, the distinction between a property interest and a money judgment may be important, because such claims are made to supplement statutory matrimonial property entitlement in some way. However, with common law couples, there's not much practical difference between the two types of relief. Both provide a financial entitlement that would not otherwise exist. And, assuming there's some asset (like an RRSP) from which payment can be made, most common law spouses are content to receive a money judgment. The exception to this is when the property to which contributions are made is the only asset. In that case, if a money judgment is granted, the property is the only source of payment. A spouse who succeeds in getting a money judgment would then be required to register the judgment on title and either commence new proceedings to have the property sold or wait for a sale of the property before the judgment is paid. On the other hand, if a property interest is granted, the successful spouse becomes part owner of the property and is immediately entitled to have his or her interest purchased or to have the property sold.

The amount of the money judgment may be difficult for the court to determine. It may reflect strict market value of the contribution to the property, if such can be ascertained. If the contribution involved household services or childcare, the court can be more flexible and grant a money judgment based on an appropriate percentage of the total value of the property at issue (often one-third to one-half). The money judgment may be secured against property. It's a good idea to make all-encompassing claims against property arising from a common law relationship, requesting a secured or unsecured money judgment or a percentage interest in a property or properties based on resulting or constructive trust, to be sure the court has complete flexibility when it comes time to consider the appropriate remedy.

Other Creative Property Claims

Trust claims are the easiest way to obtain a property interest. However, other arguments can be made either as a substitute for or in addition to trust claims. These are based on the legal principles of contract, licence and proprietary estoppel and are described in detail in Chapter 10, "Same Sex Couples," under the heading Property.

Evaluating Property Claims

As discussed in Chapter 5, it's difficult to estimate a common law spouse's property entitlement because the court has so much discretion in these matters, and because there's no simple formula for property division. Settlement discussions are therefore difficult, although they can be assisted by any of the methods described in Chapter 2, and discussed in detail in Chapter 14. Getting a legal opinion, holding a four-way meeting, or engaging in mediation or arbitration will usually give both spouses some idea of the best and worst outcomes. If, however, the titled spouse takes the position that the other spouse has no right to any property award, litigation will have to begin. Even if this is your only option, take heart: fewer than one percent of family law disputes go to trial. Usually some stage of the proceedings creates sufficient stress or financial pressure to encourage a settlement.

Many spouses who have a left a common law relationship with no property have little ability to pay legal fees, even if they succeed in obtaining an interim support award. There are several options available if you find yourself in such a situation. If you have a good case based on the facts, you can usually find a lawyer who will wait to be paid until you get your settlement. This involves some risk-taking for both the lawyer and the client. For the lawyer, there may be difficulty collecting payment from an unsuccessful client; for the client, there's a risk that the ultimate settlement will be substantially eroded by the legal fees. A good lawyer will keep you apprised of the costs and evaluate your chances of success and the corresponding risks at several points in the proceeding. Another option is to apply for legal aid, which may be available to cover your legal fees, or as a loan that's subject to repayment when the case is over. A call to the law society in your province will give you referrals to family lawyers and legal aid offices.

In some provinces, people who can't afford to retain a lawyer when their potential entitlement is unknown can bring an interim motion requesting an advance on any property entitlement or interim disbursements. These two types of motion are discussed in Chapter 5 and Chapter 15. Essentially, you must be able to show some minimal entitlement to be successful in getting an advance; whether you can do so will depend on the facts of your case and your lawyer's view of the chances of success. Of course, the final option for people who can't afford lawyers is to spend less money on one of the alternatives to litigation and hope that settlement results.

CANADA PENSION PLAN

Common law couples who separated after January 1, 1987, cohabited for a continuous period of at least one year, and have been separated for at least one year can apply for an equal division of the pension credits earned by the spouses during cohabitation. This division is mandatory (except in B.C. and Saskatchewan, where you can contract out of it) and is done automatically once you complete the necessary forms. After the division, each spouse will have a pensionable earning account to which further contributions can be made before retirement. Many common law couples don't know that they're entitled to divide CPP credits after separation and lose out only because they fail to file the forms.

CUSTODY AND ACCESS

Common law couples have the same rights with respect to custody and access, if they're the natural or adoptive parents of a child. Any stepparent who has a relationship of some permanence with a child also has custody and access rights. In fact, provincial custody and access statutes allow for custody claims by any person. (See Chapter 4.)

CHILD SUPPORT

Child support is a child's right and a parent's obligation. There's no distinction between married and unmarried couples when entitlement to child support is considered. Natural and adoptive parents must support their children in accordance with the needs of the children and the parents' ability to pay, regardless of their marital status.

FYI

If a stepparent has lived with the spouse and the child in a relationship that could be described as parental, child support will often be payable without any consideration of the fact that the child is not related by blood to the stepparent.

Stepparents, including common law stepparents, must pay child support to their spouses' children from other relationships if the stepparents have treated the children as their own or, as the law puts it, have shown "a settled intention to treat the child as a child of the family." There's no statutory duration of cohabitation that obligates a stepparent to pay child support except in B.C., where the payer must have cohabited with the parent and child for two years. In all other provinces, the test is flexible and focuses on the child's best interests. Provided the common law relationship has lasted long enough for the stepparent to have contributed to the support of the child, either directly or indirectly, child support will usually be ordered. The amount and duration of child support may be adjusted to reflect an unusually short relationship or other factors. If a stepparent has lived with the spouse and the child in a relationship that could be described as permanent, child support will often be payable without any consideration of the fact that the child is not related by blood to the stepparent. Couples can attempt to limit their exposure to support each other's children by signing a cohabitation agreement, as discussed below. While these provisions may not be enforceable, they will at least show that the stepparent did not have "a settled intention."

A small procedural hitch exists as this book goes to print. The new federal child support guidelines are regulations to the *Divorce Act* and therefore will apply only to married couples. Provincial laws govern child support payable between unmarried spouses. While the evaluation of these claims has always been identical in the past, it remains to be seen whether all provinces will pass child support guidelines that mirror the federal provisions. In provinces that do, child support will be determined by the court in the same way regardless of whether the parents are married. In provinces that pass different guidelines for unmarried child support, there could be a different amount payable under each regime. In provinces that pass no guidelines at all, child support will probably be determined according to the old method—by looking at the needs of the children and the ability of each parent to contribute to their support, on a case-by-case basis. Another option would be to consider the facts of the common law relationship and to order support with reference to the federal guidelines, regardless of the fact that they do not strictly apply. Given the unfairness to children that would arise from a situation outside their control—whether their parents are married or not—and the lack of consistency and predictability that would result from two regimes of child support, this problem may not persist for long. If it does, the distinction will probably be vulnerable to constitutional challenge based on the equality guarantees of the Charter. If you're a common law parent who needs child support, you should contact the family courts, a family lawyer or the Federal Government Child Support information line (1-800-343-8282) to determine whether child support guidelines apply to you. If two regimes exist in your province, you should discuss the issue with a lawyer. If the provincial support is lower than the federal guideline amount, consider whether you want to be the one who challenges the law and sets it straight.

Determining the amount of child support payable under the guidelines is discussed in detail in Chapter 7, "Child Support." If your province passes regulations to give common law couples the benefit of child support guidelines, the analysis in Chapter 7 will apply if you claim child support or a variation of child support. But the amounts in the provincial chart may be calculated differently and different arguments may be made about deviating from the guidelines.

DEFINITION OF SPOUSE FOR BENEFITS

All levels of government, all large corporations and most smaller employers have spousal plans that provide benefits for the common-law spouses of employees. These benefits usually involve medical and dental plans, prescription plans and survival benefits under pension plans. Misunderstanding of common law status often comes from the variety of definitions of spouse for the purpose of employment benefits. Some plans allow benefits to be paid to common law spouses after six months of cohabitation, many after one year, and some only after three or five years of cohabitation. There's no rule about the appropriate length of time, and each employer or its insurance company can make up its own requirements. Because of these discrepancies, you should find out from your personnel department the number of years of cohabitation required for spousal benefits in your plan. Remember that no legal obligations, such as property or support, flow from your status as a common law spouse under a benefits plan, except of course the benefits themselves.

PREDICTIONS FOR LAW REFORM

In 1995, the Supreme Court of Canada rendered its decision in *Miron* v. *Trudel*, a constitutional challenge to an insurance contract that denied unmarried couples the same automobile accident benefits as married couples. The Supreme Court found that the distinction was unconstitutional. The decision recognizes that there are few functional differences between married and common law couples.

Law reform advocates have suggested since 1993 that unmarried heterosexual couples who have cohabited for a requisite period or who are raising a child should have the same family law rights and responsibilities as married couples. Now, as a result of the Supreme Court's decision in *Miron* v. *Trudel*, legal distinctions between these two groups will have to be eliminated to satisfy the equality guarantees of the Charter. Any differences that aren't removed by law reform will likely be struck down by future constitutional challenges.

Family law has always held itself out as a leader in the legal system and as a fairness-based, remedial area of the law. To live up to this reputation, its statutory rules regarding division of property and matrimonial homes will have to be expanded to apply equally to common law couples. While this possibility promises fairness and equality to common law couples, it also creates uncertainty. Many common law spouses decide not to get married because they want to avoid the application of matrimonial property rules to their relationship. The possibility of law reform threatens the foundations on which these relationships were built. Family law statutes have, in the past, made sweeping changes to the rules of family relationships without giving members of the relationship time to adjust, and future law reform may well be retroactive in nature, with the new rules suddenly applying to old relationships. While this result would be consistent with family law's premises, it presents difficulties for couples who want predictability and certainty in the rules of their relationship.

PLANNING YOUR FUTURE AND PROTECTING YOUR INTERESTS

Taking Title Jointly

If you want to ensure that property you acquire during a relationship is shared equally, you can get married. If you can't or don't want to get married, you may take steps to plan your future or protect your interests. Given the potential uncertainty of common law relationships after law reform, it's a good idea to define your expectations of the relationship and make plans that create certainty in the event of the relationship's breakdown.

Since there's no automatic property sharing for common law couples, what you own is what you get on separation, unless one of you makes trust claims. The most practical way to ensure that property will be jointly owned on separation is to take title jointly at the time you acquire assets. Title is proof of ownership. It includes transfers and deeds of land, ownership papers and bills of sale. You can take title jointly to all major assets including real estate, bank accounts, cars and household contents by having joint names on bills of sale for major purchases.

In the case of real estate, you can take title in two ways. When title is taken as joint tenants, both parties are presumed to own half the property on separation regardless of contribution to the purchase price (except if a cohabitation agreement provides otherwise). On death, the surviving joint tenant will own all the property. When title is taken as tenants in common, the ownership is not necessarily equal and arguments can be made about the contributions that each made to the property on separation. On death, the surviving tenant in common continues to own half of the property and the beneficiaries of the deceased's estate own the other half.

You may not wish to take title jointly to all or any assets. If you wish to segregate assets with certainty, you need a cohabitation agreement. Even though there's no automatic sharing between common law couples, claims can potentially be made against assets. Also, property rules may change for common law couples. (Cohabitation agreements are discussed in the next section of this chapter.)

Renting and Household Contents

If you rent your home, consider whose name should be on the lease. If only one of your names is on the lease, that person will be responsible for the lease payments upon separation unless you agree otherwise. Usually that means that the other will move out. If both your names are on the lease, both of you are liable for the rent even if only one of you lives there. While notice may be given in respect to a monthly lease, and any liability can thus be limited to the notice period, a yearly lease is a different matter.

Division of household contents on separation also depends on title. If no title documents are available in the form of bills of sale, you will have to share property that you acquire during the relationship. Property you bring to the relationship or receive as a gift or inheritance during the relationship is not usually divided, although sometimes disputes arise if the parties can't agree that a particular item was brought in or received as a gift to one spouse. It's a good idea to address these issues in a cohabitation agreement, especially if you're already signing one for other reasons.

Basic Estate Planning

Common law couples receive uncertain treatment under intestacy laws; usually they're not entitled to share in property if a spouse dies without a will. You can avoid potentially contentious issues that arise on death by doing some basic estate planning and having a valid will.

Partners in common law relationships have successfully asserted trust claims and obtained licences to keep property whether or not the property is given to them in a will. In fact, trust claims between common law couples are granted regularly, but there's no certainty in this method for estate-planning purposes. If you want your partner to benefit from your will, you need a valid will and a cohabitation agreement.

Basic estate planning usually involves keeping most of your property outside of your estate on your death to avoid executors' fees, legal fees, estate taxes and lawsuits. This is why it is often wise to take title jointly and designate your spouse or another person as direct beneficiary of your life insurance, RRSPs, pensions or other retirement savings plans, as opposed to designating your estate as beneficiary.

Some other considerations for wills as discussed in Chapter 10, "Same Sex Couples," are equally applicable to common law couples. You should still seek legal advice about your particular situation and estate plans and get a will drafted for a very modest fee—usually $100 for a single will and $150 for mirror wills. You can keep the cost low by going to the meeting with a list of your assets and back-up documents and with some idea of your estate plan.

You should also consider what will happen in the event of the physical or mental incapacity of you or your partner. Common law couples often have difficulty with practical matters such as cashing paycheques or gaining access to funds if their partner becomes ill. If a property needs to be mortgaged to obtain funds for medical treatment, a common law spouse with no interest in the property can't sign the requisite forms. Common law couples are usually but not always entitled to make medical decisions in the event of incapacity. As you prepare your will, you might also consider powers of attorney for property and personal care. You can discuss your options and sign powers of attorney at the same time as your will.

FYI

You can get a will drafted for a very modest fee—usually $100 for a single will and $150 for mirror wills, especially if you first list your assets and compile back-up documents and develop some idea of your estate plan. As you prepare your will, you might also consider powers of attorney for property and powers of attorney for personal care.

Cohabitation Agreements

If you're entering or involved in a common law relationship, you should sit down with your partner and discuss your plans and expectations. In fact, I believe that the current unpredictability of the law makes a cohabitation agreement mandatory for every common law couple. Without one, you face inconsistent expectations, uncertainty and potential litigation—and becoming a hostage to law reform.

Your cohabitation agreement should set firm family law rules for your relationship, either by opting out of property sharing, establishing limited rights to property and support, or agreeing to an equal division of all assets. Even if you're holding assets jointly, you may need a cohabitation agreement to set the rules for dividing property. For example, will it be listed and sold within thirty days or will one spouse buy the other's interest? You may want to preclude trust claims by your spouse and agree that title will always determine how property is divided. If you have children or are planning on having them together, you should agree upon your arrangement. Will your spouse be obligated to support a child from a former relationship? Do you have a parental plan in the event of separation? While child support, custody and access provisions are not strictly enforceable, they do provide evidence of your intentions and may be persuasive in the event of a later dispute. If you and your spouse divide household responsibilities or if one has substantially more income than the other, you should consider spousal support obligations. You may agree that each of you will abide by the spousal support rights and obligations in effect at the time of separation. Or you may wish to set a schedule of maximum amounts of spousal support payable, or waive spousal support altogether. Years from now, a court may not respect these provisions, but they'll at least show your intentions and the financial arrangements of your relationship.

Your cohabitation agreement should state specifically that it's intended to bring certainty to your relationship in this time of imminent law reform and that it will apply regardless of any future changes in the law. If one spouse is very interested in such a cohabitation agreement and the other refuses to set the rules in this way, at least you'll both know where you stand. You can then make decisions about the path of your relationship in light of your fundamental differences.

You can find the formal requirements for cohabitation agreements between common law couples in your province's family law legislation—if it recognizes such agreements at all. Cohabitation agreements are specifically recognized in Newfoundland, New Brunswick, Ontario, PEI and the Yukon. In provinces where they're not given statutory treatment, they're still recognized under the common law rules of contract and are just as enforceable as similar agreements in other provinces. Generally, cohabitation agreements will be enforced if they're signed by both parties and witnessed; if adequate financial disclosure is given; if their terms are not so draconian as to be "unconscionable"; and if each party has independent legal advice. Financial disclosure is usually attached to the agreement in the form of a financial statement under family law rules. To enforce the agreement, you may be required to show that there was no undue influence, duress or misrepresentation.

I recently heard a story about a couple who had a cohabitation agreement drafted at the man's request. When the woman took the agreement to her lawyer, the lawyer told her not to sign it because there was no financial disclosure and the woman was financially insecure, being a landed immigrant with two young children. When she didn't sign, her spouse told her that he would have her deported unless she changed her mind. So, while the irate husband circled the block in his car, she went back to the lawyer's office and signed. That's duress. The husband also failed to give adequate financial disclosure, so the agreement is probably not worth the paper it's written on. Financial statements are discussed in Chapter 2; other matters relating to cohabitation agreements are found in Chapter 12.

FYI

Cohabitation agreements are generally enforced in all provinces if they're signed by both parties and witnessed; if adequate financial disclosure is given; if their terms are not so draconian as to be "unconscionable"; and if each party has received independent legal advice.

You can draft your own cohabitation agreement, but it's not recommended. If you're going to go through the process, you should ensure that you meet the formal requirements and that there are no unexpected loopholes. Cohabitation agreements and marriage contracts are frequently challenged in court. In fact, you can't imagine the little discrepancies or creative arguments that can threaten these agreements; often the validity of an agreement depends on a particular word. You can get a cohabitation agreement drafted by a lawyer for as little as $500 if you and your spouse have already agreed upon the terms. If you want to discuss your options and negotiate the drafting of the agreement, the cost could run as high as $3000. Given the cost of litigating later over unanticipated matters, the value of property that's usually being protected, and the potential for unpredictable law reform, this is a small price to pay for some certainty.

CHAPTER TEN

Same Sex Couples

IN THIS CHAPTER: **Marriage, or No Marriage (Yet),** **Spousal Support;** *Under Family Law Legislation, As an Equitable Claim,* **Exclusive Possession of the (Matrimonial) Home;** *Exclusive Possession as an Incident of Spousal Support, Exclusive Possession Arising from Contractual or Equitable Claims,* **Property;** *Trust Claims, Proprietary Estoppel,* **Custody and Access;** *On Breakdown of a Heterosexual Relationship, Children of the Same Sex Relationship, Joint Custody and Adoption to Create Parental Rights,* **Child Support, Definition of Spouse for Benefits, Predictions for Law Reform, Planning Your Future and Protecting Your Interests,** *Taking Title Jointly, Renting, Basic Estate Planning, Cohabitation Agreements*

IN THE PAST TEN YEARS, THE LAW RELATING TO SAME SEX COUPLES HAS UNDERGONE SWEEPING REFORM. GAY MEN AND LESBIANS HAVE CHALLENGED THE CONSTITUTIONALITY OF OVERTLY DISCRIMINATORY EMPLOYMENT POLICIES, MEDICAL BENEFITS PROGRAMS, PENSION PROGRAMS AND GOVERNMENT RETIREMENT SCHEMES. IN THE REALM OF FAMILY LAW, THEY'VE CHALLENGED INTERPRETATIONS OF MARRIAGE, STEPPARENT ADOPTION AND SPOUSAL SUPPORT. IN CANADA, THESE CLAIMS HAVE ENJOYED MIXED SUCCESS, BUT THERE'S NO DOUBT THAT THE TIDES ARE TURNING. IN MOST CANADIAN JURISDICTIONS, RECENT LEGISLATIVE REFORM HAS PROHIBITED DISCRIMINATION IN EMPLOYMENT ON THE BASIS OF SEXUAL ORIENTATION; EMPLOYMENT BENEFITS, APART FROM PENSIONS, ARE NOW AVAILABLE TO GAY AND LESBIAN SPOUSES ACROSS THE COUNTRY; STEPPARENT ADOPTIONS HAVE BEEN GRANTED TO LESBIANS IN ONTARIO; ALL ADOPTION RIGHTS HAVE BEEN GRANTED IN B.C.; AND SPOUSAL SUPPORT IS AVAILABLE IN ONTARIO, PENDING APPEAL OF THE ISSUE TO THE SUPREME COURT.

If the trend continues, we'll soon see the day when discrimination against same sex couples is part of the past. In family law, we can almost see that day on our calendars. Until then, however, same sex couples who want to order their lives and plan their futures need to understand the law as it currently stands and the reality that the future of family law remains uncertain. In some ways, this uncertainty is part of the package of family law. In the late seventies and early eighties, there were widespread changes in attitudes toward unmarried cohabitees, and the rules of entitlement on breakdown of a relationship changed dramatically. The law's attitude toward married couples has also changed substantially over the last twenty years. And, while the promise of further reform hangs over both these groups, it appears more imminent and necessary in the case of same sex couples. Whether by law reform or court challenge (and although it may take many years) we seem to be moving toward equitable treatment of all intimate partners.

A recent case in Hawaii decided in favour of same sex marriage; the U.S. Supreme Court struck down part of Colorado's state constitution that refused to protect same sex couples; many American municipalities give benefits to same sex partners; Australia gives statutory support rights and promise-based child support to same sex couples; and Denmark and several other European countries allow same sex couples to register with the state to gain most of the rights and obligations of married couples.

MARRIAGE, OR NO MARRIAGE (YET)

The federal government has exclusive jurisdiction over marriage, but the provinces have legislative power over marriage ceremonies. Parliament has not excluded same sex couples from marriage, and only the province of Quebec specifically provides that the parties to a marriage must be of the opposite sex. In all other provinces, marriage statutes are silent on the point.

Despite the absence of law on the issue, some people say that the common law (which exists outside of legislation) has its own rule, based on tradition and morality, that requires married couples to be of opposite sexes. This common law prohibition against same sex marriage was challenged in the 1993 Ontario case of *Layland and Beaulne* v. *Ontario*, after the two gay male plaintiffs were refused a marriage licence. A majority of the court found that a valid marriage can take place only between a man and a woman and stated that neither man had been discriminated against because each of them was free to marry a woman. The dissenting view, written by Madam Justice Greer, argued that the common law reflects current views in society and doesn't prohibit same sex marriage. Alternatively, she found that any denial of marriage rights to same sex couples offends the equality guarantees in our Charter. An appeal was launched but was later abandoned. The result is that same sex marriage continues to be invalid and legally unrecognized in Canada. However, another constitutional challenge will undoubtedly be brought in the future.

Even in the absence of legal recognition, large numbers of same sex couples enter into permanent relationships by marriage or commitment ceremonies every year.

FYI

Chronology of the evolution of same sex rights:

1969—partial decriminalization of anal intercourse;

1985—equality guarantees of the Charter passed;

*1986—**Anderson** v. **Luoma**, the first reported family law case involving a same sex couple. Constructive trust award granted (although low), child support for two children conceived through alternative fertilization denied because same sex couples not "parents" within the meaning of the B.C. legislation, spousal support claim denied because of opposite sex requirement; Charter challenge to same dismissed with a single sentence: "the answer is found in s. 1.";*

*1988—**Andrews** challenges provisions of OHIP after being denied family coverage for her partner and her partner's child. She loses.*

FYI

As a result of our failure to recognize same sex marriages, same sex couples have no automatic rights to share in property on separation or on the death of their partner. Most provinces don't recognize same sex couples for the purposes of consent to medical treatment. Same sex couples justifiably feel that gays and lesbians are not considered full and equal participants in our society, but stand "outside the law." All this legitimizes and perpetuates the stigma and discrimination suffered by gays and lesbians and their children.

SPOUSAL SUPPORT

Under Family Law Legislation

Only heterosexual common law couples are legally obliged to support an unmarried spouse. Recently, in a case called *M.* v. *H.,* a client of mine was successful in challenging this exclusion at trial and on appeal, with the result that spousal support is currently available to same sex couples in Ontario. The matter has been appealed to the Supreme Court of Canada, and the issue will not be settled for a year or more.

"M." and "H." were involved in a ten-year lesbian relationship. (Because of the parties' reluctance to be identified, a judge made a rare order that they be referred to by initials only.) M. pleaded that she experienced financial difficulties upon separation, arising in part from dependency created in the relationship, and claimed spousal support under the *Family Law Act*. However, M. didn't fall within the opposite sex definition of "spouse," and we were forced to challenge the constitutionality of the provision. We argued that the parties' relationship was similar to an opposite sex relationship in that it created emotional and financial dependencies. The parties had agreed that M. would focus on the domestic sphere, while H. assumed more of the direct financial responsibility. In litigation, however, H. claimed that the couple consciously avoided emulation of a heterosexual model and lived together like "best friends."

Both the trial judge, Madam Justice Epstein, and a majority of the Court of Appeal, in a decision written by Madam Justice Charron, found that the opposite sex requirement for spousal support denied same sex cohabitees the equal protection and benefit of the law. They concluded that the purpose of the legislation was to provide for those who require assistance after the breakdown of a relationship involving economic dependence. Since the exclusion of same sex couples from spousal support protections was inconsistent with the purpose of the legislation, and inclusion would in fact further those purposes, the opposite sex requirement was removed from the statute. The Court of Appeal was more cautious, however, and made their order subject to a one-year waiting period to allow the legislature time to respond. This remedy gives M. and others the right to claim support after December 18, 1997. As indicated, the matter is under appeal and will probably not be resolved for several years. It is not clear whether the government will ask the Supreme Court to "stay" the order, so that the changes will not take effect until the Court has reached a decision, but either way, claims can still be made for spousal support in the intervening period.

Lesbians and gay men will likely bring challenges in other provinces to gain access to statutory spousal support upon the breakdown of relationships. As indicated in Chapter 9, "Common Law

Couples," this will likely change in the Northwest Territories and Quebec—where opposite sex cohabitees don't have support rights—following *Miron* v. *Trudel* (as we recently saw with the *Taylor* case in Alberta). This would open the door for same sex couples to seek the same entitlement.

FYI

1989—Veysey gets conjugal visits with same sex partner in federal penitentiary;

1991—Knodel gets provincial medical benefits for his partner;

1992—Leshner persuades a Board of Inquiry to order the Ontario government to set up an off-side pension so that same sex couples have spousal pension benefits;

1992—Douglas strikes down prohibition of gays and lesbians in the Armed Forces in the Federal Court of Appeal. Haig wins in the Ontario Court of Appeal and CHRA is amended judicially to include same sex couples in its protections. (Haig had been denied promotions in the Canadian Armed Forces after coming out.)

As an Equitable Claim

If the result of the appeal in *M.* v. *H.* is that spousal support is not available by statute, equitable claims may still be asserted to obtain monthly support, and these claims might be better received with the increasing legal acceptance and recognition of same sex cohabitation.

Equity is an area of judicial decision-making that's unrelated to any statute. It is rooted in the court's ability to do what is fair according to the facts of each case. Equitable principles are invoked when unjust enrichment is claimed in respect to property, as discussed elsewhere in this book. Another principle of equity is promissory estoppel, a doctrine of law that prevents someone from acting inconsistently with a promise that was made and relied upon.

The doctrine of promissory estoppel has been put to only limited use in the context of family law, but it was recently applied in the Ontario case of *Campbell* v. *Campbell*. In that case, a husband was not allowed to reduce support when he retired earlier than he originally "promised."

W. v. *G.* is the only same sex relationship case that relies on promissory estoppel. In 1996, an Australian judge ordered a lesbian woman to pay child support to her partner. The couple had agreed to undergo alternative fertilization, and the payer of support had promised that they would both raise the two children that resulted. The judge found that it was unconscionable for the defendant to avoid contributing to the upbringing of the children. There's no need to apply this reasoning in cases of child support in Canada, because child support is available regardless of the sexual orientation of the parties. But it's easily adaptable to claims for spousal support. If a need for support arises from the way the parties agreed that they would order their lives and from promises that each would take care of the other, spousal support might well be available under the doctrine of promissory estoppel.

There are no guarantees, however. The law of equity relies substantially on a judge's subjective view of the facts, and there are some old limitations to the rules of promissory estoppel. One is that promissory estoppel can't be used to pursue a claim, but only as a defence. It's a shield, not a sword. Recent case law and academic commentary have criticized this requirement, and it remains to be seen whether the distinction will continue, especially in family law, which focuses on remedies and flexibility. Promissory estoppel for spousal support is thus an innovative claim, and the potential results of any such claim are correspondingly uncertain.

FYI

If you need support on the breakdown of a same sex relationship, you should discuss these options with a lawyer who's familiar with family law for same sex couples. By the time such an issue arises in your life, a statute may entitle you to support as a result of law reform. If it doesn't, you can either make a claim pursuant to promissory estoppel or challenge your exclusion from those rights under the Charter.

EXCLUSIVE POSSESSION OF THE (MATRIMONIAL) HOME

Possession of the home arises separately from actual ownership. If one or both married spouses own a home, either of them may apply for an order allowing them to live in the home pending the resolution of other issues. Usually, exclusive possession is for the short-term, since property will have to be divided in the long-term. If only one spouse owns the home, that spouse will eventually be entitled to get his or her money out of the property. Exclusive possession doesn't give an ownership interest in the property, but only a right to live in the property for some period.

Provincial legislation provides no matrimonial-home rights to same sex or common law couples. Instead, they can make two arguments to obtain possession of the home; either as an incident of support or pursuant to contractual and equitable principles. In either case, the general principles of exclusive possession still apply. This makes it difficult to obtain exclusive possession, because it's usually available only when one spouse can show that the other is obviously dangerous because of violence, verbal abuse or addiction. In rare cases, exclusive possession is ordered because a judge is satisfied that continued cohabitation could harm the spouse or the children emotionally. (These general considerations are discussed in Chapter 6, "The Matrimonial Home.")

Exclusive Possession as an Incident of Spousal Support

In British Columbia, Newfoundland, New Brunswick, Ontario, PEI and the Yukon, common law couples can claim exclusive possession as part of the overall spousal support package. But exclusive possession is difficult to obtain, and each case turns on its own facts.

If same sex couples become entitled to statutory spousal support, they could claim exclusive possession of a home as an incident of support in the provinces listed earlier. The remedy provides no answer, however, to a same sex partner who is financially independent. In that case, a court would probably conclude that there's no need for spousal support and thus no entitlement to exclusive possession as an incident of spousal support, regardless of the fact that a spouse might need exclusive possession for non-financial reasons. Until same sex couples receive matrimonial-home rights and protections by specific legislative reform or a ruling on a Charter challenge, the "incident of support" loophole will have limited application.

Exclusive Possession Arising from Contractual or Equitable Claims

Contractual principles also exist outside of statutes. The common law is a body of cases that have been decided in the past and that establish principles that other judges are required to follow. The rules of contract—when and how contracts are made, whether they're broken, and how breaches of contract are remedied—exist under common law. Contractual licence is one such principle, and it has some possible applications to exclusive possession, in certain cases.

A licence is permission to do something on a property that would otherwise constitute trespass. A contractual licence was granted in Canada in *Ireland* v. *Cutten*, in which the plaintiff was promised that, if she stayed in Toronto, she would have a house to live in for the rest of her life. When her benefactor died, the executor attempted to sell the property but was unsuccessful. The plaintiff was entitled to live in the home as long as she used it as a residence.

The facts of the *Ireland* case resemble a case of promissory estoppel. Promissory estoppel is based on promises, so it would apply equally to a claim for exclusive possession if promises were made during the relationship about one spouse's right to remain on the property indefinitely. As indicated above, there is an issue about whether promissory estoppel can be used as a "sword"; however, if one spouse tries to remove the other from the home by making a claim in court, promissory estoppel might be used as a "shield" to defend the claim and provide at least short-term exclusive possession.

Like the other creative arguments discussed in this chapter, there's no predictability to these claims. In the end, although the results of such claims are uncertain, there is a clear and potentially effective analogy between exclusive possession and these contractual and equitable claims, especially on an interim basis.

FYI

*1993—**Layland and Beaulne** lose their challenge to common law opposite sex requirement of marriage when majority concludes that they suffer no discrimination because each is free to marry a woman;*

*1993—The Supreme Court tells **Mossop** that denial of bereavement leave for a family member of same sex partner does not discriminate on the basis of "family status";*

1994—Ontario's Bill 167, an omnibus bill designed to remove discrimination against same sex couples, is defeated on second reading;

1995—Three same sex couples in Ottawa are granted joint custody as a means of creating parental rights;

*1995—**Re K.**: joint stepparent adoption applications by same sex couples allowed; opposite sex requirement for joint application deemed unconstitutional.*

PROPERTY

Trust Claims

Unlike married couples, neither same sex nor common law couples have any automatic right to share in property under family law. The claims that are usually made against property held in a same sex spouse's name are resulting and constructive trust—the same ones made by common law couples.

A resulting trust is a claim for an interest in property. It can succeed only if the claimant shows that money was invested directly in a property or that the parties had a clear understanding that one spouse was holding the property in trust for the other.

A constructive trust claim is one of several remedies available when direct or indirect contributions have been made to property, and when unjust enrichment is found to exist. Other remedies for unjust enrichment are money judgments and equitable liens.(See Chapter 5 and Chapter 9.)

The Supreme Court of Canada has recently analyzed constructive trust claims between opposite sex cohabitees and has shown a considerable amount of support for granting these claims when they arise out of intimate cohabitation. Such claims will likely become so frequent that they'll constitute standard entitlement between all intimate cohabitees, provided that the spouse can show the requisite amount of contribution to the property or household.

The sexual orientation of the parties has no relevance to these issues because they're based on contribution, without reference to the sexual relationship. Canadian courts have already reached this conclusion in several cases and have granted trust interests in property to same sex spouses. If a contribution has been made to a property, or substantial labour or household services are given by one to the other during cohabitation, the court will usually grant a remedy that compensates the claimant for the contribution in the form of a money payment or an interest in the property. Chapter 5, "Property" discusses equitable principles and trust claims, and the property section of Chapter 9, "Common Law Couples" illustrates the requirements of and remedies for property claims on the basis of constructive or resulting trust.

Proprietary Estoppel

Like promissory estoppel, proprietary estoppel is based on promises. However, promissory estoppel is invoked to get *possession* of property, while proprietary estoppel is invoked to obtain *ownership* of property. Also, unlike promissory estoppel—which provides only a shield—proprietary estoppel can be used as a sword, as the basis of a claim against property.

In a Canadian case decided in 1979, *Pascoe* v. *Turner,* a man bought a house for a woman with whom he was involved, but he took title in his own name. Even after dissolution of the relationship, he told her, "The house is yours." The woman spent time and money making repairs, and he said nothing to stop her. She was economically disadvantaged, older, and had made significant expenditures on the property. The man was compelled to give effect to her expectations: to perfect the gift by transferring title to her.

Proprietary estoppel might also give rise to a licence. In a British case, a father invited his son to build a bungalow on his property. The son did so, largely at his own expense. When the father died, his will pre-dated construction of the bungalow. The executors wanted to remove the son from the property, but the court held that, if the owner of land requests or allows another to expend money upon a property on the expectation that he'll be entitled to stay there, the licencee may remain on the property.

The parallels to cases involving intimate cohabitation are obvious. Many couples make contributions to a property in the form of labour or cash for improvements. Even if they don't strictly believe that they'll get an interest in the property in return, they can be seen to have formed such an expectation because they believe the relationship will be permanent and both spouses will always share in the fruits of their labour. Many spouses base further expectations on a mutual promise that each will take care of the other or that they'll be together until one dies, at which point their mutual wills will operate. While resulting trust claims are also based on promises, they're often strictly analyzed, making proprietary estoppel claims good alternatives in some cases.

FYI

*1995—**Egan and Nesbit** lose their challenge to the **Old Age Security Act**, although the application of equality guarantees to same sex couples is enshrined by the decision. **Miron v. Trudel** released the same day;*

*1996—**Rosenberg and Evans** lose a challenge to the pension provisions of the **Income Tax Act** (under appeal);*

*1996—**M. v. H.** trial decision gives same sex couples spousal support rights and obligations. On appeal, the decision is upheld, but subject to a one-year suspension to give the legislature time to make changes (this is now under appeal);*

1996—House of Commons passes Bill C-33, prohibiting sexual orientation discrimination in employment of federal employees;

*1996—**Vriend**, fired because of his sexual orientation, loses an appeal because sexual orientation is not a prohibited ground of discrimination in Alberta's human rights legislation (under appeal).*

It is my experience that promises are common in same sex relationships, because they're often perceived as the only means to structure the relationship. The law provides default rules to protect heterosexual spouses, but lesbian and gay couples have no protection except by contract and careful planning. I recently interviewed a new client whose same sex partner had made frequent promises, in front of various family members and friends, that they "each owned half of everything," regardless of the fact that a house and a ski chalet were in one spouse's name alone. My colleagues were amazed at the extent of these promises and the number of witnesses to them, since they're rarely made so explicitly between opposite sex couples.

CUSTODY AND ACCESS

A court may order custody of or access to a child to one or more persons. There's no opposite sex parental requirement; in fact, there's no requirement that either party be a parent. The only issue is whether the proposed custody or access is in the child's best interest. Parties to a former relationship can make any arrangement with respect to the custody of or access to a child without involving the courts. As I've emphasized throughout this book, resolving such issues is always in everyone's best interests, including most importantly the children's. For lesbian and gay parents, however, avoiding potential discrimination in or through the court process is another strong motivator for amicable settlement.

On Breakdown of a Heterosexual Relationship

All case law relating to custody or access claims by gay men or lesbians has been decided after one parent has left a heterosexual relationship and then advised the former partner that he or she is gay or lesbian. There are no reported decisions involving custody and access involving children of parents in a same sex relationship, probably because the fear of facing judicial heterosexism inspires same sex couples to mediate or negotiate children's issues.

There's no consistent view in the courts as to how claims for custody and access should be considered when they're made by gay or lesbian parents. Early jurisprudence on the topic saw lesbian mothers

denied access to protect the children from exposure to "people of abnor-
mal tastes and proclivities" or from societal prejudice. Gay fathers were
denied overnight access unless they became celibate. However, judicial
attitudes are changing, and there's a wealth of sociological and psychological evidence that shows that sexual orientation has no bearing on a
person's parenting ability. With the huge influx of cases in our courts
over discrimination involving sexual orientation, judges should know
that it's unacceptable to treat same sex and opposite sex couples differently or to express concerns rooted in stereotypical views. The highest
authority thus far on the subject of lesbian and gay parenting is a decision of the Ontario Court of Appeal, which states that the sexual orientation of the parties should be a neutral factor.

The most important consideration for a gay or lesbian parent
who's asserting custody is to provide the court with sufficient sociological and psychological evidence to dispel any prejudice the judge
may have. There's substantial evidence available to family lawyers, and
many judges are aware of its conclusions. Many sociologists and psychologists spend their time giving expert evidence on these issues in
court. The Ontario decision that allowed same sex stepparent adoption,
Re K., summarizes a wealth of evidence that answers the common
myths and stereotypes about same sex parenting, and should be
referred to in any same sex custody case. The bottom line is that your
advocate must negate any discriminatory assumptions about gay men
and lesbians in considerations of a child's best interests. Your advocate
must also stress that the equality of each parent creates a right to act as
a parent without restrictions.

FYI

*Some lawyers have suggested that the only way to ensure consistent results
in custody and access cases involving gay and lesbian parents is to codify a
requirement that sexual orientation is irrelevant to the best interests of the
child. Until this is done, however, addressing the issue directly with substantial evidence and positive case law and demanding unbiased judicial consideration of the issue are the only tactical answers for gay and lesbian parents.*

Children of the Same Sex Relationship

Of course, if a claim is made for custody of or access to a child and both parents are gay or lesbian, neither parent is likely to become disentitled on the basis of his or her sexual orientation. However, spouses must take care to provide the judge with evidence to show that there's no correlation between sexual orientation and parenting abilities and to ensure that no restrictions are made on the life of either parent, as referred to above.

If you have children and are entering a gay or lesbian relationship, you should remember that the court can make an order about the custody of or access to a child in favour of your partner if the relationship breaks down. There are no reported cases that have considered a claim for custody by a same sex stepparent. Courts do consider the relationship between the custody claimants and the child, including whether a blood relationship exists, but usually this factor is secondary to more basic considerations such as the bond between each parent and the child and each adult's parenting ability. Although it's an exception for custody to be granted to a stepparent over a biological parent, there are many cases in which a stepmother who has been the primary caregiver has received custody of a stepchild. In a same sex context, the same result would likely occur. A same sex stepparent might also receive custody when the biological parent has emotional problems or poses a risk to the child.

Access by a stepparent is commonplace. To be realistic, you should consider your partner to be entitled to access if your relationship breaks down.

In discussing stepparents, I'm referring to children brought to a relationship in which only one spouse is a biological parent. The law is less clear on the topic of children conceived or adopted within a same sex relationship. If a lesbian spouse conceives a child through alternative fertilization, a court would probably consider the birth mother to have some advantage in a custody dispute, because she's the biological parent. Such an assumption could be dispelled by evidence that the other parent was equally or more involved with caring for the child or is more suitable to provide care for other reasons. Same sex couples are not entitled to adopt children other than their stepchildren except in

British Columbia. In families in which one parent has successfully adopted a child, the decision is often mutual and both partners often contribute equally to childcare. Nevertheless, given the legal complexities involved in obtaining and changing this status, there would probably still be a strong presumption in favour of the sole adoptive parent.

Joint Custody and Adoption to Create Parental Rights

Several Ontario judges have given same sex parents joint custody during a relationship in which each partner is acting as parent to the biological children of one of the spouses and both wish to have rights and obligations as parents. Because there's no restriction on who may be granted custody of children, there's no reason why joint custody orders wouldn't be available to any Canadian same sex couples who wish to inject some certainty into their family relationship. Another common reason for obtaining a joint custody order is to give both spouses a right of access to information from schools and doctors and to allow a non-biological parent to pick up kids from and/or give instructions to various institutions.

FYI

Because there's no restriction on who may be granted custody of children, there's no reason why joint custody orders wouldn't be available to any Canadian same sex couple who wishes to inject some certainty into their family relationship. Although joint custody orders are usually made after a relationship ends, they are available at any time, and can be used to establish rights for non-biological parents.

In Ontario, following the decision in *Re K.*, the lesbian partners of women who have conceived a child through alternative fertilization are entitled to adopt the child, giving each spouse the status of mother. While some argue that stepparent adoption provides the most certainty and equality to same sex parents on breakdown of relationships, it may not be an attractive option if it involves a constitutional challenge to your province's adoption rules. In the end, both joint custody orders and stepparent adoptions go a long way toward removing initial assumptions and putting both spouses on equal footing.

Non-biological parents may have difficulties picking up kids from school, taking the kids to the doctor, travelling with them, making decisions in the event of emergencies, or obtaining information from various sources. Without a joint custody or stepparent adoption order, a non-biological same sex parent has no automatic right to do any of these things. A letter of authorization or permission is the easiest and cheapest solution. The permission letter usually has to be witnessed or sworn, depending on the institution, but once provided it may be effective indefinitely and can be general in nature so that it applies to all sorts of situations.

CHILD SUPPORT

In all provinces, "parents and others" must provide child support. Parents are defined as biological or adoptive parents or people who have shown "a settled intention to treat a child as a child of his or her family." Usually, the person who shows a "settled intention" is a stepparent by marriage or a common law partner who has lived with and supported the child. Although there are no reported Canadian decisions in which a same sex partner has been ordered to pay child support, a person who cohabits with a same sex spouse and kids would be considered to have a "settled intention" sufficient to create child support obligations. As more lesbian and gay couples conceive and adopt children, and as courts recognize same sex couples in all areas, we can expect to see more orders for child support made upon the breakdown of same sex relationships.

A child support claim made by a same sex spouse would be considered in the same way as any other. As we've discussed, federal support guidelines are passed under the *Divorce Act*, which doesn't apply to same sex couples; but provincial guidelines would apply if they are passed. This uncertainty also affects common law couples, as discussed in Chapter 9. The methods of calculating child support under guidelines and various other relevant considerations are discussed in Chapter 7.

As with custody and access, courts are not bound by agreements relating to the support of children. In fact, many statutes consider these agreements to be invalid. Cohabitation agreements will, however, provide the court with some guidance and evidence of your intentions during the relationship. Possible cohabitation agreements might provide that one spouse doesn't have a settled intention to treat the child as a child of the relationship or that one spouse will not have to support the other's child or that both will be equally responsible for supporting all children of the relationship. A severability clause should be inserted in all agreements that address these issues, to protect the whole contract from being set aside because it contains one void provision.

DEFINITION OF SPOUSE FOR BENEFITS

For the purpose of receiving employment benefits, same sex couples are almost always treated as spouses. Federal government employees are entitled to medical, dental and prescription benefits for their same sex partners after one year. Provincial government employees are entitled to benefits for their same sex partners everywhere in Canada but Alberta, Newfoundland, PEI, and the Northwest Territories. All federally regulated corporations and many large employers now give these benefits to same sex partners after they've cohabited for the same amount of time as required for opposite sex cohabitees. All provinces but those listed above prohibit discrimination in employment on the basis of sexual orientation. Provinces that don't include such a prohibition in their human rights legislation will probably face further Charter challenges. (Alberta will have to defend itself on this point in the Supreme Court of Canada in the *Vriend* case in the next few years.) A wealth of judicial authority has concluded that refusing employment benefits to a same sex couple treats them unequally compared to their common law counterparts and offends the equality guarantees of the Charter.

The exception to this, as the law currently stands, is any publicly funded retirement scheme or survivor pension benefit. In 1995, the Supreme Court of Canada decided a case called *Egan and Nesbit* v. *Canada*. The case involved a challenge to the *Old Age Security Act* by two men who had cohabited for thirty-seven years. In a similar opposite sex relationship they would have received retirement benefits. The Supreme Court of Canada found that laws that draw distinctions between same and opposite sex couples on the basis of their sexual orientation offend the equality guarantees of the Charter. On the issue of the *Old Age Security Act*, however, the court couldn't agree. Four judges decided the issue one way, four others decided it another way, and the ninth had the "swing vote" that determined the outcome. The conclusion was that, in the realm of publicly-funded benefits, the government must be allowed to choose between competing groups and pay benefits to those in the most need. The case has been interpreted by governments and some employers to mean that they're not required to give survivor pension benefits to same sex couples. In Ontario, there is some uncertainty on the point, because in 1992, in a case called *Leshner*, a human rights tribunal ordered the Ontario government to cease such discrimination and to establish a separate pension plan for same sex couples. This plan remains in place for employees of the Ontario government.

There are two factors to consider on the issue of employment benefits. First, you must understand that your status as spouses under a benefit plan creates no other right or entitlement and that the length of cohabitation required for benefit payments is unrelated to any other legal issue. Second, if you're currently involved in a same sex relationship and are being denied spousal benefits in your employment, you can probably obtain the benefits by retaining a lawyer with experience in same sex equality cases. In several cases that I've handled, the company was just waiting until somebody asked, and a simple lawyer's letter inspired an immediate flow of benefits. If your employer isn't so cooperative, you should get some advice about how to proceed, either from a lawyer or from the human rights commission in your province.

PREDICTIONS FOR LAW REFORM

Two recent decisions from the Supreme Court of Canada indicate promise for substantial family law reform. As discussed in Chapter 9, a recent decision of the Supreme Court in a case called *Miron* v. *Trudel* suggests that the differences in treatment between married and unmarried opposite sex couples should be eliminated. We may soon see a time when all the rules of family law apply equally to married and unmarried opposite sex couples. (Some judicial reform has already occurred; see the discussion of *Taylor* v. *Rossu* in Chapter 8, "Spousal Support.")

The Supreme Court has also suggested in *Egan and Nesbit* that distinctions between opposite and same sex cohabitees should be removed from our laws, unless the distinctions involve a choice by government about the distribution of limited funds. Family law has nothing to do with government expenditures. In fact, the government would spend less money by giving individuals responsibility for the results of a breakdown of a relationship, since fewer people would need social assistance after separation and since certain rules about how property should be divided would reduce demands on our courts. If opposite sex couples are entitled to the same rights and obligations as married couples, then *Egan and Nesbit* bridges the gap and suggests that same sex couples should have the same rights as other cohabiting couples. As I said as I began this chapter, although it may be many years away, we're moving toward equal treatment of all intimate relationships in family law.

PLANNING YOUR FUTURE AND PROTECTING YOUR INTERESTS

Taking Title Jointly

Given the lack of legal recognition of same sex couples in our laws and the uncertainty of how this will change in the future, same sex couples need to structure their relationships formally. If you want to share equally in property, you can do this in several ways.

Most practically, you can take title to assets in joint names. This goes for real estate, bank accounts, cars, even household contents. All these assets will be equally divided on separation, because they're jointly owned. They'll also be divisible in the event of death.

In the case of real estate, you can take title in two ways. As joint tenants, both parties are presumed to own half the property on separation, regardless of contribution to the purchase price unless a cohabitation agreement provides otherwise. On death, the surviving joint tenant will own all the property. As tenants in common, ownership is not necessarily equal, and the contribution made by each person to the property on separation is debatable. On death, the surviving tenant in common continues to own half the property. The other half is owned by the beneficiaries of the deceased's estate.

Division of household contents and personal effects for same sex couples is a matter of ownership. If you owned it before the relationship, received it as a gift (to you, as opposed to a gift to both of you, which is sometimes a sticking point), or can show a bill of sale for the item, you're entitled to take it in the division of household contents. Usually, people only care about the large or expensive items. For these, if you take a little time to think about it, you can obtain a bill of sale in joint names or as you decide at the time.

Renting

If you rent your home, consider whose name should be on the lease. If only one of your names is on the lease, that person will be responsible for the lease payments on separation unless you agree otherwise. Usually that means the other will move out. While notice may be given in respect to a monthly lease, and any liability can thus be limited to the notice period, a yearly lease is a different matter. If the spouse whose name is on the lease dies, the surviving spouse will lose the apartment. If both your names are on the lease, both of you are liable for the rent even if only one of you lives there, and either one of you will have the right to stay there on separation or if one of you dies. If you rent your home and are in a committed relationship, you should probably take steps to ensure that both your names are on the lease.

FYI

I recently acted for a man who had lived in an apartment with his same sex partner for ten years. He was not on the lease. When the couple split, the other man moved out and although he agreed to assist my client in getting his name on the lease, the landlord would not cooperate. In the end, my client had to move out of the apartment—an expensive and inconvenient result.

Basic Estate Planning

Everyone should have a will, and same sex couples *must* have one. Same sex couples are entirely unrecognized by intestacy laws. If one spouse dies intestate, his or her property passes in the following order: to a legal wife or husband; to children; to relatives; or to the Crown. The same sex spouse doesn't figure in the equation. Moreover, if a same sex partner dies while legally married, the heterosexual spouse can make a claim against the estate unless the parties have signed a separation agreement or are divorced. Likewise, if a same sex spouse dies with dependents and hasn't made proper provision for them in a will, they can make claims against the estate for support.

Although estate planning requires a will, the ultimate goal of financial estate planning is to have assets pass to beneficiaries outside the estate to avoid executor's fees, legal fees, estate taxes and potential actions against the estate by relatives. This is accomplished by taking title to real estate as joint tenants and designating your spouse as beneficiary under insurance, pensions (if possible), RRSPs and other savings plans. Another option is to create an *inter vivos* trust, which operates in the same way as a will, except that the property is transferred into a trust for the benefit of the beneficiaries while the grantor is alive.

Your will should then deal with other matters, as well. For starters, everyone needs to appoint an executor to handle the issues that arise on death. If you have savings, investments, a business or other assets that are not held jointly, you'll need to appoint beneficiaries. There are many stories about estranged family members refusing to recognize a same sex relationship after one spouse has died. With these stories in mind, a will for same sex couples becomes a necessity, not a luxury. If you have children, you may want to provide for them alone or for them and your spouse. You can also state your preferences in a will about who should have custody or guardianship of your children, although it will not necessarily be enforced, since every case is decided on the best interests of the children. If you've conceived children through alternative fertilization without adopting them, they'll be regarded as orphans if the biological mother dies, so you should make provisions for guardianship and custody.

A handwritten will is enforceable, but not recommended unless you want your beneficiaries to endure estate litigation. You need legal advice that's specific to your situation, and it's usually inexpensive: most lawyers will meet with you, discuss the process and draft a simple will for $100 or a pair of mirror wills for $150. Prepare yourself with a list of your property, back-up documents and your decisions on whom you wish to benefit from your will. You can then discuss your other goals and learn about your options. When the will is signed and the bill is paid, you'll know you have everything covered.

Same-sex couples also need to consider a final estate planning issue, power of attorney. If your spouse becomes incapacitated by physical or mental illness, you can't deal with property or even attend to minor financial matters without a power of attorney. And except in Ontario, you can't make decisions about medical treatment.

There are two types of powers of attorney that give your spouse rights in the event of your incapacity: a power of attorney over property and one for consent to medical treatment. You can give your partner one or both in a single power of attorney form. This too must be prepared by a lawyer, as it's enforceable only if it's in the right form. A power of attorney can be prepared at minimal cost. Most people prepare them at the same time as their will.

FYI

*1996—**Moore and Akerstrom**, two employees of the foreign services, successfully challenge the federal government's refusal to recognize them as spouses for employment benefits, including relocation costs. The CHRC tribunal orders all employment benefits be provided immediately to same sex couples and that the federal government review all of its laws and eliminate any such form of discrimination. Federal government announces a month later that it will not appeal the portion requiring payment of employment benefits, but will appeal the balance;*

*1996—**Laessoe**, an employee of Air Canada is denied pension benefits for same sex partners because sexual orientation wasn't in the Act at the time that the complaint arose;*

*1996—**Dwyer and Sims**, two employees of the Municipality of Metropolitan Toronto are successful in getting damages for employment benefits, and all municipalities across Ontario are ordered to give such benefits.*

Cohabitation Agreements

You can set the rules for your relationship and clearly establish your intentions in a cohabitation agreement. Unlike opposite sex agreements, family law doesn't provide same sex cohabitation agreements with specific enforcement powers or stipulate strict formal requirements for validity. Nevertheless, courts respect them, as they respect all contracts, and set them aside only in rare cases—usually those involving substantial non-disclosure, duress or fraud.

If you and your partner both come to the relationship with few assets and wish to share what you develop together, you will still not gain certainty on all issues by taking title jointly and conducting some basic estate planning. Even if you hold all your assets jointly or subject to beneficiary designations, you may want to provide for the division of the joint assets in the event of separation or establish rules for the method of division. One spouse may purchase the other's interest according to a strict formula, for example, or the property may be listed and sold within thirty days of separation. As an estate planning matter, you may take title to real estate jointly so that your partner gets the whole asset on your death. As a matter of separation planning, however, you may wish to share in its increase in value according to the ratio of your initial contributions, if you're dividing it after a breakup. Or you may wish to share some property by taking title jointly, but preserve other assets for each spouse to retain in the event of separation.

Even if you hold assets jointly, you may want to confirm in writing that you and your partner will share assets according to title. This will almost certainly disentitle your partner from making a resulting trust claim, a constructive trust claim or any other claim based on unjust enrichment against any of your assets. Since intention and promises are essential to the estoppel and contract claims discussed earlier in this chapter, an agreement will also go a long way toward defeating them.

If you or your spouse operate an unincorporated business, the businessperson may not wish to hold assets in his or her name to protect them from potential creditors. A cohabitation agreement allows you to agree upon shared ownership, regardless of title. Some business partnerships require partners to have cohabitation agreements or marriage contracts to protect the assets of the business from claims by spouses in the event of the breakdown of the relationship. Such agreements may not specifically include same sex spouses, but if you have such a partnership agreement and you or one of your business partners is in a same sex relationship, you should consider the need for a same sex cohabitation agreement.

If you're bringing children to a new relationship or plan to have children during the relationship, you and your spouse need to know that you're of the same mind. Discussing your arrangement for the children is crucial, even if you don't end up signing an agreement for these purposes. You may wish to protect your children financially over the interests of your spouse or simply provide certainty to avoid later disputes. You may agree that either of you will stand in the position of parent to the other's children and will have child support obligations. You may address custody of stepchildren, if only to describe your intentions, since such clauses are often considered unenforceable. (Planning options relating to children are discussed under Custody and Access and Child Support in this chapter.)

If you're considering conceiving a child by donor insemination, you may consider a donor contract. This is not a decision that should be taken lightly. Donor contracts and their enforceability are discussed briefly in Chapter 1, and in more detail in Chapter 12.

If you share household responsibilities; if one of you stays home with a child; if one of you contributes to property; if you save one spouse's income and spend the other; or even if you and your partner have substantially different incomes, you should have a cohabitation agreement dealing with spousal support. The law of spousal support for same sex couples is in limbo, and any decision on the subject could be retroactive, giving you and your partner immediate spousal support rights and obligations. Whether the law changes or not, you can grant a spouse the right to support in the form of a lump sum or monthly payments, for a limited or unlimited period, using a cohabitation agreement. Or you can use the agreement to waive support entirely. (No waiver of spousal support is iron-clad, however; see Chapter 8.)

Any change in family law relating to same sex couples could be retroactive. Whether you like it or not, you may wake up and find that you now have to share all your property and pay support to your same sex partner. Or not. We simply don't know what the law will be tomorrow. A cohabitation agreement gives you the power to establish your own law that should survive any change. The agreement should specify that you anticipate law reform and that, no matter how the law changes, your relationship will be governed by the agreement. In the process of discussing cohabitation agreements, you will have an opportunity to understand your spouse's expectations, which in itself is a good thing. If you both decide later that you need to revisit an issue, you can always amend the agreement.

For a cohabitation agreement to be binding, it must be signed by both parties and witnessed. Full and complete financial disclosure should be attached to the agreement. Both parties should fully understand what they're signing, and the only way to ensure that this happens is by obtaining independent legal advice. Although you can draft your own cohabitation agreement, gay or lesbian partners in particular should not. You want a valid and enforceable agreement, which considers all possible issues, and you want it to survive law reform. A lawyer will charge you from $500 to $3000 for a cohabitation agreement, depending on the complexity and the time required to draft and negotiate the document. Shop around and get quotes before you retain a lawyer. You can keep costs down by retaining someone with experience in the area of same sex family law, going to the meeting armed with your financial disclosure and back-up documents, and having some idea of what you want to accomplish. (Financial statements are discussed in Chapter 2; other matters relating to cohabitation agreements are found in Chapter 12.)

CHAPTER ELEVEN

Violence in the Family

IN THIS CHAPTER: **Domestic Violence Defined,**
Immediate Issues on Separation; *Emergencies and the Police,*
Community Resources, Making a Separation Plan, **Criminal**
Remedies; *Peace Bonds, Criminal Charges,* **Family Law Remedies;**
Restraining Orders, Exclusive Possession of the Matrimonial Home,
Custody and Access; *Interim Interim Custody, Interim and Permanent*
Custody, Access, **Division of Property, Child Support, Spousal**
Support, Damages, Criminal Injuries Compensation,
Children as Victims

FAMILY VIOLENCE IS A PREVALENT PROBLEM IN OUR SOCIETY. AT LEAST
ONE IN TEN WOMEN IS ASSAULTED BY HER INTIMATE PARTNER. OF ALL
WOMEN MURDERED IN CANADA, SIXTY-TWO PERCENT ARE KILLED BY
THEIR SPOUSES. THIS CHAPTER ADDRESSES THE LEGAL RIGHTS OF VIC-
TIMS OF DOMESTIC VIOLENCE AND PROVIDES SOME BASIC STRATEGIES
PARTICULAR TO CASES INVOLVING VIOLENCE. IT DOESN'T DISCUSS THE
MANY SOCIOLOGICAL AND PSYCHOLOGICAL MATTERS THAT MUST BE
ADDRESSED BEFORE VICTIMS, LAWYERS, AND JUDGES CAN UNDERSTAND
THE ISSUE, SINCE THEY ARE TOO DETAILED AND COMPLEX TO RECEIVE
ADEQUATE TREATMENT HERE. IF YOU WANT THIS KIND OF INFORMA-
TION, THE COMMUNITY RESOURCES OUTLINED IN THIS CHAPTER ARE A
GOOD PLACE TO START.

Much of the discussion in this book about avoiding litigation, settling
your own family law case and mediation does not apply to spouses who
have suffered domestic violence. The imbalances of power and threats of
continuing harm inherent in such situations make settlement and mediation inappropriate and risky for victims of violence. Turning to the
courts is often the only answer. There are many options, complications
and costs, but most victims of domestic violence find the courts to be
sensitive and responsive to their needs.

DOMESTIC VIOLENCE DEFINED

For the purposes of this book, domestic violence is any violent word
or deed, usually directed by a man against a woman and/or children.
Domestic violence may also be perpetrated by women, and it can
occur in same sex relationships. But the vast majority of cases of
domestic violence involve men attacking women, and this chapter will
proceed on that assumption. Domestic violence includes assault, assault
with a weapon, sexual assault, forcible confinement, harassment, infliction of mental abuse, threats and other forms of intimidation. Assault
may involve hitting, slapping, punching, kicking, pushing, hair-pulling
or other violent conduct. Assault with a weapon includes the use of a

gun, knife, bottle, belt, boot, or other household object. Sexual assault includes grabbing the breasts or genitals, forced sexual activity and rape. Forcible confinement involves confining or imprisoning someone and threatening physical violence if they don't comply. Threats and intimidation are criminal offences, and they're evidence of mental abuse for the purposes of civil claims.

In listing various forms of violence, I do not mean to categorize or minimize domestic violence. Even one incident of the conduct described above is reprehensible and gives cause to consider the issues outlined in this chapter. The reality is, however, that many victims of violence live in a truly vicious circle of power and control involving repeated assaults, emotional abuse, isolation, threats and intimidation, economic control, denial, self-blame, guilt, forgiveness and false hope.

FYI

Before 1983, it was not illegal to rape your spouse. However, married and cohabiting individuals can now be charged with raping their partners.

IMMEDIATE ISSUES ON SEPARATION

Domestic violence presents its own set of issues in the context of separation. Many women have endured years of threats about what will happen to them if they tell anyone about the abuse or if they leave the relationship. They often lack the financial independence to pay legal fees, find alternate accommodation, or support their children. Many women feel responsible for the violence they've suffered and are immobilized by fear or guilt. They feel that they should stay with their spouse in the interests of the children. Many hold continued hopes that the violence will end, fueled by the "honeymoon" phase that often follows an abusive incident. For all these reasons, the decision to leave the relationship is particularly onerous for a battered woman. The following discussion provides basic considerations and answers to assist abused women who are considering separation.

Emergencies and the Police

If you can safely get to a phone during or soon after an assault, you should call the police. Many women report that the police take a long time to arrive at their home, especially if they indicated that the abuser was their spouse or if they had called police to the residence before. You should not indicate in a 911 call that the perpetrator is your partner. Instead, stress that this is an emergency that requires immediate attendance by the police.

When the police arrive, they can lay charges without having witnessed the assault, if they have reasonable and probable grounds to believe that an offence has occurred. Many police forces have strict policies that require charges in every case of domestic violence. Others continue to take a non-interventionist approach, treating domestic violence as a private matter. Sometimes police will ask a victim if she wants charges laid. This can be a difficult decision, because a victim may fear further violence or reprisals, especially if the man or children are present when the question is posed.

Counsellors, lawyers and feminists agree that criminal charges should be laid in every case, and victims of violence should request them whenever possible, for several reasons. First, a criminal charge sends a strong message to the perpetrator that the conduct is intolerable. Second, this message is sent by the state, not by the victim. In the absence of such a message, the victim may feel responsible for the event and may be reluctant to call the police in the future. Third, the state takes responsibility for the conduct of the criminal case; if no charges are laid, this responsibility shifts to the victim. And fourth, the charge can provide grounds for a subsequent civil action.

If the police don't lay charges, or if they're not called at the time of the incident, the victim may go to the Justice of the Peace and lay a complaint, called an "information." This process is discussed in more detail under Peace Bonds.

If the police lay charges at the time of the incident, the abuser may be released later the same day or detained overnight and released only after a bail hearing. This depends on the police's judgment of the seriousness of the assault, the risk of a further incident, the risk that the abuser will not appear at the bail hearing, and whether there have been other charges. A victim who fears that release will result in further violence should make that concern patently clear to the police at the time of the arrest. It is also a good idea for the victim to attend the bail hearing to make such concerns known to the government lawyer handling the case.

Whether or not charges are laid, and whether or not you intend to immediately separate from your spouse, you should consider visiting an emergency department, hospital or private physician after an attack. Apart from your need for medical assistance, the medical practitioner's documentation may be important evidence for a later lawsuit, criminal case or application for public housing and assistance. You should also have some photographs taken of your injuries in the first few days after an assault. They may be Polaroid or regular photographs, and they may be taken by a friend in private or by a doctor. Such photographs provide powerful evidence of abuse. Even if you're not ready to separate, they'll give you some security and reliability if you decide to leave in the future. Finally, you should keep written notes of the event and any subsequent assaults and of the exact words of any threats or other comments. All this evidence will be useful in criminal or family proceedings, such as custody, and the history that you compile may help you focus on the extent of the violence and how it affects you.

Community Resources

Whether or not separation is inspired by a violent incident, police involvement or simply a considered decision to leave, many battered women require assistance to effect the actual separation. There are many facilities designed to meet this need. Immediate concerns are usually finding other accommodation, custody of children, financial issues, and finding and retaining a lawyer.

Finding other accommodation may be a thorny issue for a victim of repeated violence and threats. Extended families may provide immediate refuge, but many victims are afraid to tell their families about the abuse or expose them to the violence. Or they know that the abuser will find them if they go to a family member's home. In such cases, there are two alternatives: obtaining protective family law or criminal remedies (discussed below); or moving to a women's shelter and then finding other accommodation after you've sorted out your immediate financial concerns.

A list of women's shelter associations is included in Appendix E. A call to the appropriate provincial association will give you a list of shelters in your area. Many shelters have restrictions about who can move in and how long they can stay. Most allow children to accompany the victim of abuse, although some have age restrictions for children. The third option, although not immediately available, is to apply for public housing.

If you have children, you should bring them with you when you leave and their custody should be addressed immediately upon separation. You'll need a lawyer or community legal service to assist you with this process. The law societies of every province provide free legal information and assistance through a dial-a-law service, a lawyer referral service, community legal clinics and/or legal aid plans. (Law societies are listed in Appendix C. Provincial lawyer referral services are listed in Appendix D.) If you have the means to retain a lawyer, or you and your spouse have property that will be subject to division and that can provide some security for your legal fees, you should retain a lawyer specializing in domestic violence and family law before you decide upon the logistics of separation. If you don't have the means to retain a lawyer, you can obtain information from a community legal clinic about how to proceed, or you can go directly to a legal aid office and request coverage. If you're denied coverage despite the fact that you can't afford to pay for a lawyer, contact a community legal clinic. The clinic may assist you in pressuring the legal aid plan or appealing the refusal of coverage. Or it may assist you without a legal aid certificate. You should consider all these options before separation, unless the separation is initiated by an emergency, in which case you should attend to them as soon as possible. With a call to your provincial law society, you can obtain a list of community legal clinics and legal aid offices. Women's shelters and assaulted women's groups can also provide information and assistance on legal help.

If you have immediate financial needs on separation, you can address them in several ways. If your spouse has income or property, a family law action can bring fast financial relief in emergency situations. If you don't have this luxury, either because you can't find a lawyer to help you or because there's no family income to tap into, you can consider turning to family members for immediate help and/or applying for public assistance. Women's shelters, community legal clinics and battered women's support groups will assist you with these issues.

Making a Separation Plan

If you've decided to leave an abusive relationship, it's a good idea to consider all the issues before you separate and to make a separation plan. Most shelters and battered women's support groups distribute a separation checklist. You should consider this checklist even if you don't intend to leave immediately. Such lists usually include the following advice:

- Withdraw any money you can from a bank account, and keep your bankbook, bank cards and charge cards with you. If you don't intend to leave immediately, consider opening your own bank account to give you financial independence in the future;

- Assemble your passport, birth certificate, health insurance card, social insurance card, and the same documentation, plus school and medical records, for any children that you'll take with you;

- Assemble special documentation, such as immigration papers, marriage and divorce certificates, work permits, insurance papers, lease agreements, house deeds, mortgage documents;

- If you're going to make custody and support claims on an emergency basis, you'll need to complete a financial statement as soon as you meet with your lawyer. You should review the discussion of financial statements in Chapter 2, and ask yourself what documents you may need to support your income, expenses and property values. If you have any of these documents handy, you should include them with the papers described above;

- Bring clothing for you and the children for a few days, along with other personal items of sentimental value (pictures, small saleable items, your address book);

- Bring bottles, diapers, blankets and favourite toys for the children;

- If you don't intend to leave immediately, you should have all of these items ready or keep copies of the documents, extra keys, and a small bag of clothing and personal items with a trusted friend or family member, so that you can leave quickly if you decide to do so;

- Decide where you'll go if there's a "next time." If you intend to go to a shelter, keep directions to the shelter and bus fare in the same place as you keep the other emergency items. If you want to stay in the home and can afford to, see the discussion of exclusive possession and restraining orders below;

- Teach your children how to call the police in case they find themselves in danger, witness further abuse or are kidnapped by the abuser;
- Consider when and how you can actually leave the home, even if you haven't yet decided to separate;
- Identify for daycare workers or teachers exactly who can or can't pick up or visit your child. If you're separating and taking your child with you, tell them that your partner isn't entitled to pick up or visit the children;
- Investigate possible lawyers or legal clinics in advance, if possible. If you don't intend to act on your plan immediately, you should still consider discussing your options with a lawyer or legal clinic;
- Make a plan for your ongoing safety after separation, including peace bonds or restraining orders; safety on the job such as screening calls and having a plan for leaving work with a co-worker; using different grocery stores and other services and using them at different times; and using a different bank.

CRIMINAL REMEDIES

A violent situation may become criminal in nature if the police are called and charges are laid. If no charges are laid, the victim has a right to file an information with a Justice of the Peace and to have a hearing in which, at a minimum, a peace bond is requested. Other criminal charges may also be laid by the victim pursuant to an information. As mentioned earlier in this chapter, there are many good reasons to proceed criminally and to request that charges be laid following an assault, including the fact that criminal proceedings are more effective deterrents, that responsibility will then be on the Crown to compile the case, and that the fact of a criminal proceeding may assist with family law proceedings. Many women are afraid to invoke the criminal law, because they feel that the punishment and stigma associated with criminal charges are too harsh; because they have little faith in the criminal justice system and don't want to get involved in a futile process; or because they'll be in dire financial difficulties if the abuser is incarcerated. A lawyer specializing in domestic violence will discuss these issues with you and help you decide whether to proceed in the criminal or family law sphere.

Peace Bonds

A peace bond, although administered by the criminal courts, doesn't create a criminal record. It's an order requiring the perpetrator to keep the peace and be on good behaviour. In domestic violence situations, it usually includes specific provisions preventing the abuser from visiting or coming within a certain distance of the residence, from contacting the victim and/or the children and from visiting schools or places of employment of the abuser's spouse or children. It's a criminal offence to breach a peace bond.

The peace bond is obtained through a Justice of the Peace. You have to make a statement that you fear that another person will cause injury to you, your children or your property. You include the grounds for your fear in detail, including words used and dates of violent or threatening incidents. Before you go to the Justice of the Peace, you should obtain legal or other assistance. The setting can be intimidating, unfamiliar, and often unpleasant, and an experienced advocate will make sure that the matter goes smoothly. Once you've provided your sworn statement before the Justice of the Peace, a hearing must be set up before a judge of that court.

The matter may not proceed at the first hearing date, but if the perpetrator agrees to sign a peace bond at that time, the matter will end there. If not, the victim will have to prove on the hearing date that she fears for her safety, and she'll need evidence to support her fear. If she requests specific restrictions—such as a prohibiting the perpetrator from coming to the home—she'll require enough evidence to convince the judge that the restrictions are necessary. Peace bonds are usually granted if the woman establishes that explicit threats were made or there has been a pattern of violence in the relationship.

You must get a certified copy of the bond, and keep it with you at all times. Additional copies should be kept at home, work and the children's school or daycare facility. Tell your neighbours about the bond and ask them to call the police if they see the perpetrator on or near your property. If the bond is breached, call the police immediately. A breach of the bond could result in a fine, imprisonment, or both.

A criminal conviction for domestic violence usually results in the same protections for the victims. Since a peace bond is faster to obtain, it's a good alternative to criminal proceedings, especially if the perpetrator is the sole source of family income, which poses a problem if he goes to jail. You may obtain a peace bond and pursue criminal proceedings simultaneously.

The same restrictions on conduct and criminal sanctions for breach are available through family law proceedings by obtaining a restraining order. The advantage of a family law restraining order is that it requires only one attendance in court, and most judges are available for emergency hearings on short notice and will make restraining orders without notifying the abuser. Apart from the theoretical reasons for proceeding criminally, I believe that a family law restraining order is more suitable in most cases of domestic violence, because of the speed at which one can be obtained, and because custodial and other issues can be considered at the same time. The practice in Toronto, for instance, is to hear emergency motions every day, if required, and to make restraining orders, custodial orders and exclusive possession orders in all cases in which there's evidence of violence.

Criminal Charges

The police may decide to lay a criminal charge. If they decide not to, you may appear before a Justice of the Peace and swear an information. This will automatically result in a criminal hearing, notice of which will be served on the accused by the police or a sheriff. (Attending before the justice of the peace is described under Peace Bonds.) Once you lay the charge, you'll be responsible for compiling the necessary evidence and preparing for trial. For these reasons, it's more essential than ever that you retain a lawyer to assist you when you request a criminal charge. Legal aid covers the filing of an information and the criminal proceeding in cases of domestic violence.

FYI

If you're laying an information, you'll need to decide what charge to lay. Some of the usual charges in domestic violence situations are: assault, assault with a weapon or causing bodily harm, aggravated assault, sexual assault, sexual assault with a weapon or causing bodily harm, forcible confinement, false messages or indecent phone calls, intimidation, or threats to do any of the above.

FAMILY LAW REMEDIES

If you're married, every province provides family law remedies designed to protect victims of violence. You can pursue these remedies along with claims for divorce and division of property in a petition for divorce, or separately from the other issues by statement of claim. Assaulted women frequently wish to secure protective measures, custody and support, but aren't ready to claim divorce or deal with property matters. If you're in that situation, you should proceed by statement of claim and leave the other matters to be dealt with later.

If you're in a common law relationship, you'll not have protective remedies if your province doesn't include common law couples in its family law statutes. (Quebec, Alberta and the Northwest Territories don't.) In such cases, your only protective remedy will be available through the criminal courts, although you'll be entitled to make civil claims for damages and other relief separately from the criminal proceeding. The same currently holds true for same sex couples.

If your province's family law covers your situation, you'll find the judicial system sympathetic and prompt to respond to your concerns about domestic violence. Protective measures are granted freely and regularly in cases involving allegations of violence.

Restraining Orders

All provinces include provisions for restraining orders that may be made in favour of married couples. All provinces that recognize unmarried couples for support purposes allow restraining orders to be granted in their favour.

Few guidelines are given in the statutes, but these orders are regularly made based on fears of violence, even when there has been no actual violence in the relationship. If there's a history of domestic violence, restraining orders will be made. In general, the court's attitude is to err on the side of caution. The wording of the restraining order is at the discretion of the court, and terms restricting telephone calls and visits within a certain number of feet of residences, daycare facilities or workplaces may all be included. Sometimes mutual restraining orders are made as a form of judicial compromise.

Emergency orders are often made in cases of domestic violence, without notice to the other spouse. These can usually be made even before the other spouse receives notice of the commencement of an action. If the claim for a restraining order is part of a proactive separation plan, without notice to the other spouse, the restraining order may be made along with orders for exclusive possession of the matrimonial home, custody and support. While these remedies aren't available in the average matrimonial case, they're readily granted if there's a pattern of domestic violence.

Once you get a restraining order, you should have it processed by the court the same day and obtain a certified copy of the order and a few other copies. You should give copies of the order to your local police station and advise them of your immediate concerns. You should also keep copies at home, work and your children's daycare or schools.

Exclusive Possession of the Matrimonial Home

Married couples have a right to claim exclusive possession of the matrimonial home. Unmarried common law couples may have such rights (see Chapter 6). No province currently provides matrimonial home protections to same sex couples. (Chapters 9, "Common Law Couples" and 10, "Same Sex Couples" present alternative claims that you could make to obtain exclusive possession of a home.)

Exclusive possession of the matrimonial home is discussed in detail in Chapter 6, "The Matrimonial Home." Much of the procedural content of that chapter is applicable to cases of domestic violence, with a major difference: exclusive possession is almost always granted when it's requested by a victim of abuse. In fact, it's readily granted without notice to the other spouse as a short-term measure that will be subject to a rehearing on notice. Exclusive possession is granted so regularly in Ontario to victims of domestic violence that you should seek it immediately without notice, provided that you can afford to live in the home after separation. As long as your spouse is employed and can contribute to the support of you and your children, the court will order interim support to assist with the expense of maintaining the home and other immediate costs.

An exclusive possession order should direct the local police force to enforce it if required. If such a provision is included, you can take the order, once it's processed and you obtain certified copies, to the police station, and ask to be escorted to the home. The police can effect the abuser's removal from the home or, if he's not home, stay until the locks are changed. You can then ask them to keep a copy of the order at the station and be ready for your call if the abuser returns. If the abuser hasn't been served with the order by the time he returns home and finds himself locked out, you can call the police to serve the order. If you're in an extremely violent situation, you should consider installing an alarm system, replacing wooden doors with metal ones, and putting fire alarms and extinguishers on each floor.

CUSTODY AND ACCESS

Custody and access are discussed in Chapter 4, "Custody." For a complete understanding of the topic, review that chapter. Some specific considerations for domestic violence cases are presented here.

Interim Interim Custody

Emergency custody orders that allow a battered woman to move out with the children or give her custody along with restraining orders and exclusive possession orders are regularly made in violent situations. They may be made without notice and be subject to rehearing a later date. These are called interim interim orders, because they're made before an interim order. Courts generally don't look favourably on spouses who take the children from the home without a court order, but they make exceptions for assaulted women. If your situation doesn't afford you the opportunity to seek the court's permission before you leave the home, you shouldn't hesitate to take the children with you, provided you make a claim for custody *as soon as you can* after leaving. You must apply quickly to preserve the court's view of you as a responsible parent and to protect your children from being taken back by your spouse. In the absence of a court order, both parents have a right to custody.

Even when protective orders or peace bonds have been granted, the police can't intervene if a violent spouse takes custody of the children unless there's a custody order in place. You should not leave the children behind and move out, even if there are practical reasons for doing so and even if you intend to seek custody later. Judges often interpret this conduct to mean that you can't care for the children or have no real concern about their safety in your partner's care. If you leave the children with your violent spouse for a brief period, to dispel these presumptions you should immediately make a claim for custody and include detailed explanations of why you left them behind.

Interim and Permanent Custody

Interim custody is custody pending a final trial or settlement of the issue. In longer cases, it may last for two or three years. Interim custody is decided on a motion, on notice to both parties, on the basis of affidavit evidence from the spouse and any third parties. Permanent custody is ordered at the end of a trial or upon settlement.

Interim and permanent custody are decided on the same criteria in domestic violence cases as in all other cases, on the basis of the best interests of the child. Do not presume that your spouse won't get custody because he has been violent. In many cases, outdated as they may be, courts have given abusive men custody because the woman is suffering from battered wife syndrome or other repercussions of abuse, or judges have found that "although he occasionally assaulted his wife, there's no evidence that he will harm the children." That being said, if your materials are detailed and include a comprehensive review of your fears for the children if they're in your spouse's care, you'll probably succeed in obtaining interim or final custody, because courts are reluctant to place children in the care of abusive parents. You'll need to show that the violent spouse's conduct poses a risk of harm to the children and interferes with his parenting ability.

Children of violent relationships live in constant fear and suffer from various forms of distress and disability if they witness violence in the family. There's also some evidence that an abusive spouse will turn his violence toward the children if the other spouse is no longer around. Including this kind of academic evidence in your interim and permanent materials will be persuasive. Third-party affidavits from daycare workers and teachers about your child's conduct away from the home and evidence from other experts such as child psychologists also provide strong evidence. If the custody battle is hotly contested, you should seek an assessment or the involvement of the Official Guardian or Children's Lawyer. These considerations are discussed in Chapter 4.

Access

One of the criticisms of the focus on access as a right of the child is the court's reluctance to deny access in cases of domestic violence. However, in most districts, supervised access is the normal judicial response to claims for access by parents who have been accused of domestic violence. Other conditions for access, such as not consuming alcohol or drugs, or seeking counselling for substance abuse, anger management or domestic violence, may be ordered. The court may also continue to monitor the access over a longer period of time, requiring the parties to report to the court every six months. The supervisor may be a family member, a professional or an access centre. A mental health professional is a particularly good choice in cases of domestic violence. The parent and child—and their relationship—can be assessed during these visits, and the child can be eased into the access based on the professional's judgment. If there's evidence of longer-term domestic violence, the access may be ordered to be supervised on a permanent basis. Supervised access is also discussed in Chapter 4, "Custody." In rare but extreme cases, access may be denied.

If access is ordered, whether supervised or unsupervised, there must be no contact between the parents at the time of the exchange, and the place of exchange should be safe and neutral. Staggering times so that one parent drops the child off fifteen minutes before the other arrives is the usual practice if access is supervised. If it's unsupervised, you can request that, at a minimum, the transition be supervised by a neutral third party.

DIVISION OF PROPERTY

Courts in all provinces have the power to order something different from equal division of matrimonial property if it would be inequitable or unconscionable not to do so. Some statutes, however, specifically indicate that conduct of the spouses is not relevant to this determination. However, the court has occasionally invoked this provision to make a favourable property order for an abused woman.

FYI

In 1993, an Alberta Court awarded seventy-five percent of the family assets to a wife who had tolerated forty years of abuse.

The most common property issue for victims of domestic violence is their desire to waive property entitlements to avoid continuing conflict with their spouse. Many feel that if custody and child support are in place, they have no other real needs, and they'd rather avoid further negotiation or contact with their spouse than pursue their entitlement. If you're considering taking such a position, think carefully about your future and assess the value of the property that you're walking away from. If your entitlement is minimal, it may make sense to waive it. However, if you have equity in a home or if there's a sizable pension to be divided, it's a good idea to at least preserve your right to make a property claim by commencing an action, and then putting it off for a while until you're ready to deal with it.

CHILD SUPPORT

Child support is discussed in detail in Chapter 7. A claim for child support is evaluated in the same way in each case, and domestic violence is irrelevant to the determination. However, child support will be awarded on an interim interim basis, without notice to your spouse, if you're in an emergency situation. It will then be reheard on notice to your spouse, who will have an opportunity to make arguments about his ability to pay child support and other arguments under federal or provincial guidelines.

When you're making a claim for interim child support, a financial statement in the form prescribed by your province must accompany your motion materials. This can be an onerous task, especially if you're proceeding on an emergency basis. As discussed earlier, bringing documents with you to the lawyer's office will save you time and legal fees. If you don't have these documents, don't fret. Your initial financial statement can contain estimates, subject to later revision. Estimates of your expenses will also be necessary if you're living with relatives, in a shelter or in some other temporary situation. While expenses will probably not be relevant if child support is decided pursuant to guidelines, your financial statement can include both your current expenses and your estimated future expenses once you get into more permanent accommodation. In emergency applications, you'll only need child support for a brief period to meet your basic needs until an interim motion can be heard, at which point you can revise your financial statement if your situation has changed.

Whenever child support is ordered you should be sure that enforcement measures are in place that minimize contact between you and the violent spouse. If your provincial enforcement authority will garnish child support directly, you should request this. If such a remedy isn't available, annual provision of post-dated cheques to a third party or to your lawyer may be the best answer.

SPOUSAL SUPPORT

Spousal support is discussed in detail in Chapter 8. The considerations are the same for all spouses. Misconduct is generally not considered when awarding support, although some provinces have specific provisions that allow the court to consider conduct that amounts to "an obvious and gross repudiation of the relationship." In these provinces, an abused woman may receive more generous support to help her recover from the relationship. Even where such a provision doesn't exist in the statute, however, all support is compensatory in nature, and considerations of the effect of the relationship on the woman's future earning capacity and her current health are considered in every case. In many cases, a woman's earning capacity is dramatically affected by a violent relationship. She may have lost her job or lived in isolation for many years because of her spouse's control. She may suffer from emotional difficulties, she may have reduced self-esteem and confidence, and she may have expenses associated with counselling. She may have permanent disabilities that preclude her from ever obtaining or maintaining full-time employment.

If you're making a claim for spousal support, consider the realistic effects of the violence on your future earning capacity and current expenses. Refer directly to all of these issues in your claim for support. Consider how the support should be paid. If you have specific expenses, such as repairs to the home or counselling, a lump sum may be ordered. Lump sum orders may also be made if there's a risk that the payer will not meet his obligations. You should also request the enforcement measures discussed above under child support that are aimed at minimizing contact between the spouses. Finally, if there are issues about whether or when you will become self-supporting, you should vehemently request that support not be time-limited. This request will be thoroughly supported by current attitudes toward spousal support, as discussed in Chapter 8.

If you're making a claim for spousal support, consider the realistic effects of the violence on your future earning capacity and current expenses.

DAMAGES

Spouses can sue each other for damages arising from assault, sexual, assault, battery, false imprisonment, intentional infliction of mental suffering and breach of fiduciary duty. Damages can compensate for pain and suffering, past and future economic loss (including the cost of therapy or lost earning capacity) or punitive damages. Women who have been out of the workforce for some period because of control exerted over them by their abusive partners may have substantial damages relating to lost earning capacity. Economic evidence will be necessary to quantify these and other damages. Consideration should be made of physical and emotional injuries at the time that the claim is made, as well as the long-term effects of the abuse that often include lack of self-sufficiency and ongoing counselling costs. In the majority of cases, damage awards are in the range of $20,000 to $100,000.

You may make a claim for damages arising from domestic violence along with other claims in any family law action, or by separate action. If you make them in a family law action, they may be reflected in the total award granted by the court, allowing one spouse to retain all of a home or receive a larger share of the property. If they're made between married spouses, claims for unequal division of property should also be made so that the anticipated award isn't included in the property of the battered spouse or otherwise eroded by property division. If you're making other claims arising from separation, it's most efficient to incorporate damage claims in that proceeding, and enforcement of the award may be easier if this method is employed. However, some advocates believe that a separate action is best, because it provides a record of violence in our society and focuses on the violence separately from the family relationship.

Most homeowners' insurance policies cover liabilities of the insured that include bodily injuries and property damages suffered by others, in which case insurance companies may be required to pay damages for domestic violence. Any policy should be reviewed in detail to determine if there are exclusions or limitations that may apply.

You should discuss claims for damages with your lawyer immediately after separation. There are limitation periods for making these claims and other complex considerations about how the claims should be made and the amounts that should be requested under each heading of damages. It's essential that you retain a lawyer with extensive experience in domestic violence cases and family law so that all these issues and strategies are brought to your attention.

CRIMINAL INJURIES COMPENSATION

In all provinces but Newfoundland, Saskatchewan and the Yukon, victims of crime may seek compensation from the state. The criminal injuries compensation board in each province comprises three appointed members who hear complaints and make monetary awards to people who have suffered some direct personal injury as the result of a violent crime. These crimes include assault, murder and attempted murder, arson, rape, indecent assault and others.

The basic rules of criminal injury compensation are that the injury must have occurred in the province whose board hears the matter, a report must have been made to the police at the time of the incident (but charges don't have to have been laid), the required forms must be completed, and expenses and other damages must be proved with supporting documents. The decision may be based on live testimony or on the submission of documents and written argument. In all provinces except Ontario, the offender is not notified of the proceeding and does not attend.

There are maximum awards that may be granted, and there are often set or customary amounts awarded for common crimes. For example, in Ontario, the maximum award is $25,000 or $1000 per month, and these awards are usually reserved for the most severe cases. The usual payment for sexual assault in Ontario is $10,000. The awards are paid by the province, and the perpetrator is not accountable to pay or defend the claim.

Each province has its own limitation periods during which claims must be made following a criminal incident. Usually it's one year, but boards have the discretion to extend the limitation periods on various grounds.

The main advantage of the criminal compensation system is that it is an informal and inexpensive way of obtaining some relief for victims of crime. Although only one attendance, if any, is required, it usually takes about two years from the date of application until an award is received. Most boards don't encourage claimants to have legal representation because the system is designed to be accessible by the public. However, many victims of crime prefer to have representation in the process. Legal aid is available for victims who wish to retain counsel, and many community legal clinics have substantial experience with criminal injuries compensation claims.

CHILDREN AS VICTIMS

Children who have suffered from domestic violence, including sexual assault and incest, assault, and witnessing violence in the home, may make claims against the perpetrator. The claims may be criminal in nature, or for criminal injury compensation, or for damages. If a child is a minor, a litigation guardian will have to be appointed to act on the child's behalf in the litigation. Claims may also be made for compensation by a parent against the perpetrator under the family law statutes in most provinces. If you're a victim of domestic violence as a spouse, you should discuss other claims that may be made on behalf of your children. If your child alone has been a victim of domestic violence, you should retain a lawyer who specializes in that area in order to discuss the claims that could be made by or on behalf of the child. You should also consider immediate counselling for the child.

CHAPTER TWELVE

Domestic Contracts

IN THIS CHAPTER: **Marriage Contracts, Cohabitation Agreements, Common Reasons for Domestic Contracts;** *Marriage Contracts, Cohabitation Agreements,* **Separation Agreements;** *Interim Separation Agreements, Separation Agreements Settling Defined Issues,* **Donor Contracts, Enforceability of Domestic Contracts;** *Compliance with the Agreement, Setting Aside a Domestic Contract*

IN ALL PROVINCES, THE FREEDOM OF CONTRACT AND THE DESIRE FOR SELF-DETERMINATION RECEIVE GREAT RESPECT. ALL PROVINCES ALLOW INTIMATE PARTNERS TO PICK AND CHOOSE FROM THE STATUTORY RULES, TO OPT OUT OF MOST OR ALL OF THE REGIME, OR TO SETTLE MATTERS BETWEEN THEM FOR ALL TIME BY CONTRACT. THIS CHAPTER SUMMARIZES ALL TYPES OF DOMESTIC CONTRACTS AND THE RULES THAT GOVERN THEM ACROSS CANADA. IT SHOULD BE READ ALONG WITH THE MORE DETAILED DISCUSSIONS OF PROPERTY, SUPPORT, COMMON LAW AND SAME SEX COUPLES FOUND IN CHAPTERS 5, 8, 9 AND 10.

MARRIAGE CONTRACTS

Two people who intend to marry, who are married, or who have separated and intend to reconcile can enter into a marriage contract that changes the rules of property division between them, either by modifying the existing family law rules, excluding some assets from sharing, making a new set of property rules, or opting out of property rights entirely (except in Quebec, where a basic entitlement may not be waived by marriage contract). As long as formal requirements of the contract are met (which usually means that it's signed by both parties and witnessed), the marriage contract will become the "law" of that particular marriage, regardless of the family law regime that prevails in the province. It will apply whenever the agreement so provides—during the marriage, on separation, on divorce or on death.

In most provinces, marriage contracts deal with more than just property issues. Spouses can address any matter in a marriage contract, except custody of or access to children and possession and encumbrance of the matrimonial home. Spousal support may be addressed in all provinces but PEI, where you can't limit spousal support rights. In all other provinces, spousal support provisions may be subject to review by a court at a later date and set aside if they're unfair or unconscionable.

"Old" marriage contracts signed in the 1970s or earlier or contracts signed in jurisdictions beyond Canada may or may not be respected by Canadian courts. If the contract satisfies all the legal requirements and if the agreement was clearly meant to exclude conventional matrimonial property-sharing, a court may be inclined to hold the parties to their bargain. However, while judges consider modern Canadian marriage contracts to be iron-clad and almost always respect them, they give old or foreign ones almost the opposite treatment and usually set them aside. The most common justification for setting aside old or foreign marriage contracts is that the parties never contemplated such a generous property regime as the one currently in place and never meant to contract out of it. Considering that marriage contracts by their very nature involve looking into the future, this rationale makes little sense; it's clear that the contracts are really set aside out of the court's notion of fairness and sympathy for the spouse who would otherwise be left with nothing.

COHABITATION AGREEMENTS

Cohabitation agreements are marriage contracts for the unmarried. New Brunswick, Newfoundland, Ontario, PEI and the Yukon specifically address cohabitation agreements in their family law legislation, and they give cohabitation agreements establishing rules for sharing property and spousal support almost complete respect. In the provinces where there's no specific statutory recognition of cohabitation agreements, they will nevertheless receive respect from a court arising from the general rules of contract, especially if claims are later made that contravene the agreement. Cohabitation agreements between same sex couples, while not currently recognized by any Canadian statutes, are also respected by courts under the general law of contract.

Family law doesn't provide for property division for unmarried couples. Instead, they must make trust claims against property. As a result, cohabitation agreements that address property usually involve waivers of all such claims. Some unmarried couples use a cohabitation agreement as a more equitable planning instrument designed to remedy the fact that property sharing isn't available and to provide for the division of certain property according to each partner's contribution or on an equal basis. In most provinces that recognize cohabitation agreements, the rules provide that it becomes a marriage contract if the parties later marry, unless the agreement says otherwise.

Common law couples have spousal support rights in most of Canada (except Quebec and the Northwest Territories). Same sex couples have support rights only in Ontario, and this is currently under appeal. In provinces where spousal support claims are potentially available, cohabitation agreements may address spousal support, either by total waiver or by limiting the duration or amount of support. Again, where they're not available, couples can waive the rights or choose to make them available—either by court application or according to a set formula—in their cohabitation agreements.

FYI

In 1993, an Ontario court upheld a marriage contract that gave the wife a total settlement of $8000 if the couple separated within the first year of marriage. Without the agreement, the wife would have received a much more generous property settlement.

COMMON REASONS FOR DOMESTIC CONTRACTS

Marriage Contracts

People sign marriage contracts for a multitude of reasons. Some people don't believe that the property regime in their province is fair and wish to create their own rules. Many, especially the rich, wish to protect the increase in value of gifts or inheritances received during the marriage from sharing with their spouse. In Ontario, Newfoundland and Saskatchewan, the rule that a matrimonial home brought to the marriage automatically becomes equally owned or subject to sharing after separation is often altered by a marriage contract. If one or both spouses have been married before, they may wish to opt out of sharing their assets to protect themselves or their children in the event of a divorce. Mature couples or those who come to the marriage with a strong asset base often wish to protect themselves or their families from the financial loss caused by separation. Many people who bring a business to the marriage wish to protect that asset out of concern for business partners. In fact, many business-partnership agreements require all partners to have marriage contracts to protect the business from spousal claims. Some couples wish to establish clear guidelines for spousal support—many agreements specify the income that will be considered in a spousal support claim, provide for increasing support payments for each year that the parties are married, or waive spousal support altogether.

I find that many clients are reluctant to sign marriage contracts because they spoil the romance of marriage and contradict the promises that are about to be made. I think that the best answer to this concern is to think of a marriage contract as a planning document, much like a will. It's not pleasant or romantic to think about your death, but when you die, your family will be glad you spent the time on it. Although divorce is only about half as likely to happen as death (current divorce rates exceed fifty percent), you'll be glad to have a marriage contract if you ever separate. You can sign the agreement long before the marriage, then put it aside and out of your mind unless you ever need it.

Cohabitation Agreements

I believe that cohabitation agreements are essential for common law and same sex couples, because of the current uncertainty of the law. At present, trust claims may be made against property that was acquired or that increased in value during the relationship. Although courts have shown an increasing tendency to grant such claims, there are no guarantees. As I've said before, there is no certainty in the law relating to unmarried couples. Where spousal support claims are available, courts don't address them with a consistent attitude, and several important cases have suggested that we need widespread changes to the law to give common law couples treatment equal to married couples. No doubt we'll see sweeping changes in the family law rules relating to cohabitees over the next ten years, and such changes are very likely to be retroactive, suddenly changing all the rules. For these reasons, cohabitees must understand that the law prevailing when the relationship begins will probably not be the law if and when the relationship breaks down. Predictions for law reform are discussed in Chapters 9 and 10. A prudent couple should discuss these issues, and evaluate each spouse's expectations and contributions. If you're worried that this process is unromantic, a review of the comparison between marriage contracts and wills in the last section might persuade you otherwise. If you want to insulate yourself from unexpected changes in the law, you must have a cohabitation agreement.

As discussed earlier, people sign cohabitation agreements for both individual and planning reasons. Individual reasons include protection of assets by waivers of trust claims over property and waivers to or limitation of spousal support. Planning reasons include the creation of rights to share in property, entrenchment of support claims or provision of both couples with security and rules for the relationship. Many couples feel that such agreements provide the foundation for cooperation, trust and interdependency that are essential for a healthy intimate relationship. (More detailed reasons for considering a cohabitation agreement are found at the end of Chapter 9 and Chapter 10.)

SEPARATION AGREEMENTS

Separation agreements are the final word on the breakdown of intimate relationships. They contain provisions for the division of assets, mode and timing of property payments, child and spousal support terms, insurance and other security for these payments, and various releases against property and other claims. The result of a separation agreement is that no further claims may be made about issues arising from the breakdown of the relationship, except to enforce the agreement and vary the terms in limited, defined circumstances.

As indicated in Chapter 2, you should get legal advice about the form and substance of your separation agreement. Legal printing companies and some stationery stores stock standard-form separation agreements that can assist you in preparing a draft, but it's still worth ensuring that your agreement provides all the rights and protections you need.

The following are clauses that often appear in a separation agreement. They will give you an idea of the issues you should consider and discuss with your lawyer when you're contemplating such an agreement.

Recitals/Background

Recitals provide the background facts to the agreement. These usually include the date of marriage or commencement of cohabitation, the names and birthdates of children, the date of separation, the fact that there's no chance of reconciliation, the roles assumed by the parties during the relationship, and any continuing assumptions, such as a statement that the mother will remain at home with the children until they're in school on a full-time basis. In light of recent case law on variation and child support, the reasons for and assumptions behind the agreement are essential. Such assumptions may include statements about how the agreement was reached (i.e., one spouse is receiving substantial property in exchange for lower monthly support).

Choice of Laws

A choice of laws clause provides that the agreement and the parties' relationship will always be governed and interpreted under the laws of some place, usually the province in which the agreement is signed. This protects the spouses from claims raised in other jurisdictions. It's especially important if one or both spouses have lived in another province or country.

Separate and Apart

The standard provision states that the parties will continue to live separate and apart and that neither will molest, annoy or harass the other or attempt to compel the other to cohabit. Like many standard provisions, this provision is often offensive to spouses who say they would never molest or harass the other, but the standard-form language makes it easy for judges and police to interpret if necessary.

Property Payment

These clauses usually contain two parts. The first deals with the property payment owed by one party to the other and how and when it will be paid. The second addresses sale or buy-out of real estate interests and transfers of cars, savings and other assets.

Debts

Provisions for debts usually state who's responsible for paying any joint debts, and provide that, in future, neither party will contract or incur debts in the other's name.

Income Tax Matters

The tax treatment of any property transfers or support payments should be spelled out in the agreement. Other tax considerations, including attribution of income, liability to Revenue Canada for tax arrears, capital gains and primary residence designations, may be appropriate in your situation and you should discuss them with your lawyer.

Property Releases

Apart from the payments provided by the agreement, the individuals release and discharge each other from any property rights or obligations. These provisions are usually lengthy and contain specific statutory references.

CPP Releases

Parties to a marriage are automatically entitled to apply to divide the Canadian Pension Plan credits that each has accumulated during the marriage. While releases of such claims are common in separation agreements, they're invalid and unenforceable in all provinces but British Columbia and Saskatchewan.

Parenting Plan

Custody, residential schedule and/or access terms are included under this heading. It should also cover holiday times, decision-making rules, options for resolving disputes and terms for communication over issues and changes.

Change of Name

Many agreements contain waivers of all applications to change the name of any child of the marriage. Under the courts' interpretation of these provisions, they completely prohibit such an application.

Travel Issues

It's a good idea to include provisions that address who can apply for a passport in the child's name, who will hold the passport, how to handle consent to trips, and any other travel rule that's appropriate in your circumstances, such as notification of the addresses at the destination and posting of security to ensure the child's safe return.

Child Support

Always include the amount of child support payable per child and the duration of child support. The new guidelines provide for annual disclosure, which cannot be waived by agreement, but rules about annual disclosure and attempts to resolve child support annually by negotiation and/or mediation are still recommended. Specific reference should be made to add-ons. All underlying assumptions of child support, such as how the amount was reached and whether property transfers altered the settlement, must be included.

Spousal Support

There are a number of options for the form of spousal support, as discussed in Chapter 8. The form, amount and duration of spousal support are all essential elements to the agreement. If there's no support payable or if it's time-limited, this paragraph will also include specific and detailed releases from spousal support that the agreement excludes. The assumptions of the spousal support arrangement, including references to how the amount was determined, the expectations for the recipient to care for children and the expectations for the recipient to retrain or attempt to become self-sufficient, should all be included.

Security for Support

There are various ways to provide security for support payments, such as a mortgage over property or terms that provide for lump-sum payments in the event of non-payment. The most common security terms provide for irrevocable designation of a life insurance policy in a set amount in favour of the other spouse, either for that spouse's use or in trust for the children. Provision is usually made for claims against the estate of the deceased in the event that the security isn't in place at the time of death. The agreement can also specify that one spouse must receive a set amount of money under the terms of the payer's will.

Variation

All separation agreements should set out the parties' expectations about variation—either that the agreement is entirely non-variable or that certain provisions such as custody and child support will be variable in the event of a material change of circumstances. Regardless of the agreement, the law currently allows variation of these terms in many cases.

Dispute Resolution

Many agreements require the parties to advise each other in writing of any issue that arises in the future under the agreement and to attempt to resolve it by various methods before taking it to court. Such alternatives to litigation include negotiation through lawyers, mediation and arbitration. Some provisions, especially ones relating to parental issues, require mandatory mediation for both spouses if one spouse ever requests it. Mediation and arbitration clauses should contain a requirement that one person will pay both people's costs of the dispute resolution process if the mediator or arbitrator decides that person has acted unreasonably.

Releases

Clients are usually overwhelmed by the detail and volume of standard-form waivers of property, support, estate claims and all issues arising from the relationship or its breakdown. A property release alone can consume two or three pages of an agreement. Of course, releases are crucial and, while some lawyers may be overcautious, it's appropriate to be careful and err on the side of over-inclusiveness. Because the law is always changing, it's dangerous to rely on preprinted agreements or to lift releases from an outdated separation agreement. It's always a good idea to get a lawyer to review your separation agreement if only to ensure that you've included all of the necessary releases.

Divorce

If the parties are married, the separation agreement usually settles the issue of who will apply for the actual divorce and how the cost of the divorce will be paid. Unless you agree otherwise, the person who seeks the divorce judgment pays the costs, which can be as much as $1500 after court filing fees and legal fees are paid. A standard provision is usually included stating that the agreement will survive a divorce judgment. It's a good idea to require incorporation of the operative terms of the agreement into the divorce judgment and to require both parties or their solicitors to agree to the form of the divorce judgment.

Reconciliation

Most agreements address reconciliation, because the law makes agreements invalid if the parties have reconciled for more than ninety days. These terms usually allow for a reconciliation of less than or more than ninety days and provide that transfers of property made under the agreement will continue to be valid even if reconciliation occurs.

Joint Preparation

There is an old doctrine of law that interprets an unclear provision of an agreement against the interest of the person whose lawyer drafted the agreement. Most agreements specifically contract out of this doctrine by providing that both parties jointly prepared the agreement and that the agreement will be interpreted as if neither party was the sole author.

Severability

This is a standard-form clause stating that if any provision in the agreement is invalid, it will be severed from the balance of the agreement. This prevents one invalid provision from rendering the whole agreement void.

Financial Disclosure

The agreement should specifically describe the nature and extent of financial disclosure. The best way to do this accurately is for both parties to attach their financial statements to the agreement as Schedules "A" and "B."

Independent Legal Advice

The agreement should confirm that each party has received independent legal advice, with lawyers' certificates attached. If one spouse doesn't get independent advice, the agreement is still valid, although its enforceability may be challenged later. If one spouse refuses to get independent advice, the other should require a waiver indicating that the person was advised to get it, but chose not to, and that the person understands the nature and consequences of the agreement.

FYI

A separation agreement that gave child support to a wife was set aside when the court discovered that the wife had failed to tell the husband that the child was not his. In another case, a wife failed to disclose that she was unsure whether the husband was the father, and the agreement was upheld.

Interim Separation Agreements

Interim separation agreements contain short-term provisions. They're often signed shortly after separation to resolve custodial and financial issues pending final resolution. They may address any interim issue, from custody and child support, to financial disclosure and scheduling of a settlement meeting.

Interim agreements often contain terms that make the interim agreement "without prejudice," which means their contents can't be disclosed to the court. This is intended to prevent arguments that the interim agreement has created some status quo: that one party has been able to pay under interim agreement, for example, or that payment provided by the agreement is adequate and no further change should be made. Different judges have different views about such non-disclosure provisions: some respect them, others demand to be informed of the interim arrangement.

Another common interim agreement allows one party to move out of the home and leave the children in the care of the other parent without prejudicing an anticipated custodial claim. I recommend these to my clients who are reluctant to move out only because they don't want to compromise their custody claim, but who otherwise find continued cohabitation difficult, stressful or hard on the kids. Judges usually respect the without-prejudice nature of these agreements, because they recognize that reducing conflict is often necessary and in the best interests of the children.

Separation Agreements Settling Defined Issues

It's possible to sign a separation agreement that resolves some of the issues on a completely final basis, and leaves the balance of the issues to be adjudicated or settled at a later date. If property or support issues remain in dispute, but the parties have agreed upon a parenting plan or other custodial arrangement, the custodial issues can be reduced to an agreement and taken off the table. The reverse situation, in which custody is the only unresolved issue, is also an appropriate case for an agreement settling defined issues.

FYI

A wife who had recently given birth and was ignorant of her rights signed a separation agreement without independent advice after being told that she would get no support if she didn't sign. She succeeded in having the agreement set aside. In another case, a court found duress when a wife who had recently recovered from a nervous breakdown signed an agreement after being threatened with a long court battle.

DONOR CONTRACTS

In a donor contract, a man agrees to donate his sperm for the purpose of alternative fertilization on the understanding that he will have no parental rights or obligations to the child. These agreements are quite common in the lesbian community, but they're totally untested in the courts and are not mentioned in provincial laws—except in Quebec, where they're void. (Some theoretical considerations of donor contracts are found in Chapter 1, "Formation of the Family," under the heading Self Insemination.) The basic legal issues are discussed here.

There are two big problems with donor contracts. The first is that they may not only be unenforceable, but illegal as well. It's illegal to pay for the purchase of human tissue. It's debatable whether sperm qualifies as "tissue," but many lawyers believe that it does. At the time that this book goes to print, federal legislation is in the works that will make any payment for sperm illegal. The second problem arises from the first—if the agreements are not respected by the courts, then the contract clearly establishes the identity and paternity of the donor. In the United States, donor contracts have been disregarded and the donor has been given access or custody rights to the child.

Reproductive technology has developed more rapidly than the law of the family. Many provinces have studied the topic, and their reports recommend sweeping changes in the areas of birth registration, private contracts and regulation of sperm banks. A federal task force has also considered the issues and recommended legislation that would, among other things, recognize and enforce donor contracts. While such a term is not included in the proposed federal legislation discussed earlier, Newfoundland and the Yukon have included a reference in their children's laws that say a sperm donor is not the father of a child unless he's married to or living with the mother.

A good donor contract should acknowledge that the legal questions are unsettled in current law and that the parties nevertheless choose to be bound by it. The safest option is to provide that no dispute over the contract will ever be taken to court, but will instead be referred to binding mediation by a panel selected by the parties (either in the contract or when the dispute arises). Of course, the contract should also say that no support will be claimed from the donor and that the donor will not have any parental rights and thus will make no claims for guardianship, custody of or access to the child. To be safe, no payment should be made for the sperm, or at a minimum, no mention of payment should be included in the agreement.

Some donor contracts allow for some access to the child by the donor, although it may be described as a friendly visit rather than parental-type access. Most agreements address how the parties will deal with the identity of the donor when the child is old enough to understand. Some state that the donor's identity will never be disclosed, while others provide for disclosure when the parents feel it's necessary. The marital status of the parties, the right to name the child and references to the father on the birth certificate are also factors that the contract can include. If you're considering a donor contract, you must get experienced, knowledgable and up-to-date legal advice about the current law to assess your options and, if you decide to proceed, draft the agreement.

ENFORCEABILITY OF DOMESTIC CONTRACTS

Compliance with the Agreement

In most situations, provisions in domestic contracts must be enforced by court application. If a release in a marriage contract, cohabitation agreement or separation agreement is being ignored—usually by a claim made contrary to the release—the usual method of enforcing the agreement is by defending the claim with reference to the agreement or by commencing an application to prohibit the former spouse from pursuing the claim.

Family law in most provinces allows parties to shortcut the enforcement of domestic contracts by filing domestic contracts with the court. Once the domestic contract is filed, it has the same effect as an order of the court. If one party to the contract ignores a release, the other may have to make a court application. However, if one party merely wants to enforce a term such as the payment of spousal support, the document on file simplifies the process. The party merely has to appear briefly in court to prove the amount of arrears or non-payment, and the court will order enforcement measures, such as seizure of property.

Enforcement of child support is now being given priority across the country. Methods of enforcing child support are discussed in Chapter 7.

SETTING ASIDE A DOMESTIC CONTRACT

The courts generally respect domestic contracts. Marriage contracts and cohabitation agreements that establish the rules of a couple's relationship are relied upon during the relationship and are usually upheld on the basis of our freedom to contract. Separation agreements are respected out of a general desire to encourage settlements. The theory is that if parties don't believe their agreements will be enforceable, there is no incentive to settle out of court.

That being said, all domestic contracts may be set aside in the event of fraud, undue influence, duress, and material misrepresentation. This arises if one party puts significant pressure on the other or holds out other inducements to enter an agreement, or when one party has signed an agreement because the other has threatened to withhold all support or engage in a custody dispute if the agreement isn't signed. If one party fails to obtain independent legal advice, the agreement may or may not be set aside, depending on the facts. If the party who didn't obtain independent advice expressly waived all claims to set the agreement aside for that reason, or if the party clearly understood the nature and consequences of the agreement without legal advice, that party will usually not succeed in setting aside the agreement. If, on the other hand, the agreement was drafted by one spouse's lawyer and signed by the other spouse in the living room on the day of separation, it will be vulnerable to being set aside. Material misrepresentation in a domestic contract usually involves non-disclosure or misrepresentation of a significant asset or liability. Most domestic contracts include a clause in which both parties warrant that they're satisfied with the financial disclosure in the document and have no further requests for information. Most also address other grounds for setting aside domestic contracts, and acknowledge that neither party has been induced to sign the agreement and that each understands its effects.

Any issue relating to children can never be finally settled because of the court's broad jurisdiction to protect children. All agreements are subject to the children's best interests, and child support and all custodial issues are thus always open to further variation. This protective principle has even been used to justify the setting aside of the entire property settlement when the child was suffering from his parents' bargain.

The courts used to give total respect to waivers of spousal support and did not set them aside unless a significant change had occurred that was not foreseen at the time of the agreement. Recent decisions of the Supreme Court of Canada have criticized the principle as being too restrictive. A total waiver of spousal support or a provision that terminates spousal support at some set date in the future without taking a fresh look at the recipient's financial situation is now subject to serious scrutiny. Time will tell exactly how such cases will be decided, but it appears that on an application to set aside such a provision of spousal support, the court will simply treat the matter as a fresh application and consider whether there's a need for support under the prevailing general principles. (These principles are discussed in Chapter 8, "Spousal Support.")

Family law in most provinces provides additional ways to set aside domestic contracts. In most provinces, for example, domestic contracts may be set aside if one party failed to provide significant financial information or if one party didn't understand the nature of the agreement. Even in provinces where such rules are not contained in a statute, the flexibility and remedial nature of family law, combined with the common law rules of contract, often inspires judges to set aside agreements that have created grossly unfair results.

CHAPTER THIRTEEN

Divorce, Religious Divorce and Annulment

IN THIS CHAPTER: **Grounds for Divorce;** *One-Year Separation, Adultery, Physical or Mental Cruelty, Deciding What Ground to Assert,* **Getting a Divorce Before All Issues are Resolved, Incorporation of Settlement Terms, The Certificate of Divorce, Removal of Barriers to Religious Remarriage;** *Jewish Get, Islamic Talaq or Khulu, Catholic Annulment,* **Civil Annulment**

MANY PEOPLE HAVE MISCONCEPTIONS ABOUT WHEN THEY CAN GET DIVORCED AND WHAT CONSTITUTES THE GROUNDS FOR DIVORCE. MANY ARE INTERESTED IN ANNULMENT, ALTHOUGH THEY GENERALLY MISUNDERSTAND ITS MEANING. THIS CHAPTER ADDRESSES THESE ISSUES AND OTHER CONSIDERATIONS ENTERTAINED BY COURTS ON MOTIONS FOR DIVORCE AND IN ACTIONS FOR ANNULMENT.

GROUNDS FOR DIVORCE

The *Divorce Act* allows a court to grant a divorce on the ground that there has been a breakdown of the marriage. A breakdown of the marriage will be established only if:

- The spouses have lived separate and apart for one year immediately before the commencement of the proceeding, or
- The spouse against whom the claim for divorce is made has committed adultery or treated the other spouse with physical or mental cruelty of such a kind as to render continued cohabitation intolerable.

Many people who have recently separated think that they need a "legal separation." This is not a term used in Canada and there is no need for any document to establish that you've separated. If you want to be sure that your spouse knows your intention to separate, you can send a lawyer's letter indicating your wishes—and unless you reconcile for more than ninety days, you can be sure that the one-year period starts to run from the date of the letter. Most couples do need to have an interim financial and custody arrangement in place, and if necessary, this can be formalized by an interim separation agreement. These agreements are discussed in Chapter 12, "Domestic Contracts."

One-Year Separation

If you're proceeding for divorce based on a one-year separation, note that you can live separate and apart—even though you're under the same roof—as long as there's no reasonable chance of reconciliation. The one-year period begins to run when one or both spouses has the intention to live separate and apart from the other. The time will not stop running if reconciliation is attempted, provided that the attempt doesn't last for more than ninety days.

You don't need to go to court to get a divorce based on a one-year separation. You can simply file an affidavit in a standard form, along with a request for a divorce judgment, in the court office and wait for the signed judgment to be returned to you in the mail. The normal waiting period for such over-the-counter divorces is two to three months, depending on the workload of family law judges. If there's a big backlog in your province or if you don't want to wait another three months, you can appear before a judge on a scheduled day for divorce hearings and give evidence. Your divorce judgment will be signed that day and, like all divorce judgments, it will become effective thirty-one days later.

Adultery

You can get a divorce sooner than one year after separation if you prove that your spouse committed adultery. To do this, you must make the claim for divorce based on adultery in your Petition for Divorce. You must then give notice to your spouse that you intend to seek a divorce on this basis. Your spouse doesn't have to answer direct questions that would implicate him or her in the adulterous conduct, so the court will have to rely solely on your evidence and any other third-party evidence. You must be able to satisfy the court that the adultery, on a balance of probabilities, actually occurred. Every judge's standard is a little different, but most don't require much more than the evidence on which you base your own conclusion that you're sure it happened. While mere speculation is not enough, the court is entitled to draw inferences from the evidence, so it's often enough if your evidence allows the court to draw a reasonable conclusion that the adultery occurred. Third-party witnesses are helpful, but they are not necessary in every case. If someone else can attest to the adultery, it is usually easiest to bring that person with you to court. Other corroborating evidence, such as proof that a spouse has contracted a sexually transmitted disease after the date of marriage, is usually persuasive.

A claim for divorce on the grounds of adultery will not succeed if the claimant has condoned the adultery by knowingly allowing it to continue or by forgiving the adulterous spouse and continuing to cohabit for an extended period after learning about the adultery. Nor can you connive with your spouse by agreeing that you'll obtain a faster divorce on the basis of adultery. You have to state that you haven't condoned or connived in the adultery when you give your live evidence at the time of the divorce hearing.

FYI

Although a divorce based on adultery is available earlier than one year after separation, it is subject to the same waiting period as all other divorce judgments; it becomes effective thirty-one days after it's signed or proclaimed by the judge.

Physical or Mental Cruelty

A divorce on the grounds of physical or mental cruelty is also available earlier than one year after separation, and also becomes effective thirty-one days after it's granted. It's obtained in the same way as a divorce for adultery; by making a claim in the Petition for Divorce and by giving live evidence at a trial or on a motion for divorce.

There's no concrete definition of cruelty. It's generally a disposition to inflict suffering or to enjoy or show indifference to the suffering, and it must be of such a grave nature as to render continued cohabitation intolerable. It's not necessary to show that the offending spouse intended to be cruel, but only that the spouse intentionally committed acts that others would reasonably consider to be cruel. The cruelty must be exhibited toward the other spouse and must occur during the marriage, not before it. Cruelty that occurs only after the parties have separated will usually be grounds for divorce. Whether or not the conduct rendered continued cohabitation intolerable is a subjective test based on the personal feelings of the spouse who suffered the cruelty. However, something more than incompatibility, displeasure or irritation is required.

Physical cruelty usually involves one or more incidents of physical or sexual assault inflicted on the spouse. Mental cruelty is more broadly interpreted and includes various types of behaviour. Generally, there must be some active form of conduct, deliberately directed at the spouse, which is designed to injure the mind or feelings in a serious manner; alternatively, if no such intention is shown, there must be a careless disregard for the consequences of the action or deed. The only standard requirement is that the mental cruelty be something more than evidence of incompatibility. Examples of mental cruelty are: threatening physical violence toward the spouse or the children, threatening to harm oneself, alienating children, making false accusations, uttering vulgar abuse, constant nagging or denigration, and violent outbursts or scenes in the presence of others.

Deciding What Ground to Assert

Because it often takes spouses about a year to adjust to the idea of separation and because many don't want a divorce until all issues have been resolved—which takes time—almost all divorces proceed on the basis of a one-year separation rather than on the grounds of adultery or cruelty. Unless the adultery or cruelty is relevant to some other issue in the action, such as a claim for damages (see Chapter 11, "Violence in the Family"), most lawyers recommend proceeding on the basis of a one-year separation to avoid reliving the emotional distress of the offensive conduct.

FYI

Some feminists have suggested that the practice is causing us to lose a record of cruelty against women, but in most cases it's unnecessary to proceed for divorce on the basis of a matrimonial offence. This is especially so when the increased cost of attending a live hearing is considered. It can cost twice as much to have your lawyer attend with you in court to prove a matrimonial offence than if you proceed with a one-year separation divorce by filing your documents in court and waiting for the judgment to be mailed to you.

Some clients hold firm to the idea that a judgment based on a matrimonial fault would provide revenge, and many wish to mar the record of their spouse. But few people ever bother to determine the grounds for another person's divorce (although they're on the public record), so these motivations are usually unfounded, especially when the cost of the revenge is considered.

GETTING A DIVORCE BEFORE ALL ISSUES ARE RESOLVED

You can obtain a judgment for divorce, based on any of the acceptable grounds, before you've resolved all the issues arising from the break-down of your marriage. The result is the dissolution of your marriage, while all other issues continue unresolved until trial or settlement. This is referred to as "severance of the divorce from the corollary issues." If you are attempting to settle matters without litigation but have become impatient to actually get the divorce, you can commence an action for divorce only and get the divorce while you continue to resolve the other issues.

Courts will refuse motions to sever the divorce from the corollary issues only if one of the following limitations exists:

- If reasonable arrangements have not been made for the support of children of the relationship, the court will not grant a divorce, or
- If as a result of the divorce your spouse would lose medical, dental or pension benefits available through your employment, and this result would be particularly onerous to your spouse—for example, your spouse is very ill and has no other coverage available, or would lose survivor pension rights if the divorce were granted—the court may choose not to grant the divorce.

You can sever the divorce from the other issues by filing a Notice of Motion for Divorce, supported by an affidavit in standard form. If the other side consents to the divorce, the matter can proceed over-the-counter as discussed above. If the other spouse refuses to consent, the contested motion will be heard by the court and oral evidence will be given by both parties. Courts will refuse motions to sever only if one of the limitations set out above exists. Some judges interpret the first requirement, about reasonable arrangements for the children, to require a final separation agreement on the issue of child support. But most are satisfied if there's an interim arrangement and the payer is in good standing. Generally, contested motions for divorce are successful and you should think twice about contesting a claim for severance of the corollary issues. If you're unsuccessful in contesting the divorce, you may be ordered to pay your spouse's costs of the motion.

INCORPORATION OF SETTLEMENT TERMS

Many separation agreements require that certain terms of the settle-ment—usually property and support provisions—be included in the divorce judgment. This provides increased security to the recipient of such payments and simplifies enforcement procedures. If a divorce judg-ment is to contain such provisions, the motion for the judgment must include such a request, and the affidavit in support must include a copy of the executed agreement. Most agreements also provide both parties or their lawyers with the right to approve the form of such a judgment to ensure that the provisions are accurately incorporated.

THE CERTIFICATE OF DIVORCE

Thirty days after the divorce judgment is proclaimed, it becomes effec-tive. The rationale for this rule is to make the parties go through a waiting period to be sure that they actually want to be divorced. Once the divorce becomes effective, either party can apply for a certificate of divorce by filing the required documents with the court. Once the cer-tificate is signed, an original will be mailed directly to each spouse. This is the document that actually proves the divorce for all purposes. An original must be presented to obtain a marriage certificate, if either party ever remarries.

REMOVAL OF BARRIERS TO RELIGIOUS REMARRIAGE

If a spouse doesn't cooperate with the other's request to obtain a reli-gious divorce, the court usually will punish the uncooperative spouse by dismissing his or her claims or striking out his or her pleadings. This is a recent change in divorce law that accords equal respect to religious issues arising from the separation and provides a remedy that wasn't previously available to people faced with outright refusals to cooperate. The details of any anticipated religious divorce or annulment should be considered and negotiated before the divorce judgment is granted, so that the *Divorce Act* remedy continues to be available in the event that one spouse is uncooperative.

Jewish Get

Under Jewish religious law, the right to remarry is governed by the giving and receiving of a contractual release of marital bonds, called a Bill of Divorce or a Get, in the presence of a rabbi. The Get must be given and received of each party's own free will. Both parties must attend; the Get document is prepared by the Scribe on the husband's instructions; it's witnessed by two qualified witnesses and is presented to the wife and filed with the rabbi. A certificate indicating that the Get was properly completed is given to the parties. There is a nominal cost for obtaining a Get.

If either spouse refuses to cooperate with the Get, the *Divorce Act* provisions will be invoked to require cooperation.

Islamic Talaq or Khulu

An Islamic divorce involves either a Talaq, initiated by the husband, or a Khulu, initiated by the wife. A Talaq is an oral statement by the husband to the wife in the presence of witnesses that he divorces her. Alternatively, he may, without witnesses, sign and deliver a Letter of Talaq indicating that he divorces her in accordance with Islamic law. The Talaq must be done of the husband's free will. A Khulu requires the repayment of the dowry that the husband paid to the wife's family to marry her, the acceptance of the repayment by the husband, and the preparation of a document called the Khulu by a gadi. If the husband refuses to accept the return of the dowry, the wife can apply to a gadi. If the gadi considers the husband's position to be unreasonable, the Khulu will be granted.

In either case, if one spouse makes religious divorce impossible, a court application should be brought to dismiss that spouse's claims on the grounds that he or she is creating barriers to religious remarriage.

Catholic Annulment

A Catholic annulment, which declares the marriage to have been a nullity, lies solely at the discretion of the church—and not with the spouses themselves. An annulment must be granted before remarriage, or the remarriage will not be recognized in the church.

The basic application process for a Catholic annulment involves presenting proof of a civil divorce or civil annulment. Forms are completed, and both spouses are interviewed. An applicant must have at least three witnesses who knew the applicant prior to, during and after the marriage. These witnesses indicate and reinforce the circumstances of the request for the annulment. The information is received from the parties and the witnesses by three canon lawyers, two of whom are usually priests, who then render a decision. The decision goes automatically to an appeal tribunal, who render the final decision and provide the certificate of Catholic annulment.

Annulments are granted by the church in cases of addiction, violence, refusal to have children, adultery, non-consummation of the marriage, and misrepresentation before the marriage. The tribunal will consider the allegations and claims carefully, may request more information, and may want to be particularly satisfied about the innocence or truthfulness of the person claiming the annulment.

Unlike Jewish and Islamic practices, the lack of cooperation by one of the spouses doesn't necessarily frustrate the Catholic annulment procedure. However, a spouse can make annulment proceedings very difficult by refusing to cooperate or to give evidence on the hearing. Such a refusal, if proved, would be sufficient to invoke the *Divorce Act* protections regarding religious divorces in order to inspire an uncooperative spouse to assist with the process.

CIVIL ANNULMENT

A civil annulment is a declaration of nullity of a marriage that has no religious basis. Civil annulments are court orders that dissolve void or voidable marriages, treating them as though they never occurred for remarriage purposes. An annulment doesn't terminate the rights and responsibilities of marriage, such as property division, matrimonial home protections, and spousal and child support. However, since many void or voidable marriages don't last long, property, matrimonial home and spousal support rights may be limited in amount or duration or refused entirely, depending on the practice and procedure in each province. All provinces will order child support for a child of a void or voidable marriage.

A court will grant a civil annulment only in the following situations:
- where there was some misrepresentation or concealment of a material fact before the marriage, such as a lie about the capacity to have children, or a failure to advise that the spouse has a sexually transmitted disease or a criminal record (creating a void marriage);

- where the parties never had the legal capacity to marry—for example, because one was already married or was under the legal age to marry (creating a void marriage);
- where one of the formal requirements of marriage wasn't met, as prescribed by the province and described in Chapter 1, "Formation of the Family" (creating a void marriage); or
- where there's an inability or refusal to consummate the marriage (creating a voidable marriage).

FYI

There is one procedural difference between void and voidable marriages. Any court can annul a void marriage, but only the courts of the husband's domicile may annul a voidable marriage. If the husband is living in another country, the annulment of a voidable marriage must be sought in that country.

If you think you're a party to a void or voidable marriage, consult a family lawyer. If you fail to do so and commence an action for annulment, you may restrict your other matrimonial rights or get caught up in a procedural mess that you could have avoided.

CHAPTER FOURTEEN

Alternatives to Litigation

IN THIS CHAPTER: Legal Opinions, Accounting
Opinions, Four-Way Meetings, Mediation, Arbitration

By this point, the many reasons for avoiding litigation should be perfectly clear. Litigation is hard on you and your kids, it costs a fortune, and it often yields the same or a worse result than you could achieve if you and your partner could just sit down and sort things out. Introductory comments about alternatives to litigation and getting set to resolve issues are found in Chapter 2, "How Anyone Can Settle a Family Law Case (or Almost)." Once you've gone through the process described in Chapter 2, you'll be ready to evaluate the options set out in this chapter.

LEGAL OPINIONS

A family lawyer can tell you objectively how a judge might handle the contested issues that arise in your case. Usually, however, concerns about conflict of interest prevent a lawyer from acting on behalf of both spouses, so one spouse should retain the lawyer to provide a written legal opinion. Once you receive the opinion, you and your spouse can review it. In many cases the objectivity and reliability of the opinion will give you the framework you need to resolve the issues. You might seek a second opinion if one of you doubts the correctness of the first. Even if you succeed in reaching an agreement in principle you should still obtain legal advice—so you shouldn't consider an opinion to be an unnecessary expense if you're having trouble settling. Advise the lawyer that you'll probably see her or him again, ideally to put your agreement, based on the opinion, in writing.

Opinions can address issues of support or property. Property opinions may resolve an issue by advising you whether an asset should be shared or whether one party should be entitled to certain deductions under matrimonial property rules. If a property claim involves a trust issue arising from a common law or same sex union or from a legal marriage, an opinion will address the odds of success. If the claim has no merit, the opinion will say so; if it has some merit, the opinion will estimate the chances of success and the likely amount of recovery. This may not provide an entirely conclusive answer, but the odds and amounts indicated should give you the background you both need to reach a compromise.

You can handle the cost of the opinion in several ways. You can agree to share the cost; the person who's pushing the settlement along may simply pay for it; or, if you both get opinions, you can each pay for your own. The cost of the opinion will reflect the time that the lawyer spends on it. In most cases, the cost will cover a few hours of the lawyer's time (usually less than $500, plus GST). An opinion involving a complex issue that requires consideration of a number of facts or conflicting case law may be more expensive than a simple question of law. Because you're trying to be efficient, you should retain someone with substantial experience in family law. That experience and reputation will also help you when the time comes to discuss the reliability of the opinion in the context of settlement.

FYI

The cost of a legal opinion will reflect the time that the lawyer spends on the issue. In most cases, the cost will cover a few hours of the lawyer's time, usually less than $500, plus GST.

ACCOUNTING OPINIONS

In some cases the outstanding issue is more financial than legal, such as a dispute about the value of a privately owned business, a concern about the tax treatment of support, or evaluation of the most cost-effective way to resolve the property division in complex cases. In such situations, you may know all you need to know about the law, and you'd settle on an equal basis if you knew how to determine it or if you could determine the most tax-effective solution. Many accountants spend their days dealing with family law issues. You should retain one to give you an objective, informed opinion. Your spouse's accountant, your business accountant, or the person who prepares your tax returns—while they may be familiar with the facts—aren't usually the best choices to give you tax advice on settlement.

You can retain the accountant and pay for the opinion jointly or individually. If only one of you attends the meeting with the accountant, you should ask for a written opinion to refer to when discussing settlement.

FOUR-WAY MEETINGS

A four-way meeting is a settlement discussion involving both spouses and each spouse's lawyer. If you've done the legwork described in Chapter 2 and have attempted settlement but haven't been able to resolve matters, it's often advisable to retain lawyers for the express purpose of engaging in a four-way settlement meeting. The presence of the lawyers brings a modicum of civility and objectivity to the discussion (well, most of the time!) and allows both sides to hear and appreciate the legal issues that separate them. People who want to settle but find their discussions degenerating into emotional disputes or who feel overpowered by their partner often find four-way meetings to be especially useful. People who have retained lawyers but find the process is moving too slowly or that the letter-writing seems futile and endless should also consider a four-way meeting.

Before the meeting, most lawyers will review your financial situation and the facts with you in detail. This is where you can really save money in legal fees by preparing your own financial statement and compiling the back-up documents, as discussed in Chapter 2. If you have these materials ready, your lawyer can spend an hour or two with you, then schedule the four-way meeting shortly afterward. If you have no disclosure ready, it may be weeks or maybe months and thousands of dollars later in legal fees before the meeting is scheduled.

MEDIATION

A mediator is a skilled professional who is retained by two parties to facilitate settlement. Once you complete certain procedural forms to give the mediator authority to assist in resolution, the mediator will discuss with you and your spouse the issues at hand and try to move you toward settlement. In family law, there are generally two types of mediators: psychiatrists, psychologists or social workers who mediate custody and access issues, and who may include meetings with children in the process; and lawyers, retired judges and other skilled professionals, who mediate financial matters. Some members of the second group know about custodial issues and will address all family law issues in mediation. If you're considering mediation, the choice of a mediator is crucial, and you should shop around and get some advice on suitable professionals.

Once you've identified a few potential mediators, you should find out whether they have any biases, especially if the mediator is going to address children's issues. In such cases, you should select the mediator in the same way as you'd select an assessor in custody disputes, as discussed in Chapter 4, "Custody."

Most lawyers and counsellors agree that mediation of custodial issues has a high success rate. People who seek mediation usually have the right focus, so some education and discussion about children's issues usually promotes settlement. Mediation of financial issues meets with less predictable success, since parties can become more readily entrenched in positions relating to money. Nevertheless, an agreement to mediate is still a promising indication of some incentive to negotiate a settlement.

Mediation can be open or closed. If it's open, the matters that are discussed, the behaviour of the parties and the conclusions of the mediation can all be disclosed in court if settlement fails. If it's closed, everything about the mediation is confidential and may never be referred to in court. Most practitioners agree that closed mediation is preferable, because it allows the parties to be themselves, to discuss their concerns openly, and to make concessions that move the matter toward resolution, all without any risk that they'll later be prejudiced by their conduct. Open mediation is often seen as offensive to the spirit of settlement, since litigation hangs over the process. Many people refuse to engage in open mediation for this reason, believing that, if the intention is really to avoid litigation, there's no need for open mediation.

Many separation agreements, whether or not they've been reached by mediation, require the parties to mediate issues that arise later. Such provisions may be specific to an issue (such as mandatory mediation of custodial matters), or broadly worded, applying to any dispute. A common provision requires the parties to mediate any issue about decision-making for their children, no matter how minor, and requires both parties to attend if either requests the mediation. The mediator is often empowered in such cases to determine if one party has taken an unreasonable position that required the mediation and to make that party responsible for the costs. This can be an attractive provision to couples who both wish to be involved in decision-making but fear being excluded or overpowered by the other spouse.

Mediation is usually billed on an hourly basis, with a retainer paid up front. Some mediators require the parties to pay after each session. Several provinces offer publicly funded mediation services. To avoid any unpleasant surprises, you should discuss these choices, along with the anticipated cost and payment methods, with a lawyer or the mediator before you proceed.

ARBITRATION

In arbitration, you appoint your own private judge. The difference between mediation and arbitration is that the mediator pushes parties toward settlement, while the arbitrator decides the issues in the same way as a judge, after hearing evidence and legal arguments by the parties and/or their lawyers. If the issue relates to children, the arbitrator will be a psychiatrist, psychologist or social worker; if the issue is financial, the arbitrator will be a retired judge or experienced family lawyer. If all kinds of issues are involved, the arbitrator will usually be a retired judge or a lawyer. The parties must select the arbitrator together. This is crucial and should be decided upon according to the same method described earlier with respect to mediators and in Chapter 4, "Custody," with respect to assessors. Once you've chosen the arbitrator, you sign documents giving the arbitrator authority to perform either advisory arbitration, which results in an opinion, or binding arbitration, which is a final decision that binds the parties. You also have to decide if you can appeal the arbitrator's decision, and in the case of advisory arbitration, whether it is open (and discoverable) or closed (and confidential).

In single-issue cases involving only one outstanding matter—the amount of spousal support in light of the payer's substantial debts, for example, or whether midweek access visits should be overnight—arbitration is a suitable option. It's preferable to taking the matter to court for several reasons:

- The issue will be resolved quickly, which benefits both spouses and any children of the relationship in many ways. You can usually go before the arbitrator immediately after deciding to arbitrate, and the arbitrator's decision can be rendered within thirty days or less;
- In custodial situations, it prevents the creation of a status quo and, to the extent possible, limits mudslinging and the prolonged uncertainty and resentment that go along with a custody dispute;

- It allows consideration of the children's views without the formality and pressure of a court appearance, and the parents don't necessarily have to know every detail of the children's views;
- While lawyers for both parties are usually present, the nature and speed of arbitration and the fact that interim motions and examinations will be avoided make it substantially cheaper than litigation;
- It occurs in a more comfortable, informal setting; and
- You get the judge you want—not the luck of the draw, as with litigation—and your judge will be attentive and interested.

CHAPTER FIFTEEN

If You Must... The Structure of the Action

IN THIS CHAPTER: **Legal Fees, The Originating Process;** *Petition for Divorce, Statement of Claim, Application and Variation, Family Court Documents,* **Without-Notice Motions, Pleadings, Interim Motions, Offers to Settle, Affidavits of Documents and Voluntary Disclosure, Examinations for Discovery;** *Some Basic Dos and Don'ts,* **Expert Reports, Settlement Conferences, The Trial, Enforcement of the Judgment, Appeals**

IN MANY CASES, LITIGATION BECOMES THE ONLY VIABLE OPTION, IF ONLY
TO ESTABLISH SOME INTERIM RULES AND PROMOTE RESOLUTION.

This chapter is an outline of the litigation process. It's organized by the
order in which tasks must be completed, and provides general guidelines.
It's not intended to provide the basic elements of an action from start to
finish. You need a lawyer if you're litigating, and you can discuss all other
issues with your lawyer as the matter progresses.

The first section of this chapter discusses legal fees, and references to
ways to keep your legal fees low are made throughout. Just having a basic
understanding of the process will go a long way toward saving you money.

LEGAL FEES

Usually the first order of business when you start an action is a consideration of legal fees. Most lawyers will want a retainer that will cover some
or all of the costs of preparing the documents and paying filing and
process server fees. If you have a fairly certain entitlement to receive a
property payment, many lawyers will act for you without money up front,
provided that you sign a document (called a Direction) in which you
indicate that your lawyer will get paid first when you receive any settlement proceeds. If the first lawyer you meet with refuses such an arrangement, shop around. Be sure to try some of the bigger firms in your city,
which usually have a greater capacity to carry a client in this way.

When discussing legal fees, you should clearly understand how your
potential lawyer bills clients. You should sign a retainer form that sets out
the billing practices and your understanding about how and when you'll
be billed. Retainer forms usually provide that you pay on an hourly rate
for all services, including telephone calls. They also give hourly rates for
the lawyers and law clerks who may work on your file. Most firms
include secretarial services in the package, but be sure that this is the
case, because some secretaries' time is also billed at an hourly rate. Some
lawyers will agree to work for you for a flat rate, which involves giving
you a quote for the total fees up front and sticking to it. Although this
practice is becoming popular with commercial lawyers, it's not so suitable in litigation, since it's difficult to predict how much time the litigation will require or when the matter might settle.

You must incur legal fees with your eyes open. If you're not charged for secretarial time, you can save yourself some fees by using the secretary as your initial contact when issues arise. You should also try to keep your fees down by insisting that law clerks and junior lawyers do as much work as possible on the file, rather than have your lawyer spend time on such things as financial statements and draft affidavits. Most important of all, you must stay on top of the unbilled legal fees that have accrued at all points during the action. You'll want to know the approximate costs to compare them to the predicted outcome and assess your settlement options. The last thing you want is to recover $30,000 and owe $40,000 in fees.

If you're concerned about your ability to pay for legal services, contact your provincial legal aid office and see if you qualify for assistance. There are generally two types of legal aid: contributory certificates, which require the recipient to pay legal aid back some or all of the money that is lent once a result has been obtained; and non-contributory certificates, which cover all your legal costs. Each province has its own requirements for legal aid entitlement. They're all broadly based on the applicant's income and assets.

If you're rejected by legal aid and still can't pay for legal services, contact a community legal clinic and get some advice. You may succeed in getting legal aid if a clinic worker puts some pressure on the legal aid office or assists you with an appeal of the decision. If that doesn't work, the community legal clinic will discuss other options with you. You can get referrals to legal aid offices and community legal clinics by contacting the law society in your province.

THE ORIGINATING PROCESS

The originating process is the document that starts the action. It makes the claims and sets out the basic facts supporting them. It is completed and filed with the court, a fee is paid for its issuance and the court assigns a file number to the case. It is then served on the other spouse in accordance with specified rules, and proof of service is filed with the court. There are three types of originating process when family law matters are brought before the court for the first time: the Petition for Divorce, the Statement of Claim and the Notice of Application.

Petition for Divorce

Married couples may choose to begin an action by Petition for
Divorce. The petition is the document that must be completed at
some point in every case to obtain the actual divorce judgment. All
other claims, under both the *Divorce Act* and provincial family legislation, may be included in a petition for divorce. I recommend this
route for all married spouses who know that the marriage is over,
unless they feel that they might settle their case more easily if their
spouse is not emotionally upset by the claim for divorce itself. Going
with the petition at the outset is usually the most efficient method
of proceeding, since a divorce will have to be sought at some point,
and you'll save legal and court filing fees by doing one document
instead of two.

The filing fee for the petition varies from province to province, but
it's generally around $100. You must pay a further $10 at the same time
to obtain a Clearance Certificate from Ottawa to ensure that there are
no other proceedings pending between the spouses.

A provincial court has jurisdiction to determine a divorce proceeding if either spouse has resided in the province for at least one year
before the proceeding begins.

The completed petition is filed with the court and then served on
the other spouse. The method of service will be either personal (providing the document to the spouse directly, usually by process server and
never by the other spouse) or service by registered mail. The cost of a
process server for a single service varies, but is around $50.

If claims are made for property division, child support or spousal
support, a financial statement in the form prescribed by provincial rules
must be served and filed along with the petition. The more documents
you compile and the more work you do on the financial statement
before you meet with a lawyer, the better off you'll be. This is covered in
more detail in Chapter 2.

If you're settling or have settled all issues and just want a divorce,
you can claim divorce only in the petition. The process of getting an
undefended divorce is discussed in Chapter 13, "Divorce, Religious
Divorce and Annulment."

Statement of Claim

An action between married spouses for property division, support, custody and access can be commenced under provincial family legislation without making a claim for divorce. Common law and same sex couples usually proceed with claims by this route.

A statement of claim begins by requesting various grounds of relief and then sets out the facts to support the claims. The facts include the date of marriage or commencement of cohabitation, the date of separation, a list of any children and their birthdates, and other facts that are relevant to the claims. For instance, if a claim is made for exclusive possession of the matrimonial home, the statement of claim gives the reasons why exclusive possession is required and usually says that the defendant has alternate accommodation available.

The claim is obtained by attending at the court office, paying a fee, and getting a court file number. The claim is then served by personal service, usually by using a process server.

If claims are made for property, child support or spousal support, a financial statement must be completed, filed and served along with the statement of claim.

Application and Variation

If matters are not overly complicated and oral evidence of the parties will not be required, you can proceed by Notice of Application, supported with an affidavit containing all the evidence to support the claims. An application is heard and disposed of without a trial, on the basis of written materials and out-of-court examinations. A Notice of Application is the usual route for variation proceedings, in which one party seeks to change an old order.

You must take care to ensure that an application is the correct route based on the facts of your situation, since an application will be converted into an action with live evidence if the court feels that evidence is necessary. In some provinces, there's a penalty for proceeding with an application when an action is the more appropriate route. An application is heard by the court and determined more quickly, with the benefit of lower costs to the parties, so it's an attractive option for the right cases. But if credibility is in issue, or if you think that you'll benefit from appearing in person before a judge, an action may be more attractive. You should discuss the option of proceeding by application with your lawyer.

An application is obtained by attending at the courthouse, paying a fee and getting a court file number and a date for the hearing of the application. The application is then served by personal service, along with the affidavit and other documents required by the court.

Another way of varying an old order, which is available to divorced couples, is a Petition for Corollary Relief. Although the divorce has been granted, there may be an issue that needs to be revisited. Procedurally, there's no difference between a Petition for Divorce and a Petition for Corollary Relief, except that no divorce is sought.

Applications and Petitions for Corollary Relief must be accompanied by a financial statement if claims are made for property division, child support or spousal support. If custody or variation of custody is in issue, no financial statement will be required.

Family Court Documents

The final route available to commence an action is to use the forms provided by your province's family court. In every province but New Brunswick, PEI and Quebec, special family courts provide easy and inexpensive access to justice for uncomplicated cases. One of the benefits of family courts is that they're designed to allow people to act on their own behalf without lawyers, and the legal forms required for proceedings are usually simple, fill-in-the-blank documents. I still don't recommend that you act for yourself in a family law matter if you can possibly obtain legal assistance. The idea of accessible justice notwithstanding, matters can get quite complicated and contentious. In a hearing, you'll have the opportunity to give evidence and cross-examine your spouse. The outcome is so important—and depends so much on the court's impression of you—that you're always better off getting help with the process.

Family courts usually have their own form of financial statement that must be completed if financial claims are being made. These are often simplified versions of the standard documents in the province. They're also available from the provincial court office.

WITHOUT-NOTICE MOTIONS

In some cases, it's possible to get an interim order from the court before the originating process is served on the other spouse. Courts are very reluctant to make orders before the other side has had an opportunity to respond and without giving both sides a chance to make submissions on the issue. However, in cases when a spouse is afraid to serve documents without some protections, a court will sometimes make an order without notice.

PLEADINGS

Once an action is commenced, the respondent must reply to the claims within twenty days, or longer if the respondent lives outside the jurisdiction. The document, containing a response to the claims and factual assertions, is called an Answer or a Statement of Defence. If a financial statement has been served along with the original process, the respondent must also file a financial statement at the same time. If no defence is filed, the matter is considered to be undefended, the respondent is deemed to admit everything in the defence claims, and the claimant can bring a motion for judgment and get everything requested. If a counterclaim is filed, the claimant then has twenty days to respond in a document called a Reply. These three documents are collectively called the pleadings, and they frame the issues in the case.

INTERIM MOTIONS

An interim motion is an attendance before a judge to obtain relief on a temporary basis. Each province has its own rules about the service of notice of a motion and obtaining a date for the motion. The other spouse is usually given time to prepare responding materials if the motion is served with minimum notice.

This book discusses each type of interim relief in the chapter that addresses the broad subject. For example, interim custody is found in Chapter 4, "Custody."

OFFERS TO SETTLE

An offer to settle that addresses all issues should be served on the other side as soon as possible after the action has been commenced. There are two reasons for this. The first is obvious—the offer establishes a dialogue that may result in exchanges of offers and, ultimately, settlement. The second is cost-related. All provinces have rules about the legal costs of the action. Usually, if a reasonable offer is rejected, and the offerer receives an equivalent or better result at the trial, the rejecting party must pay a proportion of the other's legal fees. The rule is designed to encourage an exchange of reasonable offers and promote settlement.

AFFIDAVITS OF DOCUMENTS AND VOLUNTARY DISCLOSURE

After the pleadings are exchanged and any interim motions have been dealt with, further information must be obtained so that the spouses have an idea about the value of assets, along with the documentation to support their positions. In contentious litigation, the first step in the disclosure process is the exchange of affidavits of documents. An affidavit of documents is a sworn statement that describes every single document in the spouse's possession that's relevant to the issue, including pay stubs, tax returns, proof of the receipt of gifts, financial statements from businesses, deeds of land, and so on. You must include all relevant documents, because you can't later rely on a document that wasn't included in the affidavit of documents unless the court gives you special permission. Once the affidavit of documents is served, the other side will be given an opportunity to review the documents described in the affidavit.

If the spouses hope to resolve the action amicably, they often agree to voluntary disclosure of the relevant documentation. If you choose voluntary disclosure, your next step should be to have a four-way meeting or exchange settlement offers.

EXAMINATIONS FOR DISCOVERY

Unless you settle, examinations for discovery follow the exchange of affidavits of documents. Examinations for discovery involve the attendance of one spouse to be questioned by the other's lawyer, under oath, before a licensed court reporter. The examination is usually held in a boardroom at the court reporter's office or, if there are a lot of documents, at one lawyer's office. The setting is fairly relaxed; there's no judge, and your lawyer can assist you in answering questions.

Often the lawyers agree to examine both spouses on the same day or on consecutive days. The party that conducts the examination first is entitled to finish the examination and receive all answers and follow-up documents before being examined, although this procedural requirement is often waived by the lawyers or the spouses in the interests of efficiency.

You have to pay for the services of the court reporter for the transcripts. The total cost depends on the length of the examination but can run from a few hundred dollars to over a thousand dollars. Both spouses' lawyers attend the examinations, and legal fees for preparation and a whole day in examinations can be as much as $2000 for each spouse.

Some Basic Dos and Don'ts

The following guidelines for examinations are taken from a standard letter that my boss and mentor, Malcolm Kronby, prepared. He sends this letter to all his clients before he meets with them to prepare for an examination. An excerpt is reproduced here with his permission and my thanks.

Please be guided by the following 'dos' and 'don'ts' all of which are *extremely important*.

1. **DO** listen *carefully* to each question. **DO** wait until the question is completed before you answer it.
2. **DO** answer only the question that is asked. **DON'T** volunteer extra information, or guess or speculate—you have no obligation to do so.
3. **DO** answer questions truthfully and accurately. If you do not know the answer, or do not remember, **DO** say so—there is nothing wrong with that.
4. **DON'T** answer any question unless you fully understand it.
5. **DON'T** try to be persuasive or argumentative. **DON'T** try to "sell" yourself on the justice of your case.
6. **DON'T** be concerned if the whole story is not coming out. *That is not your problem.* **DO** let the scope of the Examination simply be determined by the questions put to you.

EXPERT REPORTS

Some cases will require expert evidence before they can be settled or before a trial. The most common expert witnesses in a family law proceeding are accountants or business valuators who have reviewed the records of a business and have an opinion of its value; and assessors (a child psychologist, psychiatrist or social worker appointed by the parties or the court), who give an opinion about the parenting plan that meets the best interests of the children. If there are medical issues in the case, a doctor may be an expert witness. If there's a rich pension at issue, an actuary who has valued it will be a witness. Any complicated factual matter may require an expert to clarify the facts and assist the court. In most cases, a party who disagrees with the contents of the expert report will be entitled to cross-examine the expert and will be given extra time to retain an expert to reply to that evidence, if required.

SETTLEMENT CONFERENCES

Ninety-nine percent of all family law cases settle before trial. If you're involved in litigation that's still alive after examinations for discovery and undertakings, you're ready for a trial. The time has come to reevaluate your settlement options. Most courts require that spouses have a meeting with the judge to hear the judge's view on the case before a trial date is set.

THE TRIAL

We all know about trials from television. Family law trials are similar to the trials we've seen on TV, except they're not so brief or so cheap. They're long and detailed. The average family law trial takes a week, and each spouse spends a day or two on the stand. They can cost anywhere from $20,000 to $100,000 in legal fees, in addition to any expert fees.

The spouse who commenced the action (either the plaintiff or the petitioner) is entitled to make his or her case first. This involves calling all witnesses, hearing their chief evidence, and presenting them for cross-examination by the opposing party. Prior inconsistent statements made during examinations may be used during cross-examination, and any important admissions from examinations may be read into the record as part of the case. The other side then leads all of his or her evidence in the same way.

All documents that are referred to are filed with the court and given an exhibit number. A court reporter records or takes down every word that's said during the trial. The transcript of the proceedings and the exhibits are referred to as the record. If there's a later appeal, the record will be transcribed and the appeal court will review it all.

When the evidence is complete, the lawyers make oral arguments, summarizing the evidence and quoting from relevant case law. When the argument's finished, the court may give an oral judgment from the bench or may reserve and release a written judgment later (as much as five or six months later in some cases). If the parties are married and haven't obtained an earlier divorce, an order dissolving the marriage will be included with the other relief. The written reasons are then summarized into a divorce judgment that is approved by both sides and filed with the court.

ENFORCEMENT OF THE JUDGMENT

Once you get a divorce judgment that provides for financial relief, you may still have to take steps to enforce it. If you and your lawyer are organized at the trial, you'll have requested enforcement assistance, such as the sale of property to satisfy the judgment, and those terms will be included. Even without specific enforcement terms, most spouses know that the judgment ends the matter, and they cooperate with conforming to its terms. Sometimes, however, the parties or the court don't consider all enforcement issues, or the parties don't cooperate, making further enforcement proceedings necessary.

Enforcement can be costly and complicated, but sometimes automatic enforcement measures are available through the sheriff's office or other provincial authorities. Talk to a lawyer immediately if you think you have an enforcement problem, and get your lawyer to provide you with a list of your enforcement options and the costs. You may be able to do some or all of it yourself if you get the right information.

Enforcement of child and spousal support can be an ongoing problem. Every province has its own enforcement agencies that are available to provide inexpensive—if not free—assistance in enforcing support.

These options are discussed in Chapter 7, "Child Support" and Chapter 8, "Spousal Support." A list of provincial enforcement agencies is found in Appendix B.

APPEALS

The trial judgment and enforcement may not be the last word. There's an automatic right of appeal from a trial judgment in each province. An appeal must be launched within a certain number of days after the judgment is released. All payments of money, except for child and spousal support, are stayed, meaning that they don't have to be paid, pending the outcome of the appeal, unless the court of appeal orders otherwise on a motion to lift the stay.

Appeals may be tactical or based on a genuine belief that an error was made. Some spouses appeal as a tactical matter to encourage the other spouse to take less than the judgment provides, thereby avoiding the appeal process. As awful as it sounds, this tactic often works, after the potential costs and timing of an appeal are considered. If an appeal reflects one spouse's belief that an error was made, that spouse may not want to compromise and may insist on dragging the matter out for another year or two. Appeal courts are busy, and they take the most pressing cases first, often leaving the family law cases waiting for long periods. Even if the matter is heard quickly, it takes months to obtain transcripts of the trial and file all the required documents. However, if you're defending an appeal, take heart—appeal courts are very reluctant to interfere with the findings and conclusions of a judge who has had the benefit of seeing all the witnesses and hearing all the evidence. The success rate of appeals is marginal indeed, and costs usually follow the result.

There are lawyers who specialize in family law appeals and focus on little else. You should retain one, if only to get an opinion about the merits of an appeal. Many lawyers who specialize in appeals will quote a flat fee for acting on your appeal. If they don't offer a flat fee, you should request one. Shop around and get a few opinions. In retaining a new lawyer, you have to pay him or her to learn your case. Sometimes you'll do better by keeping your old lawyer for the appeal and simply adopting the advice you've obtained from the other consultations.

AFTERWORD

When I was looking for closing remarks for this book, I wanted a real-life, honest overview of the family and family law. And it so happened that I remembered sitting enraptured during a speech that Madam Justice Abella gave at the 1994 National Family Law Conference. I managed to find the text in my files, as I had previously relied on a short excerpt from it in another case. It did contain just the kind of insightful summary I was looking for, but more than that, I was delighted to find that its content was so reflective of the themes of this book. And so I leave you with the thoughts of, in my view, one of Canada's most creative and family-focused jurists.

> Family law is the legal system's metaphor, the crucible where so much else in law intersects. It offers some of the most dynamic layers through which to examine the role of the law generally, and the role of those professionals who function on its behalf. It is also, because it is the area of law by means of which most people will come into contact with it, the area by which the legal system will be judged by most people. If we undertake the exercise of scrutinizing the law of the family through the eyes of the public it serves, we will soon appreciate the confusion and frustration they all too often feel....
>
> ... [T]he 1968 *Divorce Act* ushered into this generation a tidal wave of seemingly endless reform which more than made up for the quiescence of the previous century. Why, all of a sudden, so much reform so quickly and so constantly and so urgently?

I think the answer lies in the decade of the sixties. The sixties hosted breathtaking social changes. The election of John F. Kennedy at the beginning of the decade sent a message of change and youth and difference all around the western world. The riots in the ghettos, the civil disobedience spawned by the Vietnam War, the flower children who resisted everything but non-conformity, and the general impatience with everything that had gone before, were all translated by the late sixties and early seventies into a demand for a revolutionary revision of all aspects of the social contract.

Children demanded both more and less from their parents, women demanded more from everyone, persons with disabilities demanded access, minorities demanded an end to discrimination, aboriginal people demanded self-government, and Quebec demanded independence. It was very clear by the end of the sixties that no institution would be untouched by the performance appraisals from this new generation, and it was also very clear that every appraisal would find every institution wanting. It was impossible not to respond to the demands for change, and it was impossible to ignore the cry that what appeared to work for some was no longer working for most.

This generation, I suspect, will go down in history as the transition era between the lifestyle that ended in the fifties with Father Knows Best and may end this century with Where *is* Father? It is in the nature of transitions that they are difficult. They involve the tentative and some-time reluctant abandonment of prior practices in favour of new and imperfectly understood objectives and strategies.

And it is particularly difficult for *this* transition era because of the contemporaneous transitions in the world around us. What we have in this transition is a proliferation of responders and responses: the family responding to shifting social realities; the economy responding to shifting political realities; the political environment responding to shifting economic realities; and individuals responding to all of the above.

How did the law of the family respond? We went from separate property to equal property to pensions as property. We went from *dum casta* clauses to causal connections to clean-break theories and finally to *Moge* v. *Moge*. We went from women upon marriage having to quit the paid labour force, to the overwhelming majority of mothers with children under six being *in* the paid labour force. We went from no divorce, to over a third of all Canadian families divorcing, to the new phenomenon in the United States of the possibility of children divorcing their parents. We went from pre-marital virgins to accessible birth control to the sexual revolution to surrogacy and reproductive technology. We abolished the unity between husband and wife, introduced the constructive trust, extended it to common law relationships, extended common law relationships to spousal relationships, and almost extended spousal relationships to same sex couples.

We moved from children being given to the least blameworthy spouse to children being given to the better parent. We gave children lawyers to speak for them, and we gave them the possibility of being given to both parents jointly. We went from the tender years doctrine to the best interests principle. We gave children access to the criminal courts to prevent their sexual exploitation from people they had trusted and we stopped caring whether their parents were legitimate.

We have seen women's shelters, increased violence, the debate about "recovered memories" and "mommy tracks," the spread of AIDS, multiculturalism, political correctness, deficit preoccupations, the rise of religious fundamentalism, the *Charter of Rights and Freedoms*, Quebec and western nationalism, free trade agreements, global pressures, Nintendo, and the cultural trinity of Madonna, Michael Jackson and O.J. Simpson. What's wrong with this picture?

The truth is there is nothing wrong with this picture. It is undoubtedly a *very* complicated painting, but we should not be embarrassed to admit that we painted it. Any art gallery would be proud to hang it in their post-modern section. But just one glance at the cluttered canvas, at the different textures and colours and shades, at the sharpness of some of the images and haziness of others, and we instantly understand why families today are so confused about how they and their law are supposed to respond to all these realities in the social environment after having spent nearly a century ignoring them....

The *substance* of family law should be nourishing and expeditiously available; the *process* should be lean and fair. To the extent that procedural reliance unduly delays legitimate entitlements and arbitrarily blocks access to them, it ought not to be tolerated by the system.

Are we entitled to be confident that the over-judicialization and justiciability of family law is producing greater fairness to those who are between families? What we should be thinking about instead is how to minimize the possibility that family disagreements find their way into the courtroom at all, and help former families get on with their lives. It would be interesting to interview persons at the end of multi-year disputes to see whether their satisfaction increases with the amount of procedure they have been exposed to, or whether it varies with the result.

Everyone wants their days in court, not their years. We have lost the punitive substantive approach in family law which sought to prevent departures by penalizing the wayfarer, but we have replaced it with a punitive procedural approach which penalizes everyone.

If the law is going to be truly responsive to social realities, then it should be more responsive to the reality that most people cannot afford to go through a civil trial, and that many people who require

the assistance of the law will be unable to avail themselves of its benefit because the complications and ambiguities and procedural hurdles
make the possibility of access to a resolution unattainable.

Then there is the debate about what role the professionals involved
in family law can or should play. Should generalist or specialist judges
decide family disputes?

The implementation of theories and gender equality, theories of
matrimonial equity and theories of children's developmental welfare are
fraught with the potential for value judgments based on what one's
views are about how the world ought to unfold. Who can say at any
given moment in time what will turn out to have been best for a child?
Who can say at any given moment in time when or if a spouse will
become self-sufficient? Who can say what self-sufficient means when the
unemployment rate is at 11%? Who can say whether a spouse really does
or does not have the assets or deficits claimed?

Someone has to say, and traditionally that someone has been a judge.
Yet there is nothing magic about the judicial function that automatically
equips a judge, particularly a generalist judge, with the insight to divide
the equities and children. Family law is very much, and necessarily very
much, the preserve of judicial discretion, and judicial discretion is very
much a breeding ground for controversy. And it is particularly fertile
ground for controversy since a judge being judgmental over a family
about whose pre-dissolution decisions the state has been almost entirely
unjudgmental. And now, through the courts, what was aggressively private
has become aggressively and embarrassingly public, not to mention
expensive, protracted, and incomprehensibly inaccessible....

There you have it. One person's assessment of how the controversial
heart of family law pumps controversy to the rest of the body. What's the
prognosis? Do we need a transplant or a by-pass? Will the patient survive? Is there a less detrimental alternative? What is in the best interests
of the public?

Curiosity. Open-mindedness. Creativity. Empathy. Wisdom. These
are the five characteristics, in my view, with which family law can best
implement its premises. And in so doing, it can offer intellectual guidance for other parts of the legal system. Family law is and should be a
leader in the legal system because it matters so much to so many. And
that is why it is worth spending the time and energy on trying to get it
as right as reality permits....

—Madam Justice Rosalie Silberman Abella, *The Law of the Family in
the Year of the Family,* Keynote Address at the National Family Law Program,
July 18, 1994. Reprinted with permission.

APPENDICES

APPENDIX A: *Financial Statements by Province*

PROVINCE	FORM NAME	FORM NUMBER
Alberta	Statement of Finances	no number used
British Columbia	Financial Statement	PFA Serial 22
Manitoba	Financial Statement	Form 70D
New Brunswick	Financial Statement	72J
Newfoundland	Financial Statement	no number used
Nova Scotia	Financial Statement	not used
NWT	Financial Statement	Form 8
Ontario	Financial Statement	69K (married spouses) 69M (unmarried spouses)
Prince Edward Island	Financial Statement	701
Quebec	État des Revenus et Dépenses, et Bilan	no number used
Saskatchewan	Financial Statement	Form D
Yukon Territories	Financial Statement	Form 2

APPENDIX B: *Provincial Enforcement Agencies*

Where there are two numbers, the second is for out-of-province callers.

Federal Orders & Enforcement
1-800-267-7777
1-800-667-3355

Alberta
Maintenance Enforcement Program
1-800-642-3803
1-413-422-5554

British Columbia
Central Enrollment Unit
1-800-663-7616
1-604-356-8889

Manitoba
Maintenance Enforcement Program
1-204-945-7133

New Brunswick
Saint John
1-506-658-2400

Newfoundland
Support Enforcement Agency
1-709-637-2608

Northwest Territories
Maintenance Enforcement Program
1-800-661-0798
1-403-920-3378

Nova Scotia
Sydney Regional Office
1-902-563-2218

Ontario
Family Support Plan
1-800-267-4330
1-416-326-1817
(Automated phone line)
1-800-267-7263
1-416-326-1818

In the Greater Toronto Area
1-416-326-1817
(Automated phone line)
1-416-326-1818

Prince Edward Island
Supreme Court: Family Section
1-902-368-6010

Quebec
Percepteur des pensionstaires
1-800-488-2323
1-418-643-6191

Saskatchewan
Maintenance Enforcement Office
1-306-787-5677

Yukon
Maintenance Enforcement Office
1-403-667-5784

APPENDIX C: *Law Societies*

The Law Society of Alberta
600–919 11th Avenue S.W.
Calgary, AB T2R 1P3
Tel: 1-403-229-4700
Fax: 1-403-228-1728

The Law Society of British Columbia
845 Cambie Street, 8th Floor
Vancouver, BC V6B 4Z9
Tel: 1-604-669-2533
Fax:1-604-669-5232

The Law Society of Manitoba
201–219 Kennedy Street
Winnipeg, MB R3C 1S8
Tel: 1-204-942-5571
Fax: 1-204-956-0624

The Law Society of New Brunswick
Suite 206, 1133 rue Regent Street
Fredericton, NB E3B 3Z2
Tel: 1-506-458-8540
Fax: 1-506-458-1076

The Law Society of Newfoundland
Atlantic Place, 5th Floor
Box 1028, St. John's, NF A1C 5M3
Tel: 1-709-722-4740
Fax: 1-709-722-8902

The Law Society of Northwest Territories
4916–47th Street, Box 1298
Yellowknife, NT X1A 2N9
Tel: 1-403-873-3828
Fax: 1-403-873-6344

Nova Scotia's Barristers' Society
Keith Hall, 1475 Hollis Street
Halifax, NS B3J 3M4
Tel: 1-902-422-1491
Fax: 1-902-429-4869

The Law Society of Upper Canada (Ontario)
Osgoode Hall, 130 Queen Street West
Toronto, ON M5H 2N6
Tel: 1-416-947-3300 or
1-800-668-7380
Fax: 1-416-947-9070

The Law Society of Prince Edward Island
49 Water Street, Box 128
Charlottetown, PEI C1A 7K2
Tel: 1-902-566-1666
Fax: 1-902-368-7557

Bar of the Province of Quebec
Maison du Barreau, 445 boul.
St-Laurent
Montreal, QC H2Y 3T8
Tel: 1-514-954-3400
Fax: 1-514-954-3407

Law Society of Saskatchewan
1100–2500 Victoria Avenue
Regina, SK S4P 3X2
Tel: 1-306-569-8242
Fax: 1-306-352-2989

The Law Society of Yukon
201–302 Steele Street
Whitehorse, YT Y1A 2C5
Tel: 1-403-668-4231
Fax: 1-403-667-7556

APPENDIX D: Lawyer Referral Services

Alberta
Lawyer Referral Service
Operated by the Law Society of Alberta
Tel: 1-403-228-1722
or 1-800-661-1095

Dial-A-Law
Telephone Information Line
Tel: 1-403-234-9022

British Columbia
Lawyer Referral Service
845 Cambie Street, 10th Floor
Vancouver, BC V6B 5T3
Tel: 1-604-687-3221
or 1-800-663-1919

Manitoba
Law Phone-In & Lawyer Referral Service
304–283 Bannatyne Avenue
Winnipeg, MB R3B 3B2
Tel: 1-204-943-2305

Ontario
The Lawyer Referral Service
130 Queen Street West
Toronto, ON M5H 2N6
Tel: 1-416-947-3330
or 1-800-268-8326

Quebec
Service de Reference Du Barreau de Montreal
Palais de Justice
Montreal, QC H2Y 1B6
Tel: 1-514-866-9392
or 1-514-866-2490

APPENDIX E: *Provincial Women's Shelter Associations*

Alberta
Alberta Council of Women's Shelters
12739 Fort Road
Edmonton, AB T5A 1A7
Tel: 1-403-456-7000

British Columbia
Society of Transition Houses,
British Columbia/Yukon
204–409 Granville Street
Vancouver, BC V6C 1T2
Tel: 1-604-669-6943

Manitoba
Manitoba Association of Women's
Shelters Inc.
Box 651
Dauphin, MB R7N 3P3
Tel: 1-204-638-8707

New Brunswick
Hestia House
P.O. Box 7135, Station A
Saint John, NB E2L 4S5
Tel: 1-506-634-7570

Newfoundland
Provincial Association Against Family
Violence
P.O. Box 221, Station C
St. John's, NF A1C 5J2
Tel: 1-709-739-6759

Northwest Territories
Sutherland House
Tawow Society
Box 908
Fort Smith, NT X0E 0P0
Tel: 1-403-872-5925

Nova Scotia
Transition House Association of Nova Scotia
Suite 311, 5516 Spring Garden Road
Halifax, NS B3J 3G6
Tel: 1-902-429-8288

Ontario
Ontario Association of Interval &
Transition Houses
Suite 1404, 2 Carlton Street
Toronto, ON M5B 1J3
Tel: 1-416-977-6619

Prince Edward Island
Prince Edward Island Transition House
Association
81 Prince Street
Charlottetown, PEI C1A 4R3
Tel: 1-902-368-8658

Quebec
Regroupement provincial des maisons
d'hébergement et de transition pour femmes
victimes de violence conjugale
5225 Rue Berri, Bureau 304
Montreal, QC H2J 2S4
Tel: 1-514-279-2007

Saskatchewan
Provincial Association of Transition Houses
in Saskatchewan
307–135 21st Street East
Saskatoon, SK S7K 0B4
Tel: 1-306-978-6654

APPENDIX F: Legal Aid Offices

Call the office listed for your province to find out where there is an office close to you.

Alberta
Suite 300, 10320 102 Avenue
Edmonton, AB T5J 4A1
Tel: 1-403-427-7575

British Columbia
Suite 1500, 1140 W. Pender
Vancouver, BC
Tel: 1-604-660-4600

Manitoba
Suite 402, 294 Portage Avenue
Winnipeg, MB R3C 0B9
Tel: 1-204-985-8500

New Brunswick
Suite 2, 403 Regent Street
Fredericton, NB E3B 3X6
Tel: 1-506-451-1424

Newfoundland
Legal Aid Commission
21 Church Hill
St. John's, NF A1C 3Z8
Tel: 1-709-753-7860

Northwest Territories
Legal Services Board (Legal Aid)
Box 1320
Yellowknife, NT X1A 2L9
Tel: 1-403-873-7450

Nova Scotia
401–5475 Spring Garden Road
Halifax, NS B3J 3T2
Tel: 1-902-420-6585

Ontario
73 Albert Street, Ground Floor
Ottawa, ON K1P 1E3
Tel: 1-613-238-7931

Ontario Divorce Law Office
Suite 540, 439 University Avenue
Toronto, ON M5G 1Y8
Tel: 1-416-348-0001

Prince Edward Island
P.O. Box 200
Charlottetown, PEI C1A 7N8
Tel: 1-902-368-6043

Quebec
2 Complexe Desjardins
Tour Est, #1404
Montreal, QC H5B 1B3
Tel: 1-514-873-3562

Saskatchewan
Central Office
Suite 820, 410 22nd Street East
Saskatoon, SK S7K 2H6
Tel: 1-306-933-5300

Yukon
Yukon Legal Services Society
Suite 167, 2134 2nd Street Avenue
Whitehorse, YT Y1A 5H6
Tel: 1-403-667-5210

INDEX